Sophia Studies in Cross-cultural Philosophy of Traditions and Cultures

Volume 20

The Sophia Studies in Cross-cultural Philosophy of Traditions and Cultures focuses on the broader aspects of philosophy and traditional intellectual patterns of religion and cultures. The series encompasses global traditions, and critical treatments that draw from cognate disciplines, inclusive of feminist, postmodern, and postcolonial approaches. By global traditions we mean religions and cultures that go from Asia to the Middle East to Africa and the Americas, including indigenous traditions in places such as Oceania. Of course this does not leave out good and suitable work in Western traditions where the analytical or conceptual treatment engages Continental (European) or Cross-cultural traditions in addition to the Judeo-Christian tradition. The book series invites innovative scholarship that takes up newer challenges and makes original contributions to the field of knowledge in areas that have hitherto not received such dedicated treatment. For example, rather than rehearsing the same old Ontological Argument in the conventional way, the series would be interested in innovative ways of conceiving the erstwhile concerns while also bringing new sets of questions and responses, methodologically also from more imaginative and critical sources of thinking. Work going on in the forefront of the frontiers of science and religion beaconing a well-nuanced philosophical response that may even extend its boundaries beyond the confines of this debate in the West – e.g. from the perspective of the 'Third World' and the impact of this interface (or clash) on other cultures, their economy, sociality, and ecological challenges facing them – will be highly valued by readers of this series. All books to be published in this Series will be fully peer-reviewed before final acceptance.

More information about this series at http://www.springer.com/series/8880

Germán McKenzie

Interpreting Charles Taylor's Social Theory on Religion and Secularization

A Comparative Study

 Springer

Germán McKenzie
St. Mark's & Corpus Christi Colleges at
    University of British Columbia
Vancouver, BC, Canada

ISSN 2211-1107   ISSN 2211-1115   (electronic)
Sophia Studies in Cross-cultural Philosophy of Traditions and Cultures
ISBN 978-3-319-47698-8   ISBN 978-3-319-47700-8   (eBook)
DOI 10.1007/978-3-319-47700-8

Library of Congress Control Number: 2016958562

Printed on acid-free paper

This Springer imprint is published by Springer Nature
The registered company is Springer International Publishing AG
The registered company address is: Gewerbestrasse 11, 6330 Cham, Switzerland

To Giuliana,
My Beloved Wife

To Hugo and María Cecilia,
My Parents

Preface

My first conscious encounter with secularization occurred when I was a teenager while living in Lima, Peru. Being part of an urban and educated middle-class family, I was a member of a fortunate, by then reduced, number of people who enjoyed much better opportunities for personal and professional development than the majority of Peruvians. During the 1970s, my peers and I were strongly influenced by pop culture imported from the United States and the United Kingdom through the media with its criticisms against the establishment of the time. Later, when I became a university student, I encountered Soviet/Maoist socialist ideology, was very much impacted by expressivism, and found a stronger critique of religion. This clearly caught my attention, and, while triggering a process of analyzing the reasons and consequences of the challenges they presented, it also made me think about the stark contrast between secularized elites and deeply religious masses.

I should say that my interest in secularization never waned but, on the contrary, did become a source of questions I dealt with through my philosophical and theological studies up until the present. My decision to enroll into a doctoral program in religion and culture was directly motivated by it. To this, however, I added a growing interest in the intersection between theology and the social sciences, particularly sociology, through my own assessment of the strengths and weaknesses of liberation theology, God's death theology, and political theology, all of them related with the phenomenon of Western secularization in one way or the other.

The study of secularization has been carried out mainly in sociological terms. Beginning in the 1960s, a corpus of scholarly texts was developed that understood such a process as the decline of religion, which was seen as endogenous to modernization. Among the more important proponents of this view were Bryan Wilson, Steve Bruce, and Peter Berger in his early thought. This characterization of the process, which I call the "orthodox" model, was predominant in academia until the 1990s, although there were always voices who called into question its assumptions and methodology. Around that time, a new paradigm emerged that proposed a completely different (and strongly contrasting) view of secularization. Scholars like Roger Finke, Rodney Stark, and William Sims Bainbridge are among the most important advocates of this approach. The "counter-orthodox" model or rational choice theory (RCT) as applied to the study of religion affirmed that secularization was an ongoing and self-limiting process. Moreover, it gave a new interpretation of the role modern religious pluralism plays in religious vitality, finding the former to be encouraging the latter, in opposition to "orthodox" theorists who claimed exactly the contrary. After that time, an intense debate ensued between the two positions, although an increasing number of empirical studies eroded the validity of the "orthodox" model. Since then, RCT has become predominant in scholarship in the matter, particularly in the United States. However, this position has also been challenged by both quantitative and qualitative studies.

A number of scholars, whom I call "revisionists," would still search for alternative explanations for secularization in the West. Among them, one should mention David Martin, Mark Chaves, and Jose Casanova. To these, one must now add that of Charles Taylor, one of the more important philosophers in the English-speaking world, who had proposed a hermeneutic method for the sciences of man based on his own philosophical anthropology and epistemology. In 2007, Taylor published his book *A Secular Age*, a massive tome in which he gives his own account of secularization by way of a meta-narrative. Although I come from a different philosophical tradition than Taylor, the thickness of the theoretical background of his account and my own sympathy for hermeneutic philosophy motivated my interest. To this, I would add the vivid realization, as a Latin American living and studying in North America, of how much of contemporary sociological research is strongly conditioned by culture through both Western modern and postmodern narratives.

Taylor's book, while making a lengthy, multilayered, and complex argument, does indeed offer a "sociological" account which is contained in about one third of its pages. In such account, he aims at explaining the social processes in Western secularization as well as the social agents that made it possible. Taylor's argument draws from the thought of sociologists, both classical and contemporary. Among them, he chooses those whose views he finds amenable of being incorporated into his thoroughly hermeneutical approach to secularization. The names of Max Weber, along with the above mentioned Martin and Casanova, as well as Robert Bellah, Hans Joas, Robert Wuthnow, Danièlle Hervieu-Lèger, Grace Davie, and Wade Clark Roof are among the more important of them.

Taylor's resulting narrative offers two difficulties to properly engaging in a conversation with other sociological theories of secularization: it supposes a particular view of how to carry out studies in the social sciences, and it constitutes a blend of history, sociology, and philosophy. However, because of the perspicuity of Taylor's views, they also appeared to me as having the potential for contributing, along with other recent scholarship, in moving the secularization debate forward. The proximate motivation of my research is to allow the just mentioned conversation to improve by elucidating the social theory operative in Taylor's account and make it accessible to the academia, something that has not been done before. It is not that Taylor has proposed a social theory of the kind, but that I have elaborated one on the basis of his meta-narrative, his sources, and others. Although the result is an interpretation of my own, I have taken care of drawing from Taylor's sources both sociological and philosophical. In particular, I have tried to make the most of his philosophical views on the methodology of the social sciences and on the human person as both a self-interpreting and ethically bound being. However, Taylor's scholarship is very well respected; I am also aware of the many criticisms *A Secular Age* and other works by Taylor have provoked. In this book, I will only take into account those that directly affect the interpretation I develop.

My thesis is that it is possible to interpret a consistent Taylorean "social theory" that explains Western secularization. The meaning of this concept goes beyond the kind of theoretical thinking that, in sociology, guides empirical research, usually validated through statistical methods, and constitutes the framework of its interpretation. It refers to an understanding of the social processes and social agents involved in secularization on the basis of Taylor's philosophical views. Speaking of Taylorean social theory does not refer to a theory that is, in a subsequent stage, applied to the study of a given social fact, but to a set of concepts, guidelines, and criteria which allow a hermeneutic understanding of such a fact in a very particularized manner, which pays particular attention to the meanings that social facts always carry, as well as to the self-understandings shared by social agents with their society at large and to those under which the social scientist abides.

Particularly important, in this context, is Taylor's position on the problem of human agency in relation to social structures and his affirmation of the inextricable linkage between the social and cultural realms. In this light, secularization in the West is better understood as religious change due to social movement dynamics, a kind of change only made possible by the appearance of a thoroughly immanent view on human flourishing which was made available to all. This change has relocated the place of religion in society and in individual experience, provoking the decline of some religious forms and the appearance of new ones, a process which is not linear but zigzag-shaped, the future of which can only be predicted under strict conditions.

As developed in this book, my interpretation of Taylor's meta-narrative in terms of social theory provides an analytical framework to the study of Western secularization, which is a macro-social process. I believe, however, that it offers the promise of being applicable to a wider number of social phenomena, including micro-social analysis, in Western and non-Western contexts.

The methodology I have used is that of textual analysis of three kinds of sources: first, the most important works by sociologists on secularization in the West; second, all the publications by Taylor on the same topic, particularly *A Secular Age*, as well as those referred to the social sciences; and, third, I read all Taylor's important sociological sources, both classical and contemporary.

In the course of this research, I had to face a number of difficulties. With the passing of time, it became clear to me that the hypothesis with which I started was very much in need of change. Reformulating the hypothesis was just a natural thing to happen, since a deeper assessment of Taylor's philosophical views and of the social theory elements of his meta-narrative of secularization allowed me to be more precise about what he was bringing to the debate and how his views would compare with those of "orthodox" and "counter-orthodox" theorists. Other difficulties were the complexity and nuances in Taylor's arguments, the variety of topics covered, and the length of his meta-narrative. As a consequence of this, I was required to carefully distinguish and follow the narrative's intertwined stories in order to avoid misrepresentation of Taylor's thought. This allowed me, I think, to give an interpretation of "Taylorean social theory" that profits from his philosophical and sociological sources. In this last task, I also found great help from the works by Margaret Archer, a British sociologist, particularly those in which she theoretically studies the relationship between human agency and social structures.

This book is mainly aimed at philosophers and social scientists—particularly sociologists—as well as anyone interested in secularization in the West. It has three parts. The first one, called "Meta-Narrative," contains a literature review of theories of secularization, as well as a balance of the debate on the topic (Chap. 1). It also gives an account of Taylor's meta-narrative in which, along with the representation of the different stories he offers, particular topics that are important to the secularization debate are more closely studied (Chaps. 2 and 3). While providing a necessary context for the book, they are mostly descriptive. Those already familiar with the secularization debate may want to skip the first chapter, while those conversant about *A Secular Age* and other related works by Taylor may want to do the same with the following two.

The second part, "Sources," is composed by the study of aspects of Taylor's philosophical thinking that are pertinent to my interpretation, specifically his views on the human person, knowledge, and the methodology of the social sciences. Besides, this part also analyzes the relationship between Taylor's meta-narrative and those by classical sociologists: Weber, Durkheim, and Marx (Chap. 4). Lastly, I carry out an overview of Taylor's contemporary sociological sources by revisiting the topics of his meta-narrative in the same order in which I had explained them before (Chap. 5). All this provided me with materials for elaborating a Taylorean social theory.

The third part, "Taylorean Social Theory," locates it in the landscape of social theory by analyzing how it fares in regard to the problem of human agency and structure, the link between the social and cultural realms, its view of social change and social stability, its understanding of the relationship between sociology and history, and its use of qualitative and quantitative methods. After doing this, I explain what Taylorean social theory looks like and recast Taylor's meta-narrative in such theoretical framework (Chap. 6). The last section in this part (Chap. 7) consists of the comparison between Taylorean social theory and the "orthodox" and "counter-orthodox" models, as well as of a critical assessment of the former, which does not pretend to be exhaustive.

Chapter 8 summarizes my findings and what is new and important in them, as well as gives information on where additional scholarship might go.

Vancouver, BC, Canada   Germán McKenzie

Acknowledgments

This research is also the result of the help I received from many people. In the first place, I owe thanks to Dr. Pedro Morandé, professor emeritus at the Pontifical Catholic University of Chile and former dean of the School of Sociology there, for introducing me to the thought of Charles Taylor. It is because of him that I chose this research topic, and it is his testimony as a sociologist and intellectual that has inspired me.

This being a book based on my doctoral dissertation, it is just natural to express my deep gratitude to Dr. William D. Dinges, my academic advisor, for all his patient and valuable guidance during the research and writing processes, and to my readers, Drs. William A. Barbieri and Enrique Pumar. Through all their comments and suggestions on my drafts, I have learned a lot about different dimensions of scholarly work.

Thanks to Drs. Charles Taylor and Rodney Stark, for responding to some questions that were key to my research.

I would not have been able to complete this endeavor without the support of the Hubbard Scholarship I was granted by the School of Theology and Religious Studies at the Catholic University of America (CUA). I want to express my gratitude to all those anonymous supporters, in my school and abroad, who made this possible, and particularly to Dr. Charles Jones for his guidance in this regard.

The Canadian Corporation for the Study of Religion (CCSR) also awarded me a travel scholarship that allowed conducting research at McGill University's libraries in Montreal on two occasions. In this way, I had access to materials in French I would not be able to obtain otherwise. I would like to thank all those in the CCSR who helped me and especially to its president, Dr. Marc Dumas.

I would also like to thank several people with whom I spoke about different aspects of my research and who offered me their insight and support: Dr. Paul Sullins, from the Sociology Department at CUA; Dr. George F. McLean, president of the Council for Research in Values and Philosophy at CUA; Dr. Ruth Abbey, professor at Notre Dame University; Dr. Chris Smith, director of the Center for the Study of Religion and Society at Notre Dame University; Dr. Lluis Oviedo, from the Pontifical Antonianum University; and Dr. Nathan Gibbard, from McGill University.

Constructive insights from the editor of Springer's Sophia Studies in Cross-cultural Philosophy of Tradition and Cultures, and from two anonymous reviewers, helped to significantly improve some parts of my argument. Thank you very much for your assistance.

James Carnegie was a great help with the editing of the manuscript in its early stages. Anita van der Linden-Rachmat and Prasad Gurunadham, from Springer, were always there to guide me, kindly and smoothly, in the publishing process. Thank you for all your good work.

Last but not least, my gratitude goes to my wife, Giuliana, for all her love, patience, and support.

Contents

Part I
Meta-Narrative

No real sense of overall argument

Chapter 1
The Contemporary Landscape of Theories of Secularization

Abstract The contemporary debate over secularization for the most part belongs to sociology of religion. Among classical sociologists, Western secularization has been generally interpreted as a process of decline of the relevance and influence of religion (Comte), of its demise as an illusion oppressive of the proletariat (Marx), of its transformation into a "religion of man" (Durkheim), or of relocation into a narrower sphere due to rationalization (Weber). At the present, it is possible to formulate an ideal type of three groups of theories involved in the conversation. The orthodox model affirms the project of modernity unavoidably erodes religion and marginalizes it, particularly because science and pluralism discredit religious worldviews. On an opposite end, the rational choice model sees secularization as fostering religious vitality due to the establishment of a "free religious market" in which religious organizations compete with each other. The debate between these positions has been strong and has led to an excessive focus on the relationship between religious freedom and religious vitality. The third group takes a different approach by criticizing the first one without espousing the thesis of the second. Although scholars in this group have different views, they all share an understanding of secularization as meaning religious change, without necessarily entailing decline nor revitalization. It is among the latter that we find Charles Taylor's meta-narrative of Western secularization. An important feature of his approach is that it constitutes the application of his philosophical ideas on the human person and on the method of the social sciences.

Keywords Secularization • Secular • Theories of secularization • Sociology • Sociology of religion • Religious decline • Disenchantment • Re-enchantment • Religious vitality • Rational choice theory

The debate over secularization has been an intense and variegated one. The question about the changes that modernity has caused in religion in the West (which still occur in other regions around the globe that are in the process of modernizing) not only has found different answers but, as the conversation evolved, the very nature of the problem has been better defined. This process has triggered a quest for further precision of several notions, among them those of religion and the secular, and of the boundary between them. It has also fostered the exploration of several new

© Springer International Publishing AG 2017
Germán McKenzie, *Interpreting Charles Taylor's Social Theory on Religion and Secularization*, Sophia Studies in Cross-cultural Philosophy of Traditions and Cultures 20, DOI 10.1007/978-3-319-47700-8_1

concepts such as "church-religion" or "official religion," on one hand, in contrast with popular, "diffuse" or "invisible religion," on the other, as well as of the consequences of differentiation, rationalization, privatization and pluralism on religion. Besides, the debate over secularization has entailed revisiting our knowledge of the history of religion in the Western hemisphere and asking about the quality of the empirical data for our analyses.

A number of theories have been proposed that intend to explain the above-mentioned changes at the societal, institutional and personal levels. The present chapter aims at briefly presenting the most relevant information in regard to the *statu questionis* of the debate and to situate Charles Taylor's account of secularization in such a context.

1.1   Secularization in Classical Sociology

In a sense, the notion of secularization has been implicitly present since the very beginnings of sociology. As David Martin has put it,

> Sociology and modernity were born together and so the focus of sociology was on what happened to religion under conditions of modernity and accelerating change. Basically, it characterized modernity as a scenario in which mankind shifted from the religious mode to the secular. Secularization was made part of a powerful social and historical narrative of what had once been and now was ceasing to be. (Martin 2005: 18)

(a) Auguste Comte, who coined the term "sociology" as referring to a particular science, expected the decline of "theological" religion and proposed *la religion de l'Humanité* (the religion of mankind). This is significant for the establishment of the narrative on secularization in sociology because in his view what is implied is the restriction of the scope of religion to fit within the limits of Positivism.

For Comte, the evolutionary process mankind undergoes takes us from the Theological Stage, to a Metaphysical one and, lastly, to the Positive Stage. This progression is defined by Comte by taking into account the kind of knowledge proper to each period, as well as the human faculties predominant in them. The Theological Stage is characterized by explaining things by attributing human qualities to them through three sub-stages: fetishism, polytheism and monotheism. Feeling and imagination are said to be dominant here. In the following Metaphysical Stage, gods are replaced by abstract ontological entities, which Comte sees as personified abstractions. Reason becomes dominant and the great medieval theological syntheses appear. Lastly, in the Positive or Scientific Stage, Reason and observation of facts come together to allow the rational study of things in order to look for the laws that govern them. Positive science reduces its focus to what is observable and promises to be useful, and knowledge is not absolute but dependent upon our own capacity and circumstances (Comte 1903: 1–79).[1] As a result, any religious view related to the supernatural is destined to be superseded by the Positive Order.

This process, which Comte develops mostly in debate with French Catholicism, gradually and relentlessly takes humanity to a greater understanding of the world, beginning with the earth—through mathematics and physics—and passing into the study of man—which is done through biology, sociology and morals. These two last disciplines were included in a broader conceptualized Sociology that aimed at the study of man, particularly his social and moral laws (Comte 1903: xvi). Sociology, in this sense, "contemplates each [social] phenomenon in its harmony with coexisting phenomena, and in its connection with the forgoing and the following state of human development." Going beyond the cognitive into the realm of the prescriptive, and "favoring the social sentiment in the highest degree, this science fulfills the famous suggestion of Pascal, by representing the whole human race, past, present, and future, as constituting a vast and eternal social unit, whose different organs concur, in theory various modes and degrees, in the evolution of humanity" (Comte 1975: 239).[2]

In Comte's view, sociology, as the queen of sciences, represents the furthest outreach of positive science to understand the world of man and nature. Even more, positive science would become into the dogma of Comte's "religion of mankind," which in turn would ask for a moral system and worship, and even the establishment of a Positive Church with its hierarchy, teachings and catechisms (Comte 1891), sacraments, liturgical calendar, devotions and ethical demands, as well as accomplishing the role of counterbalancing the role of the state (Wernick 2001: 1–21). Religion here is defined in thoroughly immanent terms as "that state of complete harmony peculiar to human life, in its collective as well as in its individual form, when all the parts of life are ordered in their natural relations to each other" (Comte 1975: 393).[3]

(b) The following generation of scholars, that of the "founding fathers" of sociology, would commit to a more scientific approach to the study of society. They would also find religion declining due to modernity. Max Weber does not use the word "secularization" very often, but he refers to the process with the terms intellectualization, rationalization and disenchantment (Hughey 1979).[4]

In a general way, Weber refers to secularization when he describes the consequence of the process of rationalization in religion. He sees the most elementary religious behaviors as "this-worldly" oriented, seeking to produce results for the present benefit of those who perform them (Weber 1993: 1–2). There are no secular/profane distinctions here. However, in time, taboo prohibitions associated with such

---

[1] This work was first published in 1844.

[2] The text is from Book VI, Chapter 3 of the *Course of Positive Philosophy*.

[3] The quote is from Vol. II, Chapter 1 of the *System of Positive Politics*.

[4] Hughey's reading sees Weber as affirming that this process would just be possible within a particular social and cultural context. Consequently, he would not think secularization is an abstract general dynamic in the world, neither evolutionary nor cyclical. One could only identify secularization *post factum*.

behaviors were rationalized in the form of laws which, in the end gave place to the rise of a religious ethics (Weber 1993: 32–45). This was coupled with the development of ethical absolutism (Weber 1958: 119)[5] and an ethics of universal brotherhood (Weber 1993: 210–14). As a result, a state of tension between religion and the world was set up, which became ever higher when the realm of the worldly was understood as having rules of its own. This notwithstanding, religious institutions could not avoid compromising in some ways to worldly values if they wanted to survive as such due to economic, social, political and cultural factors. This entailed a process of secularization, which is still present today. One of the fruits of this process is the distinction between "other-worldly" oriented religiosity—mystic or ascetic—and the secularized ascetic and "inner-worldly" oriented religions (Weber 1993: 324–26).

Rationalization, for Weber, seems to be unavoidably linked with secularization also at the societal level. "The tension between religion and intellectual knowledge definitely comes to the fore wherever rational, empirical knowledge has consistently worked through to the disenchantment of the world and its transformation into a causal mechanism" (Weber 1958: 350).[6] This is also implied in the process by which each realm of society is understood and organized into systems, each based on its own immanent laws. The greater the internal secularization of these realms, the higher its tension with religion. The nature of such tension also depends on the particular characteristics of each religious tradition (Weber 1964: 227).

Weber thought there was a process of "intellectualization," as described above, happening in the West. It came to fruition in modern science, by which one who wants to know the general conditions under which one lives could do so at any time. "This means that there are no mysterious incalculable forces that come into play, but rather that one can, in principle, master all things by calculation. This means that the world is disenchanted" (Weber 1958: 139).[7] In this light, although as a latent process, instrumental rationality and technology do the service and, in an unintended manner, erode religion. An illustration of this is Puritanism and its role in the rise of Capitalism. The fact that motivation by religious ethics disappeared in time proves, for Weber, "the steady progress of the characteristic process of 'secularization,' to which in modern times all phenomena that originated in religious conceptions succumb" (Weber 1958: 307).[8]

However, religious reactions to the disenchantment of the world also occur, particularly in religious traditions that point to redemption. "Religion claims to offer an ultimate stand toward the world by virtue of a direct grasp of the world's 'meaning.' It does not claim to offer intellectual knowledge concerning what is or what should be" (Weber 1958: 352).[9] The basis for his view is charisma or illumination. This fact is coupled with the inability of self-sufficient intellect to deal with the problem of

---

[5] The reference is to *Science as Vocation*.

[6] The quote is from *Religious Rejection of the World and their Directions*.

[7] The quote is from *Science as Vocation*.

[8] The quote is from *The Protestant Sects and the Spirit of Capitalism*.

[9] The quote is from *Religious Rejection of the World and their Directions*.

unjust suffering and the uneven distribution of personal happiness, for which redemptive religion still has at least an "other-worldly" solution to offer. Religious reaction confines itself to what is essentially religious and "becomes more alienated from all structured forms of life" (Weber 1958: 357). The more a religious tradition rationalizes its thinking about the world's 'meaning,' and the more the world's external organization is rationally organized, the stronger the bend to the religious "other-worldly" grows. "Every increase of rationalism in empirical science increasingly pushes religion from the rational into the irrational realm; but only today does religion become *the* irrational or anti-rational supra-human power" (Weber 1958: 351).[10]

(c) Emile Durkheim sees secularization occurring as a wide historical decline and, since the last stage of the Medieval Era, as happening very rapidly in the West. In the first case, he affirms that religion embraces smaller and smaller portions of social life.

> Originally, it extends to everything; everything social was religious—the two words were synonymous. Then gradually political, economic and scientific functions broke free from the religious function, becoming separate entities and taking on more and more a markedly temporal character. (Durkheim 1984: 119: Durkheim 1965: 132)

This process starts with totemism and carries on into polytheism and monotheism, particularly with the Christian distinction between natural and supernatural, which allowed the emergence of science, and with the downplaying of ritual life, while stressing ethics (Pickering 1975).[11] As a consequence, God has progressively withdrawn, his influence "becoming more general and indeterminate, [which] leaves freer rein for human forces" (Durkheim 1984: 119). In the end, this entails a gradual loss of social control on the part of traditional religions and also a decline of the use of religious symbolism in social life.

Second, in regard to the West, Durkheim claims there has been an acceleration of secularization since the Renaissance and the Reformation. Among the reasons he gives for this one finds the loss of the temporal power of Christianity, particularly the Catholic Church, expressed in the separation between church and state; the fact that religion has become the object of scientific study itself; the inability of Christianity to enforce rules regarding sacrilege and, generally speaking, to control the lives of individuals; and the fact that in the matters of truth, science is to be followed instead of religion (Pickering 1984: 447–51). From all these causes, the last one is certainly the most decisive for religious decline. This notwithstanding, science will not affect the practical (ritual) aspect of religion but just the cognitive one:

> From now on, the faith no longer exercises the same hegemony as formerly over the system of ideas that we may continue to call religion. A rival power rises up before it which, being born of it, ever after submits it to its criticism and control. And everything makes us foresee that this control will constantly become more extended and efficient, while no limit can be assigned to its future influence. (Durkheim 1915: 431)

---

[10] The quote is from *Religious Rejection of the World and their Directions*.

[11] The reference is to Chapter 1 of Durkheim's *Moral Education*.

Given that in Durkheim's view religious representations, in the end, are expressions of society, it is not possible for religion to disappear. Social changes would always entail religious changes. The decline of some religious forms would always give place to new ones. As a result, Durkheim sees the "religion of the future" as one that would be basically rational, welcoming of freedom of thought, promoting worship in whatever ways the individual may feel fit, and *laique* in appearance. This last point means that the "religion of the future" would express the unity of society, its most sacred values; hold periodical ritual meetings, refer to "objective" knowledge of society and have social justice as a key concern (Pickering 1984: 476–85).

In this new religion, sociology would provide a reasonable account of religion, turning itself into scientific "new theology" (Pickering 1984: 476–85, 463–64). From this cognitive standpoint, a new ethics would appear that would help to cure what Durkheim sees as a great peril of his time: *moral anomie* (as a result of secularization as explained above). Egoism, incarnated as a kind of anti-social individualism, would become the antithesis of ethics (Pickering 1975, 60–61).[12] In this context, old religious form would still play a limited role in providing practices, symbols and language for ritual celebrations by the community. This new religion, which is a result of a process of increasing individualism, could be called the "cult of man":

> Since human personality is the only thing that appeals unanimously to all hearts, since its enhancement is the only aim that can be collectively pursued, it inevitably acquires exceptional value in the eyes of all. It thus rises far above all human aims, assuming a religious nature. This cult of man is something, accordingly, very different from the egoistic individualism above referred to, which leads to suicide. Far from detaching individuals from society and from every aim beyond themselves, it unites them in one thought, makes them servants of one work. (Durkheim 1951: 336)

It is no surprise, then, that Durkheim actively embraced the implementation of a free, secular school system, which would replace religious topics with others drawn from his sociological insights aimed at fostering secular moral education during the Third French Republic (Pickering 1984: 70–71).

(d) In a similarly active way, Karl Marx promoted the laicization of the state and the eradication of religion, which he saw as an alienating "ideology" that worked to legitimate the exploitation of the proletariat by the owners of the means of production (Dobbelaere 2002: 19–20). At the very basis of this view, one finds a thoroughly materialistic understanding of reality, which in turn is expressed in two branches: dialectical and historical. According to this materialistic account, economics determines human behavior and human history is the story of class struggle, passing ineluctably through the stages of tribal, feudal and capitalist modes of production, which define a particular set of social structures.

Marx understood his account of society as being as objective, predictive and definitive as that of the natural sciences. His understanding of religion (Christianity for the most part) is closely linked with his view of alienation, a concept that points out the fact that men lose a true self-understanding through religion. In this, Marx

---

[12] The reference is to Durkheim's *Individualism and the Intellectuals*.

follows and goes beyond Ludwig Feuerbach's insights: "His work [Feuerbach's] consists in the dissolution of the religious world into its secular basis" (Institute of Marxism-Leninism of the C.C, C.P.S.U 1957: 70)[13] by affirming that the divine is just a projection of human characteristics onto an allegedly supernatural being (Institute of Marxism-Leninism of the C.C, C.P.S.U 1957: 41–42).[14] However, Marx also affirms that religious essence does not just come from the human essence but from society. The human essence does not exist as such but "in its reality it is the ensemble of the social relations," (Institute of Marxism-Leninism of the C.C, C.P.S.U 1957: 71)[15] and, accordingly, "the 'religious sentiment' is itself a social product" (Institute of Marxism-Leninism of the C.C, C.P.S.U 1957: 72, 134–36).[16] In consequence, at the basis of religious alienation, Marx finds economic alienation, which happens when men do not see the fruits of their labor as a self-expression but as a commodity to be sold. And this is what proletariats do in regard to the rich proprietors of the means of production.

In this view, then, religion is an illusion. "The abolition of religion as the *illusory* happiness of the people is required for their *real* happiness. The demand to give up the illusions about its condition is the *demand to give up a condition which needs illusions*. The criticism of religion is therefore *in embryo the criticism of the vale of woe*, the *halo* of which religion is" (Institute of Marxism-Leninism of the C.C, C.P.S.U 1957: 42).[17] This abolition is not just the result of a well-defined program carried out by Communists, but it is already inscribed in the course of human history. As a consequence, in Marx's perspective, secularization will necessarily occur at all levels of society. Disestablishment of religion is a must, since "the state is not to be constituted from religion but from the reason of freedom," (Institute of Marxism-Leninism of the C.C, C.P.S.U 1957: 38)[18] which religion cannot provide.

At the organizational level, a strong action against religion should be taken in order to show its alienating nature as well as the ways in which it serves the interests of the rich in keeping the capitalist *statu quo*. However, this planned action should not concentrate in the prohibition or persecution of religion, which would only reinforce religious sentiments. In contrast, such action should focus on changing the social conditions in Capitalism, which give rise to religion, and on showing how the science of society (Marxism) proves religion to be wrong: "The religious reflex of the real world can, in any case, only then finally vanish, when the practical relations of every-day life offer to man none but perfectly intelligible and reasonable rela-

---

[13] The quote is from the Thesis IV of Marx's *Thesis on Feuerbach*.

[14] The reference is to Marx's *Contribution to the Critique of Hegel's Philosophy of Right*.

[15] The quote is from the Thesis VI of Marx's *Thesis on Feuerbach*.

[16] The quote is from the Thesis VII of Marx's *Thesis on Feuerbach*; the reference is to the Book 1 of *The Capital*.

[17] The quote is from the Introduction of Marx's *Contribution to the Critique of Hegel's Philosophy of Right*.

[18] The quote is from Marx's *The Leading Article of No. 179 of Kölnische Zeitung*.

tions with regard to his fellow men and to nature" (Institute of Marxism-Leninism of the C.C, C.P.S.U 1957: 135).[19]

After this "classical stage" of the theories of secularization, a new kind of socio-logical studies came to life around 1930 through what has been called *sociologie religieuse*, which was mostly lead by Gabriel LeBras and other French scholars interested in empirical data on religious beliefs, practices, attitudes and ethos. Based on their European studies, some of these authors started to speak of "dechristianiza-tion" (Dobbelaere 1987: 110) Lastly, we arrive at the current stage of the debate, which finds its remote roots in the post-WWII era, but which formally started in the 1960s.

1.2   The Contemporary Debate on Secularization

Sociological studies on secularization started to be carried out mainly by Europeans and some Americans in a way in which secularization was seen as the decline not only of the social influence of religion but of religion itself. This became something of a dogma. Authors like Brian Wilson, Peter Berger and Karel Dobbelaere should be mentioned as conspicuous proponents of this view by that time (Swatos and Christiano 2000: 2–3). However, cautionary words on the ambiguity of the term "secularization" were also given by David Martin (1965) and Larry Shiner (1967) by then. In the end, such a term proved to be misleading and "charged" with unwanted values (Swatos and Christiano 2000: 3–6), and the course of the debate perforce included the development of conceptual precisions. More interestingly, a rival theory appeared—championed by American scholars Rodney Stark, William Sims Bainbridge and Robert Finke—that strongly criticized the prevalent view on secularization and proposed an almost opposite interpretation: secularization would not be a long-term process of religious decline but a continuous and self-limiting one in a situation of ongoing religious vitality and transformation. As a conse-quence, the sociological debate over secularization gained in intensity and complexity.

In this light, one could say that contemporary theories of secularization form a continuum between two poles: on the one hand, the "received," "standard" or "orthodox" paradigm (Tschannen 1991; Wallis and Bruce 1992; Bruce 2002: 1–44) which affirms that modernity erodes religion and leads to its decline, marginaliza-tion and social irrelevance; on the other, is what I would call the "counter-orthodox" paradigm, which says that modernity leads to the revitalization of religion by fostering religious competition, and sees secularization as a self-limiting process. However, abandoning the idea of a continuum, I prefer to speak of the rest of the secularization theories as "revisionist," since they criticize and reformulate the "orthodox" model without necessarily accepting the "counter-orthodox" approach.

---

[19] The quote is from the Book 1 of Marx's *The Capital*.

In what follows, I will present the thought of the most important representatives of each of these three groupings.

1.2.1   The Orthodox Paradigm: "Modernization Entails Religious Decline"

This paradigm affirms, in essence, that the social changes that came about in the West with modernity corrode religious beliefs, religious practices, as well as religious organizations and, overall, the social functions religion achieves. Even when some of the scholars who maintain this view recognize in theory that secularization may not be an irreversible process, they affirm that such a regression is very unlikely to occur. Because of the geographical area where it originated, this paradigm deals mainly with Christianity. This section will present the core of the "orthodox model" as it has been presented by sociologist Steve Bruce. It will also mention the particular ways other theorists have assumed it, among them Peter Berger in his early writings, Bryan R. Wilson and Karel Dobbelaere.[20]

British scholar Steve Bruce gives a good summary of this model, which he still defends at present, in his work *God is Dead. Secularization in the West.*[21] For him, secularization is a long-term process of decline of religion, specifically in its social power, popularity and prestige, as well as in its beliefs and social practices (Bruce 2002: 3). This is a consequence of the elements that constitute modernity (Bruce 2002: 2). The changes modernization brings about cause religion to mutate in such a way that it loses significance. Moreover, this decline itself carries with it a decline in the plausibility of religious beliefs. "Changes at the structural and cultural level bring about changes in religious vitality that we see in the declining proportion of people who hold conventional religious beliefs. The bottom line is this: individualism, diversity and egalitarianism in the context of liberal democracy undermine the authority of religious beliefs" (Bruce 2002: 30).

What kinds of changes were these? Bruce links all of them with the apparition of Protestantism in a way that resembles Weber. Through this phenomenon, three trends came to life. (1) At the rational level, monotheistic faith was replaced by rationality, which turned into science and technology. This does not mean that reason and religion were mutually exclusive, but that naturalistic ways of thinking about the world prevailed. (2) At the social and economic levels, Protestant ethics encouraged industrial capitalism and economic growth. These factors in turn gave rise to "structural differentiation" (in the sense of the breaking of social life into different and autonomous realms governed by instrumental reason) and "social differentiation" (meaning that the different social classes and the more fluid social mobility brought about the fragmentation of communal conceptions of the moral

---

[20] See also Yamane 1997.

[21] For a similar account see Wallis and Bruce 1992.

and supernatural orders). In this way, religious pluralism and egalitarianism appeared, leading to relativism and privatization of faith. (3) At the level of religious organizations, the trend went from Protestant individualism to a propensity to schism, leading to the phenomena of sects and stressing the fact of voluntary rather than ascribed participation (Bruce 2002: 1–30). All the mentioned factors concur as mediate or immediate causes for secularization. However, Bruce points out that each of them is not sufficient per se but requires the action of the others, and that they are not necessarily enduring, since once their consequences come to life, they continue on their own rather than remaining dependant on what originated them (Bruce 2002: 5).

In Bruce's view, the most powerful secularizing factors are religious pluralism, privatization and relativism, which he sees closely linked together. In this view he is indebted to Peter Berger's and Thomas Luckmann's book *The Social Construction of Reality* (1966). He thinks that our ideas are made more or less persuasive due to the action of social interests and social relationships. "It is a mistake to assume that ideas and observations are of themselves persuasive or that, while we need to explain why people hold some false beliefs, somehow the 'truth' stands in no need of explanation" (Bruce 2002: 26). As a consequence, the breaking down—by religious pluralism—of a common religious view shared by the whole of society and of the monopoly of religious institutions which embodied it, had a strong impact on the way we as individuals are concerned with "what standing and what reach we accord to our own ideas and how we view those who disagree with us" (Bruce 2002: 29). We are faced with a world, which flies away from authoritative assertions, in which a number of incompatible religious beliefs share the stage. Even when we try to live our own religious commitments privately (privatization), this does not preclude the appearance of doubts about our own beliefs' soundness and about their universal validity. This leads to relativism as a cognitive style since we assume that what is true for us in religious matters may not be true for everybody else, and, as a consequence, our religious commitment is weakened (Bruce 2002: 29, 140–150).

Even when Bruce sees counter-tendencies as cultural defense or cultural transition, the consequences of secularization are unavoidable. "The removal of support at the level of social structure has a corresponding effect on the social psychology of belief. The dogmatic certainties of the church and sect are replaced by the weak affirmations of the denomination and the cult" (Bruce 2002: 36).

Bruce is the author who has more thoroughly thought about the aspects implied in the orthodox paradigm of secularization because he has espoused it since the 1980s, and because of his intense involvement in the debate. He sees this paradigm much more like a set of clusters that work well together rather than a unified theory. He also takes pains in explaining what this paradigm does not affirm and clarifies some misunderstandings. Secularization is neither universal nor inevitable, nor does it follow an evolutionary path that may be liberating, nor is its methodology weak, nor must the process have an even trajectory, nor is the endpoint atheism (Bruce 2002: 37–44). However, he does think that the secularization process, once initiated, is irreversible, and leads to religious marginalization: "As I expect that ideologies that lose relevance will also lose plausibility, I see the popularity of religious beliefs as a useful index of secularization. I expect the proportion of people who are largely indifferent to religious ideas to increase and the seriously religious to become a minority" (Bruce 2002: 43).

Peter Berger and Bryan Wilson, each in his own way, helped to provide a basis for the above-described narrative of secularization. Berger's classic work *The Sacred Canopy* (1967) gave an articulated interpretation of the way human beings relate to each other in society. Berger consciously draws from the classics of sociology. His anthropological philosophy comes from Marx; his views on how the human person relates to society, from Weber and Durkheim. He says that society is a product of man, and conversely man is a product of society, establishing a dialectical relationship between both poles. It is through the processes of externalization, "objectivation," and internalization that such dialectic is carried on. In this perspective, religion is the social enterprise through which a "sacred cosmos" is established. The sacred realm is viewed as being in continuous tension with one of "chaos." It is a socially constructed view, which legitimates a given social order and gives a *nomos* to every subject. This legitimating realm has an objective social counterpart, which keeps it alive, called "structures of plausibility," for example, processes of socialization, "churches," etc.

Religion implies the furthest reach of man's self-externalization. Nonetheless, it is just a stage in the process through which modern man, through modern science and technology, conceives the entire universe as being humanly significant. "By secularization is meant the process by which sectors of society and culture are removed from the domination of religious institutions and symbols" (Berger 1967: 107). For Berger, the social action of Communism, nationalisms, and the liberal political order, as well as the spread of industrial capitalism, undermined the objective structures of plausibility for a religious *nomos*, while pluralism eroded the objective legitimation of the old religiously-inspired order. Uncertainty about belief appears, and with it, its reduction to opinions, feelings or "religious preferences." Pluralism, in Berger's view, produces secularization.

Another British thinker, Bryan R. Wilson, discusses secularization in the United States and England in his book *Religion in a Secular Society* (1966). For him also, religion is only understandable as a social product (Wilson 1966: 13). In this light, religion as a way of thinking, as performing practices, as an organization, and as a factor of societal integration is generally in decline in Western societies. Although each case is different, the fact of secularization remains the same: religion is now largely irrelevant in those societies and its role in social change is epiphenomenal (Wilson 1966: 9–20). In the case of England, secularization is expressed in the abandonment of the Christian churches on the part of people, as well as in religious compartmentalization and marginalization. In contrast, in the United States, and in spite of the high levels of religious attendance and the organizational strength of the churches, secularization has occurred since the very beginning of the nation through a process through which the churches were absorbed by society and transformed into a reflection of the American way of life (Wilson 1966: 109–49).

In spite of some reactions by the Christian churches, in Wilson's view, they have failed, and he sees religion surviving in the West in the persistence of the Christian sects, which he analyses extensively (Wilson 1966: 207–49). He concludes that even when the completely secularized society has not existed, the contemporary modern societies seem to need very little religion.

In order to explain the causes of secularization, Wilson underscores two factors that in his view are at the core of the process of secularization in the West: the passing from community (*Gemeinschaft*) to society (*Gesellschaft*), and the appearance of scientific rationality. He develops these themes at large in an article published in 1976 and titled "Aspects of Secularization in the West" (Wilson 1976)

Belgian scholar Karel Dobbelaere has kept a consistent "orthodox" position in the secularization debate, focusing on the development of religion in Europe and also comparing his findings with those of the United States. His book *Secularization: An Analysis at Three Levels* contains a 2002 update of an overview of secularization he published in 1981. He thinks it is better to speak about secularization as a process that happens at three levels: societal, organizational and individual. This is because of the complexity of the phenomenon and the ambivalence of the term "secularization." An appropriate study of the process would not only focus on the particular development of each of these levels, but also on their inter-relatedness.

Societal secularization not only refers to the disestablishment of religion or "laicization," but more importantly to social differentiation into sub-systems, each of them autonomous and without a "sacred canopy" to give them meaning as a whole (Dobbelaere 2002: 19–21, 45–103).[22] An appropriate understanding of this process has need of a historical base-line that may serve to measure religious decline, as well as a definition of religion. Dobbelaere is aware of the impact a given notion of religion would have on the very understanding of secularization, so he probes both functional and substantive definitions. He finds the former inadequate, among other reasons, because of the fact that any functional alternative becomes "religious" per se, and because the meaning systems man needs in order to live do not need to be religious in themselves. As a consequence, he prefers a substantive and exclusive definition of religion as "a unified system of beliefs and practices relative to a supra-empirical, transcendent reality that unites all those who adhere to it into a single moral community" (Dobbelaere 2002: 52). This notion, which resembles Durkheim's, is substantively different because it does refer to a supernatural reality as conceived by the individual and not to the "sacred" as a reflection of society. However, it does not preclude the possibility of a functional analysis of religion.

Second, organizational secularization refers to religious changes that happen *ad intra* churches and similar religious bodies. It encompasses what has also been called "internal secularization." It includes the impact of rationalization in those bodies, along with the appearance in them of professional specialization, bureaucracy and instrumental rationality. Also to be mentioned here are the decline and emergence of religious communities, organizational changes, as well as changes at

---

[22] In this point he builds on the insights of German sociologist Niklas Luhmann (Dobbelaere 165–66, 189).

the level of beliefs, rituals and morality (Dobbelaere 2002: 21–22, 35–38, 105–35).

Third, individual secularization is about the decline of religious involvement of persons into organized religion. This includes not only participation in religious structures but also lack of integration by the individual with church norms at the level of beliefs, rituals and ethics, as well as the decline of relevance of organized religion in the daily life of people or in the ways in which they deal with their spiritual concerns (Dobbelaere 2002: 17–19, 137–55).

Dobbelaere studies the inter-relations of these three levels of analysis and takes pains to confirm his views with empirical findings. For example, the rise of the so-called New Religious Movements is a reaction coming from the individuals who create organizations against societal secularizing forces; the appearance of religious pluralism through different churches is a consequence of the disestablishment of religion; the adaptation of the churches to the secularized societal environment is a response to societal secularization (Dobbelaere 2002: 117–33). Also, the defensive reactions from churches to societal secularization would show a pattern of relationship between the organizational and societal levels. More important, in his perspective, is the impact of societal secularization at the individual level, which not only undermines one's church commitment but also fosters compartmentalization: the refusal to give religious professionals any control over other spheres of the personal life (family, sexuality, finances, etc). This rejection also means that each individual works on his own *religion á la carte*, which amounts to the transformation of religion into spirituality (Dobbelaere 2002: 189–95).

1.2.2   The Counter-Orthodox Paradigm: "Modernization Entails Religious Vitality; Secularization Is a Self-Limiting Process in Such a Context"

The most prominent exponents of the "counter-orthodox" paradigm are American social scientists Rodney Stark, Roger Finke, William S. Bainbridge, and Lawrence Ianaconne (Swatos and Christiano 2000). They offered a very strong critique of the "inherited model." These scholars made the following points regarding secularization: (a) There is no correlation between the claims of a process of secularization and plain facts. This is true in the United States, where the rates of church membership have doubled, as well as in Europe, because there has not been a demonstrable long-term decline in European religious participation, and the levels of subjective religiousness remain high. (b) There is a sort of "myth" regarding past piety in Europe, the rebuttal of which being the claim that "Christian Europe never existed." (c) There is a strong subjective religiousness even in places where religious participation is very low. (d) Even among scientists, where there is a supposed conflict between religion and science, there has not been decline in belief in the long term. Even in the former Soviet bloc countries, a religious revival is taking place. (e)

Islam and Asian religions are demonstrating an ability to coexist with modernity. In short, these authors regard secularization theories as a product of wishful thinking (Stark and Finke 2000: 57–79).[23]

These authors, however, do more than propose an alternative understanding of secularization. Inspired by the work by American economist Gary Becker, who applied economic analysis to other realms of the social sciences (such as racial discrimination, crime and punishment, law and politics, marriage, fertility, etc.) (Becker 1976), they explore religion in a similar way. They are exponents of what is known as the "rational choice theory" (abbreviated as RCT) or the "market economy" approach to religion. Within this framework, these scholars have even formulated a general theory of religion (Stark and Bainbridge 1987).

According to this perspective, religion is thriving in our times. It is a rational phenomenon since religious choices respond to cost/benefit analysis on the part of individuals. Religion is good for mental/physical health as well as society, and should be taken more seriously by the social sciences (which address just the "human side" of faith). Rational choice scholars also contend that religion is strengthened by religious pluralism and undergoes changes that do not imply its decline (Stark and Finke 2000: 27–41).

RCT theorists developed an understanding of religion and the way it is lived by individual persons, groups, and society as a whole (the "religious economy"). In regard to secularization, an important premise this theory brought to the debate is the assimilation of churches and other religious organizations to the "supply side" of the religious economy, while identifying individual persons with the "demand side." The rational search for "other-worldly rewards" is a constant relative to the supply/demand equation (Stark and Finke 2000: 83–113). If religious decline occurs, it should be credited to organizational or societal roots.

In this light, any process of secularization is seen as a "self-limiting" process, characterized by a cost/benefit calculus. The impact of science challenges religions in a way in which they are forced to purify their own doctrines, rites and mores from all those elements that now can be interpreted in a mere naturalistic way. This is called "internal secularization." In this way, a number of spiritual compensators once offered by religious bodies wane. However, other-worldly supernatural compensators are, perforce, beyond the scope of science (e.g., the afterlife), so they remain as a patrimony of religion and are very much sought after. Other spiritual goods, such as providing meaning to life and suffering, also remain attractive in the realm of religion. In this way, churches that supply them compete more favorably in the religious market than those who have gone a long way in their internal secularization. This situation also triggers intents of renewal within churches in process of self-secularization, which are called "sects" and are aimed at the revival of those churches. It also nurtures the apparition of brand new religious bodies that create innovative religious forms, which are called "cults." In any event, self-secularization puts into work a church to sect/cult dynamic that sets limits to it. This dynamic is an

---

[23] This is a chapter by Stark titled *Secularization R.I.P.*

ongoing one, so secularization is always kept between boundaries, turning it into a self-limiting reality (Stark and Bainbridge 1985: 429–456).[24]

One of the most contrasting arguments in this theory in regard to the "orthodox paradigm" is that religious pluralism is seen as promoting religious competition among religious organizations within the "market." In the end, religious vitality is maintained and even increased, rather than diminished as the "orthodox" paradigm asserts (Stark and Finke 2000: 193–217).

1.2.3 Revisionist Approaches: "Modernity Is About Religious Change, Not Necessarily Decline Nor Revitalization"

As I mentioned before, I think it is better to group the rest of the theories of secularization under the label of "revisionists," since these authors have criticized the "orthodox" model, redefined the problem, and proposed a different alternative, which usually does not coincide with the "counter-orthodox" approach. These scholars, however diverse in their views, all share the conviction that secularization is about religious change. In what follows, I will briefly present the theories by Thomas Luckmann, David Martin, Mark Chaves, Peter Berger in his late work and Jose Casanova.[25]

German scholar Thomas Luckmann offers his own view on secularization in his work *The Invisible Religion*, first published in 1963 and which appeared in English in 1967. He criticizes the confusion between church and religion, especially in the West, a confusion he associates with (a) a too narrow understanding of social institutions, and (b) a positivistic prejudice—where religion is a primitive stage in the evolution of human reason that will be replaced by science. Distancing himself from most of the sociology of religion of his time, Luckmann says that "in the absence of a well-founded theory, secularization is typically regarded as a process of religious pathology to be measured by the shrinking reach of the churches. Since the institutional vacuum is not being filled by a counter-church—which was still envisaged by Comte—one readily concludes that modern society is non religious" (Luckmann 1967: 23). However, Luckmann points out that it is not enough to analyze how church-religion has been pushed away into the periphery of Modern society (as in the case of Europe) nor to ask how church-religion has modernized through a process of self-secularization (as in the case of the United States). The most important question, in his view, is: What in modern society has replaced the role religion once accomplished?

---

[24] This is a chapter titled *Secularization, Revival and Cult Formation*.

[25] Although I believe that the theories presented in this section give an appropriate account of the variety of "revisionist" positions and include those which are relevant for my research, there are other important works I have omitted. Among them Fenn 1978; Luhmann 2013; Smith 2003; Norris and Inglehart 2004.

According to Luckmann, secularization is the process through which religious change occurred due to modernity, one in which the function church-oriented religion played in regard to giving meaning to the lives of individual persons and to the whole social structure is now carried on by a different actor, what he calls "invisible religion." The latter would be characterized first and foremost by its private nature, lived by an autonomous individual who puts together his/her own sacred cosmos using the "old" declining one, as well as other sources. Autonomy, self-expression, self-realization, a mobility ethos understood as the climbing of the social ladder, the liberation of sexuality from social control, and familism become, in Luckmann's view, the most prevalent modern religious themes (Luckmann 1967: 107–117).

In this perspective, the causes of secularization would not simple be industrialization and urbanization per se, nor the appearance of "hostile ideologies and value-systems such as various types of 'faith' in science" (Luckmann 1967: 38). Luckmann sees this as a too immediate causal understanding and a naïve one. In contrast, he asks for a better understanding of industrialization and urbanization as forces that have led to "encompassing changes in the total social structure" (Luckmann 1967: 38). Once this transformation is deeply grasped, the reasons for the declining influence of church-religion in lending meaning to the pattern of individual life would be clarified. This means that the relationship between industrialization and secularization is indirect. "In short, the decrease in traditional church religion may be seen as a consequence of the shrinking relevance of the values, institutionalized in church religion, for the integration and legitimation of everyday life in modern society" (Luckmann 1967: 39). Interestingly, Luckmann finds that Judaism and Christianity were strong forces in promoting religious social specialization, a phenomenon which prepared specialization in general and, paradoxically, the waning of Christianity as "official" church (Luckmann 1967: 72–73, 92–95).

On its part, David Martin's theory affirms that secularization is not a "master-narrative" but a differentiated process occurring in the West and in areas of Western influence (such as South Africa, Australia and New Zealand). This British scholar has developed his views in two works. The first one, a detailed assessment of the process in regard to world-wide Christianity, appeared in 1978 under the title *A General Theory of Secularization* (Martin 1978). This was followed by another one appeared in 2005 and titled *On Secularization: Towards a Revised General Theory* (Martin 2005).

Martin sees secularization as a process comprised of different stories of secularization, depending on the specific nature of the society in which it takes place (and its predominant religion, symbols, narratives, meaning, etc). From the standpoint of theology, he finds that each large process of secularization in the West is the reaction to a corresponding process of Christianization, the missionary drive of which is intrinsic to it as a religious tradition.

Martin's sociological analysis is already found in his detailed study of 1978, which was updated in 2005. For him, religion is "an acceptance of a level of reality beyond the observable world known to science, to which are ascribed meanings and purposes completing and transcending those of the purely human realm" (Martin 1978: 12). Based on this notion—and considering religion as including beliefs, a particular ethos and peculiar institutional arrangements—he focuses on how to understand the diminishing power of religious institutions as sects and churches, and the increasing difficulty in the acceptance of religious beliefs.

Inspired by Talcott Parson's insights, Martin sees secularization as a process of religious decline at a societal level, which is mainly driven by differentiation: "I present the viable core of secularization as the sub-theory of social differentiation. Serious doubts can be raised about the sub-theory of rationalization, and… the sub-theory of privatization" (Martin 2005: 17). In this light, secularization in the West is due to the increasing autonomy of the various spheres of human activity. The geographical context of Martin's analysis compels him to concentrate on Christianity. In his work, Martin makes use of a number of empirical sources to create "historical filters" that serve to direct, deflect or inflect secularization in different ways. The more important of these "filters" are: Protestant Northern Europe, Protestant North America, Latin Europe (Western Europe inasmuch as it expresses a Catholic vitality), and Latin America (Martin 2005: 58–59).[26] In each of these cases, he carries on an analysis based on a number of interpretive keys: the variations between religious monopoly and competitive pluralism; the relationship between churches and political parties; the relationship between religion and voluntary associations; and the dynamics of center and periphery running transversally to the above mentioned elements. Other interpretive concepts are the possible connection between cultural identity and religion, especially in cases of external oppression or significant cultural minorities; the action of industrialization in the erosion of interpersonal bonds and the degree in which individual persons resist this by seeking reintegration through the family and the church; the homogenizing impact of the mass media in society along with its communication of values of comfort and consumerism; and the impact of Calvinist ethics and Enlightenment ideals in culture (Martin 1978: 56–94).

As a consequence of this approach, Martin provides a varied and complex description of religious changes in different geographical areas, explaining why in many cases there is a decline and why, in some others, religion still takes hold or flourishes (Martin 1978: 59).[27] He does not see secularization as a long-term trend, nor as one that inevitably leads to a situation in which religion is irrelevant. Changes are not mechanical and the consequences of the differentiation process in one cultural context could mean very different things for religion. For example, in some areas, religious pluralism would promote religious decline, whereas in others, it would trigger religious revival.

In 1994, American scholar Mark Chaves proposed to redefine secularization. According to Chaves, secularization should not be understood as the decline of

---

[26] In his study of 1978, the patterns of secularization are defined a bit differently due to the different historical contexts and geographical areas analyzed: (a) the American, (b) that of the UK, (c) the French Latin/South American Latin area, (d) the Russian area, (e) the Calvinist, and (f) the Lutheran areas (Martin 1978: 18–27.)

[27] The chart that appears on this page summarizes a substantial part of Martin's findings for each pattern of secularization.

religion, but as the declining scope of religious authority, since religious persistence has challenged what he calls the "classical version" of secularization. His starting point was to reassess that model with an eye toward discerning what is valuable and what must be abandoned (Chaves 1994).

Chaves proposes a different understanding of the role of religion in society by affirming a new view of structural differentiation, one in which existing institutions (such as religious agencies) do not always need to respond to a functional role. In this view, neither religion nor rationality is seen as the "glue" of society, which is no longer understood as a moral community. In contrast, society is seen as an "inter-institutional system" in which no single sector is primary in the sense of taking care of the goals of the whole society, and in which there is a political, conflictual and contingent relationship between institutions. There is not an a priori ranking of some institutions as more primary or dominant than others. As a consequence, sometimes and in some social contexts religion may decline, while at other times and places, it may be strong. There is not a presumed "master trend" for religious decline or strengthening. Significantly, while religion may decline at the societal level, religious belief, sentiments and ethos may be very much alive at the individual level. This is the case in the West. Chaves clearly asserts that "it is no longer possible to truthfully assert that "modernity" is incompatible with religious belief… Rather than inevitably undermining religion, modernity seems quite unthreatening to, and perhaps even promotes, religious ideas, sentiments, and practices among individuals" (Chaves 1994: 753).

Chaves re-conceptualizes the secularization process by shifting its object of analysis. As mentioned above, for him secularization consists on the declining scope of religious authority. Inspired by Weber's commentary, Chaves defines religious authority as "a social structure that attempts to enforce its order and reach its ends by controlling the access of individuals to some desired goods, where the legitimation of that control includes some supernatural component, however weak" (Chaves 1994: 755–56). Secularization as declining religious authority will refer to the declining influence of social structures that receive legitimation from the supernatural. At the level of society, this will be the declining capacity of religious elites to exercise authority over other institutional spheres. At the level of social organization, it will entail the declining ability of religious authorities to control the "organizational resources" within the religious realm. Finally, at the level of the individual, secularization will be seen as the decrease in the level of institutional religious control over individual actions (Chaves 1994: 764–69).

Peter Berger's later works express the change of his position in the debate over secularization. Berger basically says "that the assumption that we live in a secularized world is false" (Berger 1999: 2). That modernization has had secularizing effects is true, but it has also triggered strong movement of counter-secularization. Whereas at the level of organizations some may have lost power and influence, new religious bodies have appeared. Even those religious organizations that have diminished in membership have still played important social and political roles. On its part, individual religiosity, in the way of old and new beliefs, continues to be at work and even to thrive (Berger 1999: 3–4). The redefinition of the role of religion in society has sometimes acquired the shape of religious revolutions, but more often that of the persistence of a given religious sub-culture.

The last in my list of proponents of a "revisionist" account is Spanish scholar Jose Casanova, who does comparative sociology from the standpoint of critical theory. He argues that secularization as differentiation should be kept as the valuable element in the "orthodox" approach. However, he criticizes two other parallel accounts of such phenomenon as being contested by empirical evidence: that of secularization as religious decline and as privatization (Casanova 1994: 25–39). In proposing a plan, he would affirm: "What the sociology of religion needs to do is to substitute for the mythical account of a universal process of secularization comparative sociological analyses of historical processes of secularization, if and when they take place" (Casanova 1994: 17).

Casanova would even say that the process of differentiation should be carefully studied and not be considered as a single and teleological process. He sees that multiple patterns of differentiation have occurred in the modern West, each with diverse manners of establishing the boundaries between the diverse sub-systems, which makes him adhere to the thesis of "multiple modernities" (Casanova 2008: 103–106).

Casanova shows how religious traditions in the West, particularly Catholicism, have been able to relocate themselves, passing from a position of dependence or sponsorship by the state, into a situation in which they are disestablished and focus their ministry on civil society. This he calls "deprivatization" of religion, by which he means the resistance such traditions have shown to becoming enclosed in the private world of individuals and marginal to society. In some cases, Casanova finds that public interventions of religious organizations are possible and (passing from the analytical to the normative) even desirable:

> By crossing boundaries, by raising questions publicly about the autonomous pretensions of the differentiated spheres to function without regard to moral norms or human considerations, public religions may help to mobilize people against such pretensions, they may force or contribute to a public debate about such issues. (Casanova 1994: 43)

There are, however, conditions for religions to carry on this public function: to keep respect for the differentiated structures and to respect the individual freedoms (Casanova 1994: 218–20). Becoming "deprivatized" is a historical option religious organizations could make, deciding either to maintain themselves as private religions of individual salvation or to enter, at least occasionally, into the public space (Casanova 1994: 221). In Casanova's view, the boundaries between the public and the private, which parallel that between the secular and the sacred, are flexible depending on the models of public spaces inspiring particular institutional arrangements. He is very critical of the liberal approach, which tightly divides both realms (Casanova 1994: 41–43, 51–66, 229).

1.3 Balance of the Debate and Important Related Issues

In the light of the previous description of the conversation on secularization that has occurred from the second part of the twentieth century on, it is appropriate to summarize the terms of the debate and note some of the sub-topics that have been part of it.

The proponents of the "orthodox model" maintain that religion has lost its significance at the level of society, organizations and individuals. In regard to the social system, and due to a number of factors pertaining to the advent of modernity (the most important of them being differentiation), governments no longer need religious legitimation; members of society no longer need religious theology/theodicy since they have access to alternative meaning-bearing systems; and religion has become a less plausible explanation of man and the universe. Religion has lost its monopoly on meaning, while non-religious agencies now take care of many activities once performed by religious organizations. Religious pluralism drastically erodes personal religious commitment. In general, the process of religious decay is only temporarily halted when religion is linked with the cultural identity of a threatened society or by large minorities of immigrants.

At the level of religious organizations, some try to adapt to the secularized environment only to sharply decline in the end. Others try to resist, relocating themselves to the periphery of society.

At the individual level, there is decline in church attendance, and the acceptance of religious beliefs and religious authority has been eroded.

In contrast, "counter-orthodox" thinkers see that social differentiation and religious disestablishment at the societal level have triggered a competitive religious market in which religious organizations in lesser tension with the surrounding culture tend to secularize themselves, while sects remain in higher-tension mode. These trends counterbalance the secularizing forces, which are ultimately defeated because they do not provide the individual with ultimate otherworldly rewards. Individual persons are always seeking these "spiritual compensators," which are to be found in already familiar religious traditions, or in new forms of spiritual paths. Religious pluralism thus is enriched by and nurtures individual spiritual quests (Hanson 1997).

Lastly, "revisionist" scholars distance themselves from the "orthodox paradigm" in idiosyncratic ways, without agreeing entirely with the "counter-orthodox." In all cases, they agree on the fact that social differentiation is what has driven the secularization process, but qualify it in different ways.

What has just been described above entails commentary on a number of other topics. The more important of these are:

(a) The need for a clarification of the term "religion," not in the sense of proposing any definitive version of it, but in the sense of providing a "working definition" for the purpose of the analysis of secularization in a specific geographic area. The caveats of functional and substantial definitions have also been debated (e.g. by Dobbelaere and Chaves). Besides, notions of "official" religion (as that which is professed by the professionals of particular religious bodies), in contrast to concepts such as "popular" religion (the one lived by laypeople of the same religious organization) have also helped in understanding processes of decline (if any) in individual beliefs, rituals and ethos.

If we ask about the influence that concepts of religion coined by classical sociology have had on the above-described theories, those by Durkheim (functional) and Weber (substantive) would appear as prominent. Bruce, Wilson and Berger in his early works would allude to a substantive (Weberian) definition when affirming the decline of individual religious allegiance in regard to beliefs, rites and mores. However, they would also make use of a functional concept of religion when they understand it as a mere social construct (with reference to Durkheim and also Marx), radically affected by societal changes and surviving, marginalized in an already secularized world, by performing subsidiary social functions.

On their part, "counter-orthodox" theorists will base their approach on a Weberian understanding inasmuch as their focus is mainly on rational choices by the individual who is looking for salvation, for whom "spiritual compensators" would never stop being attractive.

Among "revisionists," Luckmann appears to be strongly Durkhemian with his notion of "invisible religion," whereas Martin, Chaves and Berger in his most recent works seem to refer to Weber's view of religion in the first place. Lastly, Casanova stresses both the functional and substantive characteristics of religion within secularization.

(b) The understanding of the concept of "secular" or "profane," corresponding to the previous point, and the ways (if any) in which this concept would be in contrast with religion. In this regard, scholars (particularly Casanova) have realized the great ambiguity when it comes to drawing the boundary between these two concepts.[28]

(c) The very content of the concept of "secularization" with its ambiguous meanings, which have been further refined (particularly by Martin and Casanova). A three-leveled analysis—societal, organizational and individual—seems to have contributed to the clarification of the analysis. The specification of the meaning of "religious decline" and "privatization" (particularly by Dobbelaere and Casanova) has also been helpful in understanding the nuances of both "orthodox" and "counter-orthodox" stances in particular.

(d) The debate on Luckmann's notion of "invisible religion," which has been linked with new understandings of individual spirituality, expressed in the "spiritual but not religious" formula, and in the appearance of the so-called New Religious Movements. In a sense, a redefinition of what is meant by "religion" has occurred. In this regard, as Danièle Hervieu-Léger shows, the appearance of a "religious modernity," particularly applied to Western Europe, refers to the paradoxical fact that whereas, on the one hand, the modern has undermined religion, on the other hand it has fostered forms of belief that are subjective, individual and constructed. What characterizes this new phenomenon is the constant flow of self-constructed

---

[28] See, for example, Calhoun et al. (2011). Defining the boundary between secular and profane is even more complicated in non-Western settings. See, for example, Asad (2003).

religious identities, in which the figures of the "pilgrim" and the "convert" are paradigmatic models (Hervieu-Léger 1999).

Marcel Gauchet, on his part, referring to the same geographical area, would see this "religion after religion" (that is, in a secularized world) as motivated by a search for meaning, the beauty and our own self. This is, however, a painful state, in which some relief could be sought either in private religious practices, without any link to religious traditions, or in substitutes for religious experience (Gauchet 1997: 200–207).

(e) The clarification of the particular religious past with which we are comparing things. Historical studies and long-trend statistical analysis have helped to better understand the ways in which religion was experienced from the Middle Ages on, and also along denominational lines within the Christian tradition.

(f) There has been a strong initiative on the part of scholars to substantiate their claims with empirical findings. This has lead to an improvement of the quality of the data on which analyses are based. Particularly intense have been the efforts to statistically measure the ways in which religious pluralism either undermines or fosters religion.

1.4   Where Are We Now and the Taylorean Position

The secularization debate has been intense, varied and complex. It has even been harsh sometimes (Tschannen 1991: 413; Bruce 2002: 1, 39, 45). What is the current state of the question? Christian Smith, while giving an overview of the field of sociology of religion in 2008, said that the debate between "orthodox" and "counterorthodox" had stalled:

> The arguments, which were frequently contentious, mobilized many forms of individual-, congregational-, county- and national-level data to try to determine whether religious pluralism increased or decreased religious adherence, whether religious competition energized or undermined religious mobilization, whether religious beliefs were eroding or maintaining stable levels, and so on. The debate produced a lot of important and valuable research and we are that much the more knowledgeable for it. But, by my reading, that debate has lost most of its energy. (Smith 2008: 1562)

The reason for this entrapment, in Smith's view (2008: 1562), is the appearance of evidence, in an article by Daniel Voas and others (Voas et al. 2002), that questions the relevance of most of the empirical studies on the relationship between religious pluralism and religious involvement.[29]

> The typical study looks at correlations between some measure of total religious participation (e.g., the percentage of people who attend religious services or are church members) and an index of pluralism based on the denominational diversity of these adherents. A negative correlation has been taken to corroborate [orthodox] secularization theory; a positive correlation bolsters the religious economies position. (Voas et al. 2002: 213)

---

[29] They refer to the exhaustive list of research on the topic provided in Chaves and Gorski 2001.

Studies have drawn different data from diverse historical and geographical settings, giving mixed results. What Voas et al. have shown is that a nonzero correlation, which may reflect a probably causal relationship between religious pluralism and religious participation, is possible to be established due to merely "mathematical associations between the pluralism index and religious participation rates. Even when pluralism has no causal influence on participation rates, the expected value of the correlation between these two variables is usually not zero" (Voas et al. 2002: 213). Furthermore, when previously examined datasets are reevaluated assuming no causal influence of pluralism, the results are strikingly similar to those correlations that have received, in the past, substantive interpretations. The consequence of this is that "nearly all the evidence that has been assembled on both sides of the pluralism debate will have to be reevaluated" (Voas et al. 2002: 213).

More recent contributions to the debate on Western secularization as a macro-social process have looked into other combinations of explanatory variables (e.g. Smith 2003; Norris and Inglehart 2004). However, there has been an explosion of new topics in the study of the secular to the point that a new field of "secular studies" has emerged, one in which philosophical, political science and sociological approaches are predominant. Charles Taylor's book *A Secular Age*, published in 2007, has provided great impetus to this scholarship.[30] Among the issues treated one finds the question about the nature of the secular, both as theoretically-grounded position as well as in the ways it becomes institutionalized. Some scholars call into question its assumed neutral character and explore its re-definition, talking about the "post-secular." Others react against any quick dismissal of "the secular" and are working on more quantitative and qualitative research about it. Other thinkers ask what would the role of religion in a pluralist democratic society in the West be, and how do cultural and religious minorities affect it. In this context, Christian theologians are reflecting on ways in which their religious tradition, still a majority in the Western religious landscape, could regain vitality and continue engaging in the public square (Cassidy et al. 2010; Barbieri 2014; Smith 2014). Furthermore, questions similar than those above are being asked about non-Western contexts, providing with a plethora of studies. Things get more complex when one adds the forces of globalization into the equation.

I think Taylor's work offers the opportunity for providing new insights and energy to carry on the Western secularization debate also by interpreting it in terms of social theory. In the following two chapters I will focus on Taylor's meta-narrative in this regard. For Taylor, the "mainstream secularization theory" is like a three-story building. The ground floor "represents the factual claim that religious belief and practice have declined," (Taylor 2007: 431) along with the scope and influence of religious institutions. The basement represents the claims about how to explain these things, which includes structural differentiation, social differentiation, the disappearance of community, the growth of bureaucracy, and increasing rationalization (Taylor 2007: 431). However, Taylor thinks one should not stop here at the level of

---

[30] For a view on how does Taylor's views relate with theories of secularization, and in particular with his points of contact with revisionist scholars, see Portier 2014.

what he calls a "thin version" of secularization. There is a richer version that includes a second floor regarding the place of religion today: "Where has the whole movement left us? What is the predicament, what are the vulnerabilities and strengths of religion and unbelief today?" (Taylor 2007: 432). Those are, in Taylor's view, the questions that matter to most people.

In this regard, there is a connection between the basement and the second floor, because when "orthodox" theorists claim that religion "is no longer an independent motivating force in conditions of modernity," (Taylor 2007: 433) they are already framing the potential answers to the question about the place of religion today. Even more, he sees this approach as affected by "powerful enframing assumptions." The following chapters will give a precise account of Taylor's understanding of secularization in the West and the nature of these assumptions.

References

Asad T (2003) Formations of the secular: Christianity, Islam, modernity. Stanford University Press, Stanford

Barbieri WA (2014) At the limits of the secular: reflections on faith and public life. William B Eerdmans Publishing Company, Grand Rapids

Becker GS (1976) The economic approach to human behavior. University of Chicago Press, Chicago

Berger PL (1967) The sacred canopy: elements of a sociological theory of religion. Doubleday, New York

Berger PL (1999) The desecularization of the world: a global overview. In: Berger PL (ed) The desecularization of the world: resurgent religion and world politics. Ethics and Public Policy Center, Washington, DC, pp 1–18

Berger PL, Luckmann T (1966) The social construction of reality: a treatise in the sociology of knowledge. Doubleday, Garden City

Bruce S (2002) God is dead: secularization in the West. Blackwell Pub, Malden

Calhoun CJ et al (eds) (2011) Rethinking secularism. Oxford University Press, Oxford, UK

Casanova J (1994) Public religions in the modern world. University of Chicago Press, Chicago

Casanova J (2008) Public religions revisited. In: De Vries H (ed) Religion: beyond a concept. Fordham University Press, New York, pp 101–119

Cassidy IL et al (2010) The Taylor effect: responding to a secular age. Cambridge Scholars Publishing, Newcastle upon Thyne

Chaves M (1994) Secularization as declining religious authority. Soc Forces 72:749–774. doi:10.2307/2579779

Chaves M, Gorski PS (2001) Religious pluralism and religious participation. Annu Rev Sociol 27:261–281. doi:10.1146/annurev.soc.27.1.261

Comte A (1891) The catechism of positive religion. Kegan Paul, Trench, Trubner & Company Limited, London

Comte A (1903) A discourse on the positive spirit. A. Bonner, London

Comte A (1975) Auguste Comte and positivism, the essential writings. Harper & Row, New York

Dobbelaere K (1987) Some trends in European sociology of religion: the secularization debate. Sociol Anal 48:107–137. doi:10.2307/3711197

Dobbelaere K (2002) Secularization: an analysis at three levels. Peter Lang, Brussels

Durkheim E (1915) The elementary forms of religious life. George Allen & Unwin, Ltd., London

Durkheim E (1965) The rules of sociological method. Free Press, New York

Durkheim E (1951) Suicide. A study in sociology. Free Press, New York

Durkheim E (1984) The division of labor in society. Free Press, New York

Fenn RK (1978) Toward a theory of secularization. Society for the Scientific Study of Religion, Ellington

Gauchet M (1997) The disenchantment of the world: a political history of religion. Princeton University Press, Princeton

Hanson S (1997) The secularisation thesis: talking at cross purposes. J Contemp Relig 12:159–179. doi:10.1080/13537909708580797

Hervieu-Léger D (1999) Le pèlerin at le converti. La religion en movement. Flammarion, Paris

Hughey MW (1979) The idea of secularization in the works of Max Weber: a theoretical outline. Qual Sociol 2:85–11

Institute of Marxism-Leninism of the C.C., C.P.S.U (ed) (1957) K. Marx and F. Engels on religion. Lawrence and Wishart Ltd., London

Luckmann T (1967) The invisible religion: the problem of religion in modern society. Macmillan, New York

Luhmann N (2013) A systems theory of religion. Stanford University Press, Stanford

Martin D (1965) Towards eliminating the concept of secularization. In: Gould J (ed) Penguin survey of the social sciences 1965. Penguin, Harmondsworth, pp 169–182

Martin D (1978) A general theory of secularization. Harper & Row, New York

Martin D (2005) On secularization: towards a revised general theory. Ashgate, Aldershot

Norris P, Inglehart R (2004) Sacred and secular: religion and politics worldwide. Cambridge University Press, Cambridge

Pickering WSF (ed) (1975) Durkheim on religion: a selection of readings with bibliographies. Routledge & K. Paul, London

Pickering WSF (1984) Durkheim's sociology of religion: themes and theories. Routledge & Kegan Paul, London

Portier P (2014) Charles Taylor et la sociologie de la sécularization. In: Taussig S (ed) Charles Taylor. Religion et sécularization. CNRS Editions, Paris, pp 83–111

Shiner L (1967) The concept of secularization in empirical research. J Sci Study Relig 6:207–220. doi:10.2307/1384047

Smith C (2003) Introduction: rethinking the secularization of American public life. In: Smith C (ed) The secular revolution: power, interests, and conflict in the secularization of American public life. University of California Press, Berkeley, pp 1–96

Smith C (2008) Future directions in the sociology of religion. Soc Forces 86:1561–1589. doi:10.1353/sof.0.0040

Smith JKA (2014) How (not) to be secular. Reading Charles Taylor. William E. Eerdmans Publishing Company, Grand Rapids

Stark R, Bainbridge WS (1985) The future of religion: secularization, revival, and cult formation. University of California Press, Berkeley

Stark R, Bainbridge WS (1987) A theory of religion. Peter Lang, New York

Stark R, Finke R (2000) Acts of faith: explaining the human side of religion. University of California Press, Berkeley

Swatos WH, Christiano KJ (2000) Secularization theory: the course of a concept. In: Swatos WH, Olson DVA (eds) The secularization debate. Rowman & Littlefield Publishers, Lanham, pp 1–20

Taylor C (2007) A secular age. Belknap Press of Harvard University Press, Cambridge, MA

Tschannen O (1991) The secularization paradigm: a systematization. J Sci Study Relig 30:395–415. doi:10.2307/1387276

Voas D et al (2002) Religious pluralism and participation: why previous research is wrong. Am Sociol Rev 67:212–230. doi:10.2307/3088893

Wallis R, Bruce S (1992) Secularization: the orthodox model. In: Bruce S (ed) Religion and modernization: sociologists and historians debate the secularization thesis. Clarendon, Oxford, pp 8–30

Weber M (1958) From Max Weber: essays in sociology. Oxford University Press, New York
Weber M (1964) The religion of China: confucianism and taoism. The Macmillan Company, New York
Weber M (1993) The sociology of religion. Beacon, Boston
Wernick A (2001) Auguste Comte and the religion of humanity: the post-theistic program of French social theory. Cambridge University Press, Cambridge
Wilson BR (1966) Religion in secular society. Penguin, Baltimore
Wilson BR (1976) Aspects of secularization in the West. Jpn J Relig Stud 3:259–276
Yamane D (1997) Secularization on trial: in defense of a neosecularization paradigm. J Sci Study Relig 36:109–122. doi:10.2307/1387887

Chapter 2
Charles Taylor's Account of Secularization (I)

Abstract In Taylor's view, it is not possible to understand Western secularization without clarifying what do we understand by religion, how was religion lived in the past with which we compare our current situation, and which is the specific geographical area we want to study. He embraces a substantial notion of religion, makes use of historical and sociological studies on how religion was lived during the last five centuries, and concentrates on the United Kingdom, France, and the United States. He sets to study secularity in three ways: as the retreat of religion from the public space, the decline of religious belief and practice, and as changes in the conditions of belief for individuals. In his view, Western secularization is better understood as a "relocation" of religion in society and in personal lives, which entails the decline of past religious forms and the appearance of new ones. In his explanation of such a process, Taylor weaves three complementary stories. The first one evolves through three historical stages: the Ancien Régime (pre-modern), the Age of Mobilization (between the nineteenth and twentieth centuries) and the Age of Authenticity (after the 1960s). During all this time, social imaginaries were radically changed through the interaction of specific elite groups and the masses. Social imaginaries are self-understandings shared by people of a given society, which are also embedded in social practices. These self-interpretations are a-thematic and also provide with explanations about how do people live together as well as how they should.

Keywords Secularization • Western secularization • Religious decline • Religious vitality • Disenchantment • Re-enchantment • Social imaginaries • Elite-masses relationships

2.1   Introduction

Within the previously described landscape of the debates on Western secularization, Charles Taylor's approach appears to take a "revisionist" position before the "orthodox model" of secularization, without agreeing with the "counter-orthodox" pole. However, his view does more than just balance differently the sociological data and

© Springer International Publishing AG 2017
Germán McKenzie, *Interpreting Charles Taylor's Social Theory on Religion and Secularization*, Sophia Studies in Cross-cultural Philosophy of Traditions and Cultures 20, DOI 10.1007/978-3-319-47700-8_2

the interpretations given by other theoreticians. His intention is to offer a different intellectual framework, one that blends sociology, history and philosophical insights on human fulfillment. Taylor's interpretation of secularization, which draws from the work of a large number of scholars, is based on such previous stance.

Taylor's account of secularization is thoroughly explained in his work *A Secular Age* (Taylor 2007). However, some sections of the book were previously published in his *Varieties of Religion Today: Willliam James Revisited* (Taylor 2002), and *Modern Social Imaginaries* (Taylor 2004), as well as in articles from 2006 to 2008 that have been collected *in Dilemmas and Connections: Selected essays* (Taylor 2011). These materials, as well as other minor works by Taylor, are pertinent to the focus of Chaps. 2 and 3 of this book, which aim to present his account of secularization in the West.[1]

Chapter 2 is divided into two main sections. The first one is about the definition of secularization and Taylor's redefinition of it as a problem. The second section, the more complex, focuses on the first of three stories that, woven together, configure Taylor's meta-narrative of secularization. Chapter 3 continues with the remaining stories, with a focus on the contemporary conditions of belief in the West. I also includes a brief summary of what he sees as the future of religion.

In what follows, I will specifically identify those sociologists that Taylor recognizes as sources of inspiration, as well as those with whom he explicitly disagrees, in order to lead into the topics on which my research will focus in the following chapters. I will also examine Taylor's use of concepts such as secular, secularization, differentiation, rationalization, elites-masses relationships, social imaginaries, enchantment, fragmentation, and privatization. Original Taylorean concepts such as immanent frame, porous and buffered self, Nova Effect, and fragilization are also explained. Precise meanings can also be found in the Glossary at the end of the book.

2.2 Defining the Problem

In Taylor's view, the issue of secularization is problematic. Part of the difficulty is due to the fact that the very definition of "secularization" depends on three changing points of reference: (a) a given notion of religion, (b) a view of the past with which one wants to compare contemporary religion, and (c) a specific geographical setting for the inquiries to take place. It may be better to start from this last point for the sake of clarity. Taylor argues that something like a decline in religion has happened in the Western part of the world.

---

[1] Dr. Bradley Thames, from University of St Thomas, keeps a website with an up-to-date bibliography by Charles Taylor, as well as about works on the Taylorean corpus (Thames 2015). He counts with the help of Dr. Ruth Abbey, from Notre Dame University, who performs an advisory role.

In regard to the geographic scenario of the specific secularization story, Taylor sets out to explain that the limits of his study are confined to North Atlantic countries. He mainly refers to the United Kingdom, France and the United States, and also mentions Canada, the Scandinavian countries, Holland and other nations. However, in his general remarks on the topic, he speaks of secularization in the West as a whole. For Taylor, there is no way to study any secularization process other than localizing it. This is because of a methodological consideration: the idea of religion we can work with is not all-encompassing enough, and the secularizing process is so complex that it is difficult to study without framing the topic in some way.

Besides, the kind of geographical localization Taylor establishes for his study corresponds to intertwining sociological and religious factors. First, he espouses the thesis of "multiple modernities," which means there is not just one "canonical" path for modernity to take flesh in a given society and culture but several variations of a similar process. In this light, North Atlantic countries share the main trends of a common pattern. Second, he agrees with David Martin's idea that secularization occurs in different places around the world according to different processes (Martin 2005; Taylor 2007: 461, note 65), which corresponds, among other reasons with the specific religious traditions predominant in a given area. In the case of the North Atlantic countries this leads him to deal with what he calls Latin Christianity (which distinction between natural and supernatural Taylor finds as a factor contributing to secularization) and the Reformation.

With regards to a definition of religion, Taylor generally shares with Steve Bruce the idea that "religion for us consists of actions, beliefs and institutions predicated upon the assumption of the existence of either supernatural entities with powers of agency, or impersonal powers or processes possessed of moral purpose, which have the capacity to set the conditions of, or to intervene in, human affairs" (Wallis and Bruce 1992: 10–11; Taylor 2007: 429, note 20). On the one hand, Taylor agrees that this definition prevents a too broad notion of religion by recognizing the role of "impersonal powers" other than subjectively created ones. On the other hand, he makes two important qualifications. The first is that there are spiritual agents that are not "supernatural" (a notion he sees coined by Latin Christianity).[2] The second one—which has utmost importance in his view—is that religion in the West is linked to a certain idea of human flourishing, one that he calls "transformative" (Taylor 2007: 430–31).[3]

Taylor expresses in different places in his work that, even though there has always existed an "enchanted world," and one that still exists now, such a realm has lost the grip it once had among most Westerners. In this sense, it is possible to speak of a decline of religion in relation to the past. In his view, we have passed from a

---

[2] Taylor several times speaks of Latin Christianity or Latin Christendom as synonyms for Western civilization (e.gr., Taylor 2007: 556).

[3] Martin Reisenbrodt points out here that Taylor seems to favor the more intellectualist understandings of religion (those related with meaning) in detriment of its practical aspects (Schweiker et al. 2010:399–400).

situation in which belief in God was unchallenged and unproblematic to a scenario in which belief has turned into one option among others for most people, and one that has also become problematic to keep.

Based on what has been said, it is possible for Taylor to affirm that, if secularization primarily refers to people's beliefs (in which he follows Bruce), something like a decline has occurred, since nowadays such beliefs are less influential in the lives of Westerners than in the past (Taylor 2007: 429). More precisely, in Taylor's view, secularization has occurred in the West in the first place as the undermining of a "transformative" view of human flourishing, this being Christian in character. According to the latter, human beings are called to participate in God's love (*agape*) in a way that eliminates any possible mutuality: it supposes a supra-human power who calls and a similar supra-human state into which we are called, one we acquire through a transformative process. In contrast with this view, a new perspective has been raised, one that sees each human being as someone who aspires to his/her own happiness on the basis of assured life and freedom, in a social context in which individuals help each other in a way that fosters mutual benefit. This novel approach had at the beginning a Deist/providentialist rationale, which was replaced in time with atheistic or agnostic explanations that considered the aspirations for a higher transformation as mere illusions (Taylor 2007: 430).

The result of these changes is a situation in which the transformative and immanent perspectives act as two extreme positions, in the middle of which a myriad of possible varieties are located, relative to the majority of Westerners.

As part of his analysis, aimed to better describe the profile of what secularization might be, Taylor begins by stating that the term "secular" was originally linked with time: there was a "secular" time which contrasted with an eternal, sacred time. "Certain times, places, persons, institutions and actions were seen as closely related to the sacred or higher time" (Taylor 2011: 304).[4] After this relationship was established, the term secular could be applied to all the elements listed above. All this occurred in the context of Latin Christianity. However, by the seventeenth century, a new understanding of the term appears which affirmed the secular by itself and was "opposed to any claim made in the name of something transcendent of this world and its interests" (Taylor 2011: 304). Later on, this position would further develop into a Deist and a post-Deist outlook.

Taylor then shifts to an analysis of the contemporary view of "secularity," of which he finds three different understandings that help to make sense of the process of secularization. Secularity 1 will be, for him, the retreat of religion from the public space; secularity 2 is defined as the decline of religious belief and practice; and by secularity 3, he speaks of the conditions of belief in a given historical time, both individual and communal. By making these distinctions, Taylor wants to avoid some misunderstandings, but at the same time he recognizes that there is an overlap between the first two meanings and the third one (Taylor 2007: 1–22, 423).[5]

---

[4] The quote is from the chapter titled *What Does Secularism Mean?*

[5] Reisenbrodt suggests to avoid using the concept of secularization/secularity here because he finds it misleading. He would rather suggest institutional differentiation, disenchantment, and de-insti-

The first misunderstanding about which Taylor is concerned is the explanation of secularization as being relative to "differentiation," the latter being understood as the process through which functions that were originally carried on together crystallize out and fall into different spheres.[6] This description is relevant, but it does not suffice to provide an entire explanation of what has happened. "The fact that activity in a given sphere follows its own inherent rationality and doesn't permit of the older kind of faith-based norming doesn't mean that it cannot still be very much shaped by faith" (Taylor 2007: 425). Thus, differentiation may explain in part secularity 1, but fails to explain secularity 2. The error here, in Taylor's view, is identifying secularization with disenchantment (Taylor 2007: 425–426, 551–54).[7]

Taylor mentions a second source of misunderstanding, which is the identification of secularization with privatization. Following Jose Casanova (1994; Taylor 2007: 426, note 7), he says that even when different spheres (as the state, economy, science) have separated and freed themselves from religion, this doesn't mean that the latter is only lived at the margins of society. On the contrary, religious traditions are reacting against such localization (Taylor 2007: 426). Taylor also states that religion *de facto* plays the role within the secular public sphere of legitimating, at the level of the particular individuals and minorities, their particular political identities, which in turn are supposed to become disengaged from confessional allegiances and be supportive of the general political identity of the country through a Rawlsian "overlapping consensus" (Taylor 2004: 193–94, 93–99). In light of this, Taylor would, in regard to democracy, insist not on the general application of the principle of separation between church and state (which he sees as just one of the possible institutional settings than can be proposed), but on a previous topic: that of "principled distance," on the part of the government, from particular religious allegiances and even from secular systems of belief (Taylor 2011: 303–325).[8]

Another misunderstanding mentioned by Taylor is the explanation of the occurrence of secularization mainly by means of urbanization. Recognizing that urbanization has had an impact in secularity 2, he argues that the opposite seems to have been true for the United States and also for the United Kingdom in some respects (Taylor 2007: 426, notes 8 and 9).[9]

Lastly, Taylor critiques what he calls "orthodox" secularization theories, which maintain a zero-sum approach which affirms that the more modernity permeates the world, the more religion will decline to the point of becoming irrelevant. His

---

tutionaliation/privatization of religion, instead of the three notions of secularity used by Taylor (Schweiker et al. 2010:398–399). I do not see how his proposal for secularity 3 would really fit its meaning.

[6] I have shown how this could be considered as the theoretical core on which "orthodox" and "revisionist" scholars agree, who in turn inspire themselves in Max Weber. Taylor himself mentions Berger 1967 and Tschannen 1992 (Taylor 2007: 2, note 3).

[7] A more developed argument may be found Taylor's piece titled *Disenchantment-Reenchantment* (Taylor 2011: 287–302).

[8] The quote is from the chapter titled *What Does Secularism Mean?*

[9] Taylor cites here works by Finke (1992), McLeod (1995, 2000) and Brown (2001).

criticism is focused in three areas: (a) The process of the undermining and sidelining of religion is not linear, but entails the decline of older religious forms and the rise of new ones. (b) A future in which religious indifference will become widespread and be taken as a given is implausible, since the view on human flourishing based on "transformation" and the view circumscribed to the immanent (*laïque* or secular) are both equally fragile and destabilize one another, while most people espouse some intermediate (and also fragile) stance. "They all remain vulnerable, in the sense that circumstances may arise in which they feel the force of the opposite solicitation. And if they don't, often their children will" (Taylor 2007: 435).

In relation to Steve Bruce and Roy Wallis' "orthodox" position (Wallis and Bruce 1992; Taylor 2007: 432, note 26), Taylor argues that such an approach is affected by what he calls an "unthought," using a term borrowed from Michel Foucault. This "unthought," which can bedevil the debate on secularization, consists of an outlook by which religion must decline, either (a) because science shows it to be false; (b) because it has been made irrelevant due to contemporary technological advancement; or (c) because it goes against a contemporary trend that favors individual autonomy, whereas religion is based on authority (Taylor 2007: 428–29).

At a deeper level, this "unthought" is nurtured, according to Taylor, by what he calls the "disappearance" and the "epiphenomenal" thesis. The former maintains that any independent motivation for religious belief and practice tends to disappear with modernity. The latter, within modernity, holds that any religious belief and practice that would eventually remain will do so because it accomplishes some non-religious social function. In contrast with these affirmations, Taylor recognizes the existence of religious motivations per se in human beings (Taylor 2007: 436).[10]

Having reached this point in Taylor's description of secularization as an object of study, it is fair to clarify his standpoint, while reserving an in-depth analysis of it for a following chapter. Taylor strongly affirms that he is not claiming for himself a position of "objectivity" free of any "unthought," but just that he wants to offer a more perspicuous explanation of such phenomenon. He confesses to be a believer, one who is moved by the "transformative" perspective described above, although he hopes to defend it with rational arguments (Taylor 2007: 436–37). Why put together a meta-narrative? He answers this by saying that "various tellings of the story of how we have become carry this sense of secularity as an inevitable consequence. To challenge this you have to tell another story. Hence the length of the book [*A Secular Age*]" (Taylor 2010: 301).

In addition, in regards to secularization, Taylor deliberately has chosen an approach which intertwines sociological, historical and philosophical discourse: "Just as sociology without history can't really get to the really important issues, so at the same time, if you don't have a deep consideration of the philosophical issues, you can't do good historical sociology" (Taylor 2008). What philosophy brings to the discussion, in his mind, is a more thorough analysis of human motivation, one

---

[10] For an analysis of this "unthought" as a particular "spin" on the immanent frame given particularly by the academia, see Taylor 2007: 550.

that challenges the assumption regarding the shallowness of religious motivation in human life.

2.3   (Re) Describing the Secularization Process in the West

Secularization in the West, in Taylor's view, consists of a decline of religion in the sense of the decline of certain "religious forms." Nowadays, religious belief exists amidst a field of possible choices, which include demurral and rejection. Moreover, Christianity exists just as a possibility to be chosen alongside other religious traditions. However, the interesting part of the phenomenon is that it "is not simply one of decline, but also of a new placement of the sacred or spiritual in relation to individual and social life. This new placement is now the occasion for recompositions of spiritual life in new forms, and for new ways of existing both in and out of relation to God" (Taylor 2007: 437).

He shares with the "orthodox" thesis a perspective of decline of previously existing religious forms, which is partly due to social facts such as urbanization, industrialization, migration, the fracturing of the earlier communities, the rise of bureaucracy, and the increase of rationalization (Taylor 2007: 431, 436).[11] These changes made earlier religious practices difficult, even impossible, and led to whole groups of people taking intellectual positions contrary to Christianity or even to religion in general. This Taylor labels as secularity 2. But it also occurred that people responded to these changes by creating new religious forms. This view helps avoid the risk of seeing the process of decline as linear and the result of the same set of causes all the way to the present. Besides, it allows us to consider how religion has changed in relation to the renewal of previous religious forms, and by the appearance of new ones.

In a similar vein, when talking about the role the appearance of the conceptions of the autonomy of nature played in secularization, Taylor argues that: "The straight path account of modern secularity can't be sustained. Instead, what I am offering here is a zig-zag account, one full of unintended consequences" (Taylor 2007: 95).

What makes our contemporary religious landscape unique and so different from any previous one is the fact that it is extremely plural in spiritual options (even non- and anti-religious ones), very dynamic in the way it changes, and characterized by instability. As Taylor puts it, such landscape "is marked in consequence by a great deal of mutual fragilization, and hence movement between different outlooks. It naturally depends on one's milieu, but it is harder to find a niche where either belief or unbelief goes without saying" (Taylor 2007: 95). A consequence of this is that belief of many kinds is more widespread than ever, even in ways that may embrace some kind of "transformative perspective." It is this change in the conditions of belief, which Taylor calls secularity 3, that is more characteristic of his approach and in which he invests much of his analysis.

---

[11] Here he cites some of Bruce's views on secularization.

2.4   How Did Secularization Happen?

At this point, Taylor narrows down the scope of his study to that of the North Atlantic countries. In order to give some explanation of the causes of secularization in this context, he defines three historical stages and describes two cultural upheavals, each with a particular set of causes: (a) The first breakdown occurred by the end of the nineteenth and the beginning of the twentieth centuries. (b) The second took place after WWII, especially in the 1960s. In each of these circumstances, earlier religious forms were undermined and new forms appeared.

This approach of Taylor triggers three lines of inquiry. In the first place, the analysis of the above mentioned historical stages. This is done from a twofold standpoint: that of their peculiar social matrices (for which the notion of "social imaginary" will become central) as the milieux where religious life took place, and that of the characteristics of the spiritual forms of which such life consisted in. Within this line of inquiry, the role of elites and their impact on the construction of the social imaginary of a given time attracts Taylor's attention.[12]

The second line of inquiry goes back in time and focuses on the narrative of the story about how a new alternative arose in the West in the eighteenth century, one that Taylor calls "exclusive humanism." This included a view of reality that was the condition *sine qua non* for secularization (in the sense of secularity 2 and 3) to occur. This view gradually came to be predominant among North Atlantic elites. Through a number of mechanisms, it impacted the whole of society through the inspiration of a shared social imaginary.[13]

Thirdly, Taylor's last line of inquiry goes deeper into the more relevant features of contemporary conditions of belief. He explains that we in the West currently live within an "immanent frame" where whole cultures experience cross-pressures between narratives of closed immanence, on one side, and a sense of their inadequacy on the other. By "narratives of closed immanence" he means stories that carry over arguments about human flourishing that *in principio* deny any possibility for humans to acquire the latter anywhere outside "this world." In spite of their efforts, these narratives are unable to provide an apodictic demonstration of their points but, on the contrary, trigger doubt about their claims and a consequential experience of uneasiness. Along with these situations, one still finds religion, in relation to which people locate themselves in a vast array of positions and distances.[14]

It is worth noting that these three courses of action for Taylor's research on secularization unavoidably overlap with each other while maintaining their own logic,

---

[12] This topic will be addressed in Chapters 12–14 in *A Secular Age*, which are reunited under title *Narratives of Secularization*.

[13] This issue is developed in *A Secular Age*'s Chapters 1–11.

[14] This is the topic of *A Secular Age*'s Chapters 15–20, gathered under the title *Conditions of Belief*.

nonetheless. In the sections that follow, I will focus on the first of these lines of inquiry. The remaining two will be the matter of the next chapter.[15]

2.5   North Atlantic Secularization

As it was mentioned previously, there is a three-staged story of secularization in the North Atlantic area, for the study of which Taylor makes use of three Weber-inspired ideal types: (a) The Ancien Régime, (b) the Age of Mobilization, and (c) the Age of Authenticity. For each of them, he introduces a description of its characteristic social imaginary and respective spiritual life outlook. His description of this process is aimed at explaining "the move from an age of some élite unbelief (the eighteenth century) to that of mass secularization (the twenty-first)" (Taylor 2007: 437). He is aware that, as ideal-types, not all concrete cases will fit nicely into his explanation. However, he finds that this approach facilitates identifying the long-term tendencies and discriminates between the different kinds of social matrices involved in such development (Taylor 2007: 461).

Taylor complements such threefold division with parallel distinctions regarding the ways in which religion and political systems relate to each other. He calls these new ideal-types Paleo-, Neo-, and Post- Durkhemian dispensations (Taylor 2007: 458–460).[16] However, each of these three ideal-types—while predominating in the phases of the Ancien Régime, the Age of Mobilization, and the Age of Authenticity, respectively—should not be considered as historical stages that succeed one another. On the contrary, in Taylor's view, they coexist and continue to compete with one another even when one of them becomes dominant. This would become clearer in what follows.

2.5.1   Ancien Régime

The first stage is called the Ancien Régime matrix (AR). It is characterized by (a) a pre-modern idea of order that is grounded in the cosmos and/or in the idea of a higher time, and by (b) "AR forms [which] pre-exist the actual human beings which belong to them, and define their status and role; they are already there 'since time out of mind'" (Taylor 2007: 460). With regard to the general profile of the social matrix, (c) "AR forms are 'organic', in the sense that society is articulated into con-stituent 'orders' (nobility, clergy, bourgeoisie, peasants), and institutions (Assembly of clergy, Parliament, estates), and smaller societies (parishes, communes,

---

[15] James Miller finds the three-staged structure of the meta-narrative as a following a "monolithic teleology" (2008). This seems to me at odds with the role human agency through elite-masses dynamics is acknowledged in Taylor's meta-narrative.

[16] A detailed explanation on this can also be found in Taylor 2002.

provinces), such that one only belongs to the whole through belonging to one of these constituent parts" (Taylor 2007: 460). Lastly, (d) the world of AR is usually an enchanted one, that is, a milieu inhabited by spiritual and moral forces with which we interact and which also present to us the meanings of things.

In conjunction with the described social matrix, Taylor finds operative at this stage what he calls a "Paleo-Durkhemian" dispensation. In this stage, society is seen as an "organ," and one's place within this "organ" whole is the essential definer of obligations and duty. The church encompasses society in such a way that everyone should belong to her. Besides, it is from the former that social obligations draw their force, which comes from the realm of the sacred as mediated by the church. "Societies organized by such a church are in this (loose) meaning 'Durkhemian', in the sense that church and social sacred are one—although the relation of primary and secondary focus is reversed, since for Durkheim the social is the principal focus, reflected in the divine, while the opposite is true for ultramontane Catholicism" (Taylor 2007: 442, 486).

All the above-mentioned elements are part of a "baroque" and Catholic-inspired social imaginary. By the latter, Taylor understands the ways people "imagine their social existence, how they fit together with others, how things go on between them and their fellows, the expectations which are normally met, and the deeper normative notions and images which underlie these expectations" (Taylor 2007: 171). This is not just to say that individuals have images through which they view society and that change in time, but refers to something deeper. For Taylor, social imaginaries are the ways in which human sociality is understood, many times in an athematic manner, one which is also embedded in social practices. It should be said that this notion draws strongly from Benedict Anderson's thought (Taylor 2004: 2, 2007: 713ff; Anderson 2006) and has points in common with similar concepts used by scholars such as Cornelius Castoriadis, Pierre Bourdieu and Bronislaw Baczco, as it will be explained in Chap. 5.

Social imaginaries, then, in Taylor's sense, shouldn't be confused with social theory. They are simply ways in which ordinary people imagine their social surroundings, which is not mainly done through theoretical language but in images, legends and stories. They are, then, shared by large groups of people. Lastly, social imaginaries allow a common understanding that gives sense to a set of common practices and produces a shared sense of legitimacy (Taylor 2007: 171–72, 2004: 23–30).[17] For example, key features of the modern social imaginary are, according to Taylor, the people as sovereign, the public sphere, and the market.

Social imaginaries also help people both to know what they should normally expect from living together as well as to understand how they fit together. In Taylor's words, this understanding is "factual" and "normative," meaning that it provides us with a sense of how things are and how they should be (Taylor 2007: 172). Along with an ideal image of how things should work, there is a wider notion or "background" of a metaphysical or moral order. Such "background" is that "largely unstructured and inarticulate understanding of our whole situation, within which

---

[17] Most parts of *Modern Social Imaginaries* are already contained in *A Secular Age*.

particular features of our world show up for us in the sense they have" (Taylor 2007: 173). A social imaginary can't be rightly expressed as explicit doctrines, since it is unlimited and indefinite. This is why it is called an "imaginary," not a theory.

Lastly, regarding social imaginaries, there is a "circular" relationship between the understanding and the practices they encompass: on one hand, understanding makes practice possible; on the other hand, practice in some way carries the understanding "within." In this light, the above mentioned moral order appears as a key element that not only gives sense to the norms underlying our social practice, but also communicates to us the idea that it is possible for us to abide by them. This may work in two ways: as a means of keeping a given social order, or as a drive towards social change.

Some may ask why the term "imagination" is included in the already described concept. Taylor sees this as a device that may point out a dual characteristic of "social imaginaries." On one hand they may be false in the sense of covering up or distorting certain important realities, working in a similar way to the Marxist notion of "ideology" as a false consciousness of our situation. However, on the other hand, social imaginaries also play a constructive role, making possible a number of all sorts of social practices. Moreover, they can have a creative function in opening up new possibilities and in building a renewed social self-consciousness (Taylor 2004: 182–83).[18]

Although Taylor doesn't expand on how, it is within a given social imaginary that the relationship between elites and the masses takes place. These are very important in the master narrative he puts together, due to the importance that "exclusive humanism" has as a theoretical and practical stance towards reality.

Within the baroque social imaginary of AR, religious life and spiritual practices are characterized by strong collective rituals. In these, "orthodox" and unofficial beliefs and practices mingle together. In the case of the latter, they did not correspond so much to "pagan" religious experience, but to unorthodox meanings given to Church feasts (e. g., Good Friday was also a good day, due to the power it carried, to plant crops). Taylor affirms that in this stage Pre- and Post-Axial religious elements co-existed at ease, borrowing a concept from Karl Jaspers and inspiration from Robert Bellah (Bellah 1970; Taylor 2007: 147, note 1, and 149, note 4).[19] Rituals related to Pre-Axial religion, "were concerned with securing human flourishing, and protecting against the threats of disease, famine, flood, etc." (Taylor 2007: 439, 2011: 367–379),[20] while celebrations related to Post-Axial religion included an aspiration to some higher good transformative of human life—which was actively sought by those Max Weber calls *spiritual virtuosi*. In a similar way,

---

[18] Gregor McLennan criticizes Taylor's use of social imaginaries as diminishing societal causality in the process leading to Western secularization, and attributes that to an influence by Hegel (2010). I would say, on the contrary, that societal causality is indeed present in his view, as my interpretation of Taylorean social theory recognizes. Besides, the idea of social imaginaries seems to denote a quite a different primary influence, that of Wittgenstein.

[19] In the last reference, Taylor explains how he is indebted to Bellah on this.

[20] The last reference is to the chapter titled *What was the Axial Revolution?*

rites of passage were related to rituals such as baptism, confirmation, marriage and funerals.

To live in an "enchanted" world means, for Taylor, to inhabit a world that (a) is filled with spirits and moral forces that directly affect human existence (Taylor 2011: 287–302).[21] By "moral forces," he means those that reside in specific objects that are capable of doing good or ill to those who get in contact with them: relics, love potions, etc. Secondly, (b) in an "enchanted world," the meanings of things reside in objects or agents which act independently of us and can impose their influence on us. This "enchanted" view is in stark contrast with a modern view of the cosmos where "thoughts and meanings are only in minds," which explains why "there cannot be 'charged' objects, and the causal relations between things cannot be in any way dependent on their meanings" (Taylor 2007: 35).

Living in this world entails a sense of vulnerability. If meanings are extra-mental, "once we can fall under the spell, enter the zone of power of exogenous meaning, then we think of this meaning as including us, or perhaps penetrating us. We are in as it were a kind of space defined by its influence" (Taylor 2007: 35). Being things like this, the distinction between "within" and "without" ourselves is blurred and our identity becomes "porous."

It is here that Taylor comes up with his notion of a "porous self" in contrast with the modern "buffered self." On one hand, the former is a self for whom the source of its more powerful and important emotions is external to the mind, and any boundary between itself and such sources is meaningless. The latter, on the other hand, is a self for whom a boundary is possible like a "buffer" that separates the mind from the extra-mental. In this way, the "buffered self" has taken away the fear for spirits or moral forces and, more importantly, sees itself as disengaged from whatever is beyond the boundary. It gives "its own autonomous order to its life. The absence of fear can be not just enjoyed, but seen as an opportunity for self-control and self-direction" (Taylor 2007: 38–39).

By defining things like this, Taylor deliberately takes Max Weber's concept of disenchantment, criticizes it, and redefines it (Taylor 2007: 446, 2011: 148, 288).[22] This point, along with others, will be expanded in the following chapters. There I will study Taylor's account as compared with Weber, Durkheim and Marx, as well as with contemporary sociologists whom are influential in his thought.

Without leaving the AR stage, Taylor sees the Reformation as a step further leading into "disenchantment." He also sees the Catholic Counter-Reformation as part of the same reforming process that aimed to "purify" religious beliefs and practices from Pre-Axial elements. This work by religious elites (Catholic bishops and priests; Lutheran, Calvinist and English reformers) engendered a process of rupture with popular religion, which, among French Catholics, produced a gradual shift of the masses away from the Church. This was radicalized by the effects of the French Revolution and the anti-Christian policies fostered by Jacobinism. The Restoration

---

[21] The reference is to the chapter titled *Disenchantment-Reenchantment*.

[22] The last two references are to the chapters *Religious Mobilizations* and *Disenchantment-Reenchantment*.

period was not able to recover the allegiance of the middle classes or, later, of the working classes. Urbanization, industrialization, and class conflict also played a role in debilitating the strong ties folk religion had with the land. They also weakened the notion of time appropriate to agricultural life, through the disruption of community life and migration to the cities and the factory work. The presence of national institutions such as the army and public schools also played its part in disseminating a secular stance towards reality. Taylor summarizes the process by saying that once the "enchanted" world either disappears or we relate to it differently, once elites depart from the guidance of the official church, and once class conflict is exacerbated due to industrialization, religious alienation occurs among the people. This, in societies where some version of Christianity has been dominant, meant that the masses tend to assume a secular humanist stance (Taylor 2007: 444).

Taylor sees the above process also occurring in Spain and in Prussia-Germany. In a parallel way, there is also a story of changes in the spiritual practices that constituted the religious life of people. Going back to the French case, Taylor explains that there is a change in the ways the Catholic Church promoted devotion. The harsh rigorist stance towards sinners was abandoned for a more compassionate one, reflected in the warmer and more emotional piety centered on the Sacred Heart and greater openness to popular forms of devotion like those occurring at Lourdes. He sees in these events the impact of Romanticism. More importantly for Taylor, new organizations established by lay people were fostered, which entailed the mobilization of persons to win members for the institutions to which they belonged, and the corresponding mobilization of people to acquire membership (Taylor 2007: 445). All these elements helped to consolidate the presence Catholicism had in the countryside and to regain some of the terrain it had lost in the cities. This process of mobilization of the laity helped to produce a significant shift in the social imaginary, one that may be considered as a turning point.

2.5.2   Age of Mobilization

Having reached the end of the 18th and the beginning of the nineteenth centuries, we are now in the presence of secularization's second stage, the Age of Mobilization matrix (AM). The key features of AM are: (a) an idea of a structured world based on the modern moral idea of order, "as a way of coexistence among equals, based on principles of mutual benefit" (Taylor 2007: 460, 2011: 146–64),[23] along with (b) a model for which we are called to work for in order to bring them into existence. In the AM matrix, "people have to be induced, or forced, or organized to take their parts in the new structure; they have to be recruited into the creation of new structures" (Taylor 2007: 460). This happens in time considered as secular. Besides, (c) AM societies are organized in a way in which the individual person is a citizen "immediately," without any reference to groupings of any kind. Group allegiances

---

[23] The last reference is to the chapter titled *Religious Mobilizations*.

are not a given, but the result of a decision and, consequently, can be withdrawn at will. (d) Lastly, the world of AM has also increasingly become disenchanted.

"Mobilization" refers here to the fact that, in this era, people are persuaded or forced by governments, church hierarchies and other elites to become part of new forms of societies, churches or associations. People were no more embedded within an order "received from above." Even though these forces were acting already at the end of AR, the difference now resided in the fact that, differently than before, mobilization had lost the backdrop of Kingdom and Church and was now aimed at building new structures that were still an ideal and were yet to be realized (Taylor 2007: 445–46).

The new social imaginary that began to rise was also characterized by the mutual interaction of the previously mentioned processes (a) and (d). On the one hand, the disenchanted cosmos still affirmed the Newtonian idea that it reflected a divine design. On the other hand, at the political level, there was also a divine design expressed in what Taylor calls Modern Moral Order (MMO) as devised by Grotius and Locke. Such order is an order aimed at the mutual benefit of its members. It is an order that starts with individuals and sees society as conceived for their sake. It supports individuals to help each other by providing security, exchange opportunities and prosperity. These goals are expressed in terms of serving the rights of individuals and these rights and freedoms are secured to all members equally (Taylor 2007: 170–71).

These new ideas of the cosmos and the polis produced smoother transitions in Protestant countries than in Catholic ones. The former, because of their rupture with elite-dominated religion and the widespread notion of acquired religious allegiances, fitted better within the model above. The latter, on the contrary, witnessed a sharp conflict between the new ideas, on the one hand, and the Catholic Church and the vast number of people whose allegiance was predominantly ascribed, on the other (Taylor 2007: 445–48).

For Taylor, another important element to take into account here is the rise of denominations as groups based on religious affinity. This fact strongly impacted the social imaginary of North Atlantic countries. "The denomination clearly belongs to the Age of Mobilization. It is not a divinely established body (though, in another sense, the broader 'church' may be seen as such), but something that we have to create—not just at our whim, but to fulfill the plan of God" (Taylor 2007: 450).

A Neo-Durkhemian setting, in regards to religion and political systems, characterizes this stage. It is God who gives a design for the political order as well as for a civilizational order. The latter means "the sense people have of the basic order by which they live, even imperfectly, as good, and (usually) as superior to the ways of life of outsiders, be they 'barbarians', or 'savages', or (in the more polite contemporary language) 'less developed' peoples" (Taylor 2007: 455, 486).

Representing this view, Taylor sees the United Kingdom and the United States in the first place. In both cases, patriotism was seen as a way of accomplishing God's plan. Their supremacy over other peoples was based on a kind of "civilizational supremacy" rooted in the end in Christendom (Taylor 2007: 456).

Religious and spiritual life during AM shared some common characteristics in the Protestant and Catholic realms. First, new or renewed forms of spirituality appeared which were deeply emotional. On one side, the notion of conversion to a loving God; on the other, retreats, novenas, special devotions (again, the cult to the Sacred Heart and the veneration of Therese of Lisieux are important examples), parish missions, pilgrimages, etc. On both sides there is a strong interest in "some special, stronger, more focused, concentrated and/or disciplined form of devotion/ prayer meditation/dedication" (Taylor 2007: 468). Resources for meeting these interests were provided by churches.

Second, both Protestants and Catholics were the object of diverse efforts aimed to inculcate the needed discipline and ethos to live in the changed economy and society. Churches also nurtured organizations and credit unions and friendly societies oriented towards providing means for economic survival.

Third, in Taylor's view, across both the Catholic and Protestant sides, there were offered special services, devotions and modes of prayer for the particular needs of individuals and groups of individuals. Protestants did this through revival experiences, whereas Catholics promoted novenas, pilgrimages, etc.

Forth, on both sides, particular ways of spirituality and self-discipline are related with specific "political identities," this meaning "the identifying common description of our society" (Taylor 2007: 455). In the case of the United States and the United Kingdom, Evangelicals saw their link with political identity as a positive one that expressed their fundamental values. On their part, wherever one found Irish and Polish Catholic minorities in those countries, their religious life nurtured political identities in opposition to the established authorities. In Continental Europe, Catholics were either struggling to participate in the definition of the country's political identity (as in France) or, where they were minorities, trying to assure an acceptable status as such (Taylor 2007: 467–470).

According to Taylor, it is possible to summarize the religious landscape of AM as waiving together four strands: spirituality, discipline, political identity, and an image of civilizational order. "These four strands have been present in elite religion in the two preceding centuries, but now this had become a mass phenomenon. They strengthened each other, made a whole" (Taylor 2007: 472).

The way towards the following stage in the secularizing process of the North Atlantic countries is described by Taylor as a path towards authenticity. The post WWII Western world witnessed the explosion of such forces from the 1960s on.

2.5.3   Age of Authenticity

Taylor names the third and current stage of secularization's story as the Age of Authenticity (AA). This is the result of a very recent cultural revolution in North Atlantic societies, which nowadays is perceived by many as the erosion of families, communities and even the polis, as a lack of willingness to participate in the building process of the common good, as a lack of trust. Why has this happened and why is it important for the process of secularization? While Taylor recognizes a number of material "precipitating factors" (extension of consumerism, social and geographical mobility, new family patterns, overwork, growth of suburbia, the rise of the media), he affirms, as indispensable for the process to occur, the apparition of an "understanding of human life, agency, and the good which both encourages the new (at least seeming) individuation, and also makes us morally uneasy about it" (Taylor 2007: 473–74).

What better characterizes this age is the rise of expressive individualism as a mass phenomenon. Although this phenomenon takes many forms, Taylor sees it as a common driving force in an understanding of life that was first proposed by Romanticism in the early nineteenth century, whereby "each one of us has his/her own way of realizing our humanity, and that it is important to find and live out one's own, as against surrendering to conformity with a model imposed on us from the outside, by society, a previous generation, or religious and political authority" (Taylor 2007: 475). This process that first captivated the youth in the 1960s and the 1970s is now ever present in the social imaginaries of North Atlantic nations.

In spite of the fact that such a process has undergone a recent transformation, one can still find commonalities between the current situation of this drive towards authenticity and that of the 1960s. Among its relevant similar characteristics, there is: (a) a search for a societal system which would stress more organic ties instead of purely mechanical ones; (b) a greater attention on the intrinsic value of things instead of an emphasis on instrumental ones; (c) an even greater promotion of egalitarianism in the face of privileges; and (d) a stance against the repression of the body by reason and for the fulfillment of sensuality (Taylor 2007: 476). More proper to our times, one may add a broader understanding of choice that now entails a highly valued element of self-expression, to the point that to typically modern "spaces," such as the economy, the public sphere and the sovereign people, a new one has been added: the realm of fashion. These four elements should be seen as constitutive of contemporary North Atlantic social imaginaries. Secondly, the understanding of people as sovereign has received a twist in the sense that tolerance has became the most cherished value for the polis. The prevalence nowadays of the application of Stuart Mill's "harm principle" downplays the ethical demands of Locke's view on political participation and promotes social atomism, which in turn weakens democracy (Taylor 2007: 484, 1991: 55–69).

Taylor is aware of the ambivalences (e. g., BoBo lifestyles, utopianism, consumerism, alienation, the so-called "higher selfishness",[24] radical relativism, etc.) that are present in these developments (in that of the 1960s and in the current one), but thinks that something valuable should be pointed out here: that fragments of the ideal of authenticity, "selectively acted on, remain powerful; and even the abandoned segments may still tug at our conscience" (Taylor 2007: 478). As a consequence, Taylor suggests to "pick up on the flattening and trivialization of many of the key terms of public discourse" as well as to "see that our actual deliberations, while distorted and partly captive of such illusions, nevertheless are always richer

---

[24] "BoBo lifestyles" and "higher selfishness" are concepts Taylor draws from David Brooks (2000).

and deeper than these allow" (Taylor 2007: 480). He shows himself here as embracing the modern ideals of authenticity.

In this new dispensation, religion and the political system relate to each other in a Post- (or Non-) Durkhemian manner, meaning that there is no necessary link any more between adhering to God and belonging to the state. This is a somewhat expected consequence of the Neo-Durkhemian dispensation: "The religious life or practice that I become part of must not only be my choice, but it must speak to me, it must make sense in terms of my spiritual development as I understand this" (Taylor 2007: 486). As a consequence, in the logic of the expressivist mode, the spiritual as such is no longer linked per se to society.

Religious life in AA, then can be characterized as something to be lived, in the first place, to the fullness of oneself. No allegiance to a given political identity or to a specific civilizational order is implied here. This has destabilized all the previous religion-state dispensations. Second, the place and nature of spirituality has pluralism as a "built in" feature, which goes in harmony with our contemporary self-understanding as "buffered selves". Experiences and emotions are much more important than any notion of theological correctness. Third, the rise of consumerism has affected both Protestant (more smoothly) and Catholic societies (more abruptly) in a way that has centered attention on the (religious) goods we may enjoy here and now. Fourth, there has been change in the way religion relates to the public space, from a plural culture in which there was a fracture between religion and a-religion, into a new situation where the possible options have multiplied in all directions and have become available to the masses. Finally, the link between the Christian faith and civilizational order is severed, specifically in regard to sexual ethics. Taylor thinks in this regard that, whereas in the past Christianity gave place to an ethics of discipline and self-denial which in turn held civilization's order, now experience shows that a certain order and an ethical stance in human life can be kept without any religious reference. Moreover, expressivism and the sexual revolution have alienated people from Christianity inasmuch as it is seen as the source of the "old sexual ethics" and of authoritarianism. The spiritual nurturing of purity as well as of moralism and of the repression of sexuality has been rejected by many (Taylor 2007: 486–504).

Spiritual life also changes (although somewhat differently in the United States than in the other North Atlantic countries) in AA. Taylor gives a detailed account of this in the last six chapters of *A Secular Age*, as explained below. In order to complete this exposition on secularization in the North Atlantic area, it is helpful to summarize its basic features. From the perspective of the individual person, the appearance of a new "spiritual profile" can be noted, which could be characterized this way: (a) Many people are dissatisfied with the immanent order prevalent in the new social imaginary; (b) religion is more and more related to a personal quest, a search that is worthy for its own sake; (c) a sense of the unity of the self and of the need for its wholesome flourishing links religion with physical health and with a greater place for the world of feelings; (d) the spiritual is seen by many as opposed to organized religion (Taylor 2007: 486–504).

Taylor finds that today most people live spirituality/religion in vastly diverse ways that include a gamut of variegated positions located between two poles which are in tension with each other: on one end, a kind of extremely privatized spirituality, which often times tends to take the form of a shallow quest, oriented towards the immanent and, on the other end, an authoritarian style religiosity. This situation expresses the fact that there are multiple spiritual itineraries with multiple outcomes as well. "If one can escape from this dialectic which propels to these extremes, it should be clear that there are other alternatives, and that much of today's spiritual/religious life is to be found in this middle ground" (Taylor 2007: 512).

From the standpoint of society, spiritual life is characterized by the breaking down of barriers between religious groups. There has also been a decline in the number of "committed practitioners" while intermediate positions in relation to beliefs and belonging, as described above, have widened. To describe this, Taylor uses notions such as "découplage de la croyance et de la pratique" (unleashing of belief and practice) and "désemboîtement de la croyance, de l'appartenance et de la référence identitaire" (lack of interlocking between faith, belonging and identity references), borrowed from Danièle Hervieu-Léger (1999), and "believing without belonging", taken from Grace Davie (1994). The number of agnostics and atheists has also increased.

Before the appearance and dominance of a Post-Durkhemian dispensation, some reactions towards a Neo-Durkhemian array have occurred, most notably among immigrants, people whose national identity gathers around some religious marker (e. g., the Irish) and, in the case of the United States, among the so called Christian Right. Taylor expands on the particularities of the American religious phenomenon in a way that will be summarized in the following section. Overall, it is not the case anymore for North Atlantic nations that Christianity deeply informs society. Christianity is mostly recognized as having significantly shaped the history of the area in the past (Taylor 2007: 514–16).

The access to a deeper practice of religion shifts, in AA, into various forms of spiritual practice that appear to be meaningful for each individual person. In a world in which Christendom has retreated and religious practice has been unhooked from any sacralized order in society, or from political or national identities and any civilizational order, people will do a lot of shopping around from one religious tradition to another. Although strongly individualist in this regard, the religious landscape according to Taylor won't be devoid of a communitarian dimension due to the prevalence of festive celebrations of different kinds.

Lastly, according to Taylor, religion today will see a much lower rate of intergenerational continuity of religious allegiances. Many previous forms (mostly Christian) will be adapted to the predicament of the new times (e. g., a new understanding of pilgrimage as religious quest). Many people will keep distance from their ancestral churches without breaking with them completely, since they also cherish them somewhat (Taylor 2007: 518–21). People "want to be there, partly as a holder of ancestral memory, partly as a resource against some future need (e.g., their need for a rite of passage, especially a funeral); or as a source of comfort and orientation in the face of some collective disaster" (Taylor 2007: 522). This may imply that, from one perspective, one could talk today of a kind of persistence via mutation of the Neo-Durkhemian dispensation: religion as linked to a national/political identity or civilizational order would not disappear but change from a "hot" to a "cold" state, just as a powerful resource in memory, retreated into a certain distance.

2.5.4 The American (or European?) Exception

Before finishing the present line of inquiry, Taylor addresses the fact that, in spite of the account of secularization he has offered so far, the current outcome of the process is so different in the United States than in the rest of the North Atlantic nations. How is this possible? Taylor recognizes this as one of the most intense debates in the field of secularization theory—one which he summarizes like this: "We are faced with a strong even if not uniform pattern of decline in European societies, and virtually nothing of the sort in the U.S.A. How can this difference be explained?" (Taylor 2007: 522). What would be in the background of this phenomenon, for Taylor, is the fact that modernity has developed differently in specific areas in the West, generating a variety of closely-related social imaginaries which, nonetheless, are different (being, for example, one of these that in the United States and another ones those present in particular Western European countries) (Taylor and Lee 2015).

Taylor gives four reasons for the above-mentioned differences. The first and most important one is that the United States, since its birth, was informed by a Neo-Durkhemian dispensation, without knowing any different previous order. No large-scale events of harsh religious conflict are recorded in its history, in sharp contrast with what happened in Europe (starting with the Wars of Religion up to WWI). In the latter, one still finds a mix of Paleo- and Neo-Durkhemian settings, with a noticeable presence of national churches against which, in turn, anti-clerical reactions are nurtured. Besides, the destabilizing role of contemporary expressivist trends in religion as a whole is stronger in Europe (where Paleo- and Neo-Durkhemian dispensation forms are still alive) than in the United States (where just a Neo-Durkhemian setting is contested).

Second, migrations into the United States did not strengthen the membership of churches per se, as Steve Bruce argues (1996; Taylor 2007: 523, note 36), but rather the ways in which the American social imaginary helped newcomers to integrate into the country. In Taylor's view, it has been the idea of diverse denominations and religious traditions united in a common "civil religion" that served as key reason for immigrants to discover they could become Americans without leaving their existing religious allegiance and, even more, through the practice of their specific religious traditions. As a result, integration occurs here through religious diversity. In contrast, in Europe, religious diversity has triggered conflicts in the past and also at the present, as it can be seen in the tensions between the national churches and their dissenters, (e.g., the Catholic French regime and the Huguenots, the Anglican

British regime and the Irish, etc.) and between church authorities and supporters of laicism (as in the case of *laïcité* France).

Third, in European countries, due to their past as hierarchically-ordered societies, secularized elites have both tended to resist religion as well as to become role models for the rest of the members of society. In this sense, the "orthodox" secularization theory espoused by such elites has worked as a "self-fulfilling prophesy" in Taylor's perspective. In the United States, in contrast, due to the strongly egalitarian ethos of the country since its inception, elites do not play such a strong role model function. Although similarly secularized as their European counterparts, and although they play an important role in the shaping of the social imaginary, American elites are also resisted by a large number of people in the Unites States.

Fourth, because in the United States the Neo-Durkhemian identity is still strong in the form of a "civil religion"—and faith is still importantly related to national/political identity, morality and family—expressivist forces have not been able to substantially erode religion. Europe, however, having experienced the Neo-Durkhemian dispensation itself, is today very resistant to it due to the fear of repeating the wrongdoings of nationalism, most noticeably in World War I and World War II. The horrors of such wars strongly dissuade Europeans from linking religion and national identities, while in contrast Americans can nurture their "civil religion" without too many problems of conscience.

Finally, Taylor explains that in the United States those who, animated by an expressivist outlook, want to push things forward into a Post- (Non-) Durkhemian dispensation are given plenty of room to express their criticism and to try more personalized spiritual explorations. This is a feature of American religious pluralism and has been characteristic of the United States' history. As a consequence, expressivism has been much more destabilizing in Europe than in the United States (Taylor 2007: 523–30). What has occurred in the latter is that "the original civil religion gradually moved wider than its Protestant base, but it has now come up to a stage where, while the link to civilizational order remains strong, the connection to religion is now challenged by a broad range of secularists and Liberal believers" (Taylor 2007: 528). This is what is commonly referred to as "culture wars" and included issues such as abortion, homosexual marriage and school prayer.

Taylor considers that the answers to the American (or European) exception provided up to the present, including his own, are not satisfactory enough because a question remains unanswered: Why were Europeans less able to come out with new religious forms as the Americans did? Why did they not even copy the latter? He thinks this may be because in Europe one still finds the presence of the shadow of the Paleo-Durkhemian dispensation, especially in the form of hegemonic national churches. These churches are related to authoritarianism, conformity to society-wide standards, division between people, and a history of violence, in sum, the opposite of what is supposed to characterize the Age of Authenticity (Taylor 2007: 530).[25]

---

[25] The topic of this section has been object of numerous studies, which has grown steadily as scholars review their understanding of secularization. I find coincidences with some of Taylor's points, as well as a recent and compelling view by well-respected sociologists, in Berger et al. 2008.

As mentioned above, let's turn now into Taylor's second and third lines of inquiry, those on the rise of "exclusive humanism" and on our contemporary conditions of belief. This will be done in the next chapter.

References

Anderson B (2006) Imagined communities: reflections on the origin and spread of nationalism. Verso, London

Bellah RN (1970) Beyond belief; essays on religion in a post-traditional world. Harper & Row, New York

Berger PL (1967) The sacred canopy: elements of a sociological theory of religion. Doubleday, New York

Berger PL et al (2008) Religious America, secular Europe? A theme and variations. Ashgate, Hampshire

Brooks D (2000) Bobos in paradise: the new upper class and how they got there. Simon & Schuster, New York

Brown CG (2001) The death of Christian Britain: understanding secularisation, 1800–2000. Routledge, London

Bruce S (1996) Religion in the modern world. Oxford University Press, Oxford

Casanova J (1994) Public religions in the modern world. University of Chicago Press, Chicago

Davie G (1994) Religion in Britain since 1945: believing without belonging. Blackwell, Oxford

Finke R (1992) An unsecular America. In: Bruce S (ed) Religion and modernization: sociologists and historians debate the secularization thesis. Clarendon, Oxford, pp 145–169

Hervieu-Léger D (1999) Le pèlerin at le converti. La religion en movement. Flammarion, Paris

Martin D (2005) On secularization: towards a revised general theory. Ashgate, Aldershot

McLennan G (2010) Uplifting unbelief. New Blackfriars 91:627–645. doi:10.1111/j.1741-2005.2010.01394_1.x

McLeod H (1995) European religion in the age of the great cities, 1830–1930. Routledge, London

McLeod H (2000) Secularisation in Western Europe, 1848–1914. St. Martin's Press, New York

Miller J (2008) What secular age? Int J Polit Cult Soc 21:5–10. doi:10.1007/s10767-008-9037-5

Schweiker W et al (2010) Grappling with Charles Taylor's a secular age. J Relig 90:367–400. doi:10.1086/651709

Taylor C (1991) The malaise of modernity. Anansi, Concord

Taylor C (2002) Varieties of religion today: William James revisited. Harvard University Press, Cambridge, MA

Taylor C (2004) Modern social imaginaries. Duke University Press, Durham

Taylor C (2007) A secular age. Belknap Press of Harvard University Press, Cambridge, MA

Taylor C (2008) Akbar Ganji in conversation with Charles Taylor. In: The immanent frame. http://blogs.ssrc.org/tif/2008/12/23/akbar-ganji-in-conversation-with-charles-taylor/. Accessed 28 June 2015

Taylor C (2010) Afterword: Apologia pro libro suo. In: Warner M et al (eds) Varieties of secularism in a secular age. Harvard University Press, Cambridge, MA, pp 300–321

Taylor C (2011) Dilemmas and connections: selected essays. Belknap Press of Harvard University Press, Cambridge, MA

Taylor C, Lee B (2015) Modernity and difference. In: Multiple modernities project. http://www.sas.upenn.edu/transcult/promad.html. Accessed 28 June 2015

Thames B (2015) Charles Taylor bibliography. http://nd.edu/~rabbey1/. Accessed 3 July 2015
Tschannen O (1992) Les théories de la sécularisation. Droz, Genève
Wallis R, Bruce S (1992) Secularization: the orthodox model. In: Bruce S (ed) Religion and modernization: sociologists and historians debate the secularization thesis. Clarendon, Oxford, pp 8–30

Chapter 3
Charles Taylor's Account of Secularization (II)

Abstract The socio-historical explanation of Western secularization Taylor proposes is complemented with two other narratives. In the first one, he analyzes the
rise, in the eighteenth century, of what he calls "exclusive humanism," a completely
immanent view of human fulfillment. This disseminates among the elites and, from
there, makes itself available to the masses. An important aspect of this story is the
passing from a theological view of the world into one under Providential Deism, in
which God ceases being personal and becomes an ordering power of a disenchanted
(impersonal) world, one that we are called to shape through this-worldly means to
accomplish the divine design. Another relevant feature is the drive towards reform
that religion assumed from the end of the Middle Ages to the present, one that promoted disenchantment, self-control, and a rationally-planned transformation of the
world. The second narrative that completes Taylor's interpretation of secularization
is his phenomenological analysis of our contemporary conditions of belief. He sees
our current situation as living in an immanent frame, which is a social imaginary
bent towards the impersonal order just described. It is de facto tilted towards the
secular, having no reference to any transcendent reality, but it can be also opened to
it under certain condition. Most people in the West lives, then, somewhere in the
middle of two poles: transformative religion and exclusive humanism, keeping a
myriad of unstable positions. None of these poles can claim victory over the
demands of the other but they fragilize each other.

Keywords Secularization • Western secularization • Providential deism •
Impersonal order • Disenchantment • History of reform • Immanent frame • Close
world structures • Cross-pressure • Fragilization • Transformative religion •
Exclusive humanism

After laying out the first line of inquiry Taylor develops to explain North Atlantic
secularization, I will present the two other complementary approaches he takes: that
of the rise in the West in the eighteenth century of what he calls "exclusive humanism," and his analysis of the more relevant features of contemporary conditions of
belief. As a consequence, this chapter deals more than the previous one with issues
related to culture (ideas, values, myths, symbols, rituals, etc.), particularly with the
epistemic conditions of belief in our times in the West. However, as it has been said,

© Springer International Publishing AG 2017   51
Germán McKenzie, *Interpreting Charles Taylor's Social Theory on Religion
and Secularization*, Sophia Studies in Cross-cultural Philosophy of Traditions
and Cultures 20, DOI 10.1007/978-3-319-47700-8_3

these three courses of action for Taylor's research on secularization unavoidably overlap with each other while keeping their own logic. The chapter closes with Taylor's views on the future of religion in the West.

3.1   The Way to Exclusive Humanism

The story told until now is paralleled, according to Taylor, by two others, one of the world's "disenchantment" and another of the emergence of exclusive humanism as a viable alternative, not just to the elites, but to the masses. Both of them necessarily interact with each other and have lead to the emergence of our contemporary secular social imaginary. This raises the questions as to why primacy should be given to the development of ideas. The answer is that the modern social imaginary originated in theory. "This is something exceptional in history. The earlier social imaginaries it displaced weren't like this" (Taylor 2010: 314). However, Taylor himself is aware of the existence of a number of material (non-intellectual) factors in operation in the process of secularization. This is why he also insists on the need for material conditions (Taylor 2007: 212ff), and contrasts his master narrative (which he also calls a Reform Master Narrative—RMN) with the Radical Orthodox story of secularization, championed among others by John Milbank and Catherine Pickstock (Milbank 2006; Pickstock 1998), that centers on the development of ideas (a position he calls Intellectual Deviation—ID). "I would see both stories, RMN and ID, as complementary exploring different sides of the same mountain, of the same winding river of history" (Taylor 2007: 775).

According to Taylor, in the processes described below in this section, the communication of the perspective and outlook rooted in exclusive humanism from the elite to the masses is not solely one of "diffusion" (Taylor 2007: 424). He says it is more complicated than that, but doesn't explain exactly how this is. What he insists on is the fact that exclusive humanism was built as an alternative, one that is crucial for the drastic changes in conditions for belief (secularity 3) to take place, which in turn explains the decline in religious belief and practice (secularity 2) (Taylor 2007: 423).

3.1.1   History of Reform

Taylor's story of "disenchantment" is introduced by his proposal of a three staged over-arching process: that of Pre-Axial, Axial and Post-Axial religion (Taylor 2011: 367–379, 2007: 146–58).[1]

(a) For Taylor, Pre-Axial (or early) religion is characterized as one that "embeds" the agent. Religious life is seen as inseparable from social life. We relate to God

---

[1] The first reference is to a chapter titled *What Was the Axial Revolution?*

religious evolution

primarily as a society. The social order, with its distinction between religious "functionaries" and "the rest", is sacred. People's identity is to live and develop within this socio-religious matrix.

In relation to the cosmos, this stage is one in which spirits and forces are woven with it. An identification of the divine with animals, plants and places occurs.

In relation to human flourishing, this is understood in very concrete terms, as obtaining prosperity, health, a long life, and fertility. What humans want to avoid is disease, early death, sterility, and the like. Our relationship with the divine occurred in our relationship with the gods, which are not necessarily well disposed to us, but may also be indifferent or hostile. This sometimes was felt by human beings as overwhelmingly stressful. Such situation also fostered propitiatory actions and even the role of "trickster" characters. In sum, human flourishing was not understood as pointing towards transcendence, but as something occurring in the realm of ordinary human life.

Although not following exactly the nomenclature American sociologist Robert Bellah uses when speaking of religious evolution, Taylor recognizes the great help Bellah's thought has given to his own approach (Bellah 1970, 2005).[2]

(b) The "Axial revolution" happened around 1000 b.c., "when various 'higher' forms of religion appeared seemingly independently in different civilizations, marked by such founding figures as Confucius, Gautama, Socrates, and the Hebrew prophets" (Taylor 2011: 371).[3] According to Taylor, the new stage in religious evolution these figures inaugurate is characterized by the beginning of a breaking in the three-level embedded order described above.

The most important change takes place in the ways in which human flourishing is conceived. The transcendent God is defined unambiguously in favor of man (as in Christianity, Buddhism, Chinese religion, Plato). Besides, the highest human goal cannot be defined just as before: Salvation is offered as something that takes us beyond what we usually understand as "human flourishing"; the divine demands from us to imitate its goodness and to alter the order of the world; our view of "evil" is changed in a way that turns it into "imperfection" and is not supposed to be accepted as such, but transformed.

As a consequence of this redefinition of human fulfillment, our drive towards achieving it takes us beyond ordinary human life. A set of vocations with special higher powers (*spiritual virtuosi* in Weberian terms) appear and embodies such flourishing. The good we are supposed to pursue is the true good for us by virtue of the way things are. It is grounded in such a way that this goal is unitary, harmonious and inner-worldly consistent.

(c) Post-Axial religion is the way Taylor sees religion in our times in the West. Our current dispensation, so to speak, combines elements of the Pre-Axial times and the Axial revolution in an unstable way.

---

[2] The first reference is to a chapter titled *Religious Evolution*.

[3] The reference is to a chapter titled *What Was the Axial Revolution?*

This is notorious in the tensions between the way religion is lived among religious *virtuosi* and among those in the larger society. For Taylor, the fact that the latter is so numerous impeded a complete disembedding of religion, even today. Different arrangements are tried to deal with this instability, in a positive way in the guise of affirming the complementarities of both groups, or in a negative manner through the reproach of the former on the latter.

Another locus of tension rises from the fact that there is a redefinition of our human flourishing. The consequence of this is the proposal of human goals as a set of specifically adequate ones for human beings (unitary) which, when achieved, provide a sense of harmony and peace. Besides, the whole cosmos is seen as harmonious, unified and aligned with the human good. A two-tiered setting makes place for the cosmic frame, on one hand, to judge human social orders, on the other. Even when the cosmos may accept the action of spirits ill-disposed towards the human good, these are destined to work as a source of purification for human beings and to be defeated or annulled in the end. This two-tiered arrangement is unstable and is not able to provide alternation between the forces oriented towards the human good and those "oriented towards evil" (as Taylor sees happening, for example, in the case of carnivals in Latin Christendom).

Latin Christendom has continued to foster the movement towards disembedding through the movements of Reformation, both Protestant and Catholic, since the sixteenth century on—which, in turn, was nurtured by the Renaissance. This leads to a change in the social imaginary in the West. The world is now seen as comprised of individuals, whose goal is to reorder human society in a way that may embody the demands of the Gospel in a stable and rational manner. In this way, disenchantment, reform and personal religion go together. In the end, the new dispensation intends to overcome the instabilities described above through the primacy of moral codes.[4]

In this perspective, when asking of the roots of our contemporary secular age, Taylor affirms two: "(1) There had to develop a culture that marks a clear division between the "natural" and the "supernatural", and (2) it had to come to seem possible to live entirely within the natural. Point (1) was something striven for, but point

---

[4]John Milbank (2009) and Collin May (2009) are in deep agreement with Taylor's claim here. Both of them, however, make some precisions about the ways in which this happened historically, both at the level of Middle Ages and Reformation philosophers and theologians, as well as on the paradoxical relationship between enchantment and religious morality.

More critical has been Jonathan Sheehan (2010) for whom Taylor's account if history has been, from the beginning, biased by his desire of creating a particular kind of "secular age" and explaining its appearance and current shape. To this, Taylor's (2010) answer has been that, that what he has done has been interpreting social imaginaries through the practices involved, which can go wrong in many ways. However, in this effort he has tried to pay attention to all relevant facts regardless of his personal convictions. However, what seems to be operative more deeply in Sheehan's criticism (as well as in others) is a Postmodern understanding by which relations of power constitute the ultimate criteria of interpretation of knowledge. Taylor, although recognizing the role of the latter, would affirm interpretive knowledge as one that allows to propose theories which actually could offer "epistemic gains" in the light of specific criteria (of which I speak in Chap. 4).

(2) came about at first quite inadvertently" (Taylor 2010: 304–5) The process, in his view, starts with the Reformation goals of promoting a more individual-oriented devotion to Christ and a greater ethical commitment derived from it. The repression and abolition of certain forms of ritual and collective behavior, more closely linked to Pre-Axial religion, such as magic and superstition, are part of this first step. A second step forward into that direction takes place when new social orders were based on Neo-Stoic ideas. The reduction of social disorder and violence this entailed, in turn, reinforced the new forms of devotion and morality both in Protestant and Catholic countries.

For Taylor, this drive towards Reform succeeded beyond what their promoters thought it would, to the point in which the "polite" order that was fostered led to a more and more immanent understanding of what a Christian order might be. As a consequence, "the understanding of good order (what I call the 'modern moral order') could be embraced outside of the original theological, providential framework, and in certain cases even against it" (Taylor 2010: 305, 2007: 90–158).

3.1.2 Providential Deism, Impersonal Order and Exclusive Humanism

Taylor tells another story that occurred in Latin Christendom that gives another view of the developments narrated above. This has to do with what he calls Providential Deism, which marks the genesis of the shift to an exclusive humanism and which constitutes an intermediate stage before the latter appears not only as a position proper of the elites, but accessible and widespread among the masses in the West (Taylor 2007: 221–95). This narrative has a strong element of history of ideas built into it.

The first facet would be that of a turnaround of the previous view on how the world is designed by God into what he calls the "anthropocentric shift". This shift occurs in a sequence of steps: (a) God becomes the essential energizer of the ordering power through which we disenchant the world, and asks for a purer worship. The latter means, in short, that we should carry God's goals (this is, our goals) in the world. (b) Grace seems less essential for our religious life than before. The moral/ spiritual resources can be experienced as purely immanent. There are intra-human sources of benevolence that orient us. (c) We are disengaged, disciplined agents, capable of remaking ourselves and in control of an awesome power. Finally, (d) public space is turned into a self-sufficient realm.

The second facet Taylor explores is the shift towards the primacy of an impersonal order. The divine "relates to us primarily by establishing a certain order of things, whose moral shape we can easily grasp, if we are not misled by false and superstitious notions" (Taylor 2007: 221). A number of changes lead from the Christian worldview to this kind of order, the most important of which is disbelief in God as a personal being.

The last facet is the appearance of the idea of a true, original religion, which was meant to be recovered. This, as a consequence, brings up a view in which religion is founded not in revelation, but on human-lived reality either as nature or reason alone.

Coupled with the three above described steps, one can also mention the appearance of the modern social imaginary, as has been described before, along with the establishment of the Modern Moral Order (MMO). The confluence of these two realities is how, according to Taylor, an exclusive humanism emerged as an alternative to the Christian faith as a theoretical alternative.

From this point on, there is a further diversification of positions that gives place to an ever-widening variety of moral/spiritual options. This, starting in the eighteenth century, extends up to the present in a way in which the fractured culture of the elites becomes generalized into the whole society during the second half of the twentieth century. Taylor explains this itinerary in great detail. He focuses on the indictments during the 1700s against traditional religion, as well as on the reactions to the immanent-oriented approach in Romanticism and in perspectives with tragic overtones. He then explores the more radical positions of exclusive humanism in the 1900s, with the appearance of evolutionary theory and the notion of universe instead of that of cosmos (Taylor 2007: 299–419).[5]

3.2   Our Contemporary Conditions of Belief

3.2.1   Living in an Immanent Frame

After explaining the argument summarized here, Taylor thinks it is possible to answer the question about the conditions for belief in our times; the issue of secularity 3. His views here develop a complex phenomenological analysis.

He sees that we are now living in an "immanent frame" which results from the process of disenchantment described in the last section (especially in its impact on the human practical self-understanding) and the rise of modern natural science. This particular frame is an order that can be understood on its own, without reference to any transcendent reality. "The life of the buffered individual, instrumentally effective in secular time, created the practical context within which the self-sufficiency of this immanent realm could become a matter of experience" (Taylor 2007: 543). More precisely, this frame is "objectivized," and appears as including a set of cosmic, social and moral orders, all of them impersonal.

This immanent frame should not be understood per se as "naturally" closed to the transcendent, but bent towards an impersonal order. As a consequence, it is in a way inclined to accept Deism over orthodox Christianity, or to devalue insights such as prayer that come from sources other than "scientific neutrality." However, the fact

---

[5] Taylor's *Modern Social Imaginaries* is almost entirely included in this part of *A Secular Age*.

that we who live within this frame perceive ourselves solicited by both the calling for immanence and the resisting attraction towards the transcendent shows how the mere fact of living within the immanent frame is not enough to tilt our stance into a specific option. Briefly said, we can give a closed or open "spin" to the way we live in the immanent frame (Taylor 2007: 555–56).

How one remains in the open spin is, according Taylor, potentially a consequence of a number of factors: our personal formation (due to family and school), our living in a society in which religion and political and national identity relate as in a Neo-Durkhemian dispensation (as is the case of "civil religion" in the United States), or our experience of a kind of "void" when living just in an immanent mode. Conversely, one could be living in a closed spin when avoiding allegiance to theological beliefs or ecclesiastical structures which are seen as opposed to the Modern Moral Order described in the last section ("fanaticism" in the Enlightenment parlance), when responding to the moral attraction of immanence (and the rejection of any "higher" instance seen as the temptation of escaping from our reality), or when espousing a naturalistic view of things based on science and the sense of power and control it can enable (Taylor 2007: 546–48).

In any event, it is not usual that people are able to give a stark and clear answer to the question about the deceitfulness/evilness of transcendence, or about its goodness. This is (a) because the immanent frame is not a set of beliefs in the first place, but a "sensed context in which we develop our beliefs" (Taylor 2007: 549), and (b) due to the fact that any of the two above described options "usually sunk to the level of such an unchallenged framework, something we have trouble often thinking ourselves outside of, even as an imaginative exercise" (Taylor 2007: 549). As a consequence, for Taylor, the immanent frame is not the only point of reference to understand the place of religion and the sacred in the contemporary West, but also the different ways in which such a frame receives a particular spin (open or closed) in specific milieux (e. g., the closed stance in the academy). In short, the immanent frame is the way our contemporary social imaginary in the West is shaped, and secularization should be understood both as a change in structures (social and others) as well as a change in the way we see and imagine those structures (Taylor 2007: 594).

3.2.2 Closed World Structures

Getting into more detail in the epistemic issue he has raised above, Taylor speaks of four kinds of "Closed World Structures" (CWS) operative in the secularized West. CWSs are "ways of restricting our grasp of things which are not recognized as such" (Taylor 2007: 551). In the present case, Taylor sees them acting as the previously mentioned "unthought," "explaining the unjustified force of the mainstream account of secularization, as well as the disinterest and contempt for religion which frequently accompanies it" (Taylor 2007: 551, 594). Borrowing from the thought of Ludwig Wittgenstein, he sees this phenomenon as being "held captive" by a "picture" (Taylor 2007: 557). If CWSs seem obvious to us, it is because "we have already taken a stance to it" (Taylor 2007: 556). But the rationality of such obviousness is nothing but illusion (Taylor 2007: 556).[6]

What is exactly involved in CWSs? Taylor himself specifies the basic elements that compose this concept:

(a) What I shall really be describing is not worlds in their entirety, but "world structures", aspects or features of the way experience and thought are shaped and cohere, but not the whole of which they are constituents. (b) I will not be describing the world of any concrete human beings. … What I'm doing is trying to articulate certain world-types ("ideal types" in a quasi-Weberian sense), which may not, will almost surely not coincide with the totality of any real person's world. (c) Thirdly, the articulation involves an intellectualization; one has to get at the connections in lived experience through ideas, and very often ideas which are not consciously available to the people concerned, unless they are forced to articulate them themselves through challenge and argument. (Taylor 2007: 557)

CWS 1 could be summarized as this: "Science undermines religion." This view has two variants. The first one is an epistemological one—Science alone explains why belief is not possible and it also establishes a materialistic understanding of things. The second variant is a moral one—Religion keeps us in a childish condition, giving us wrong and mythical explanations of the world in order to provide us with security and comfort. We are morally called to grow up and free ourselves, and courageously face the world as it is (Taylor 2007: 561–69).

CWS 2 is that of a "narrative of substraction" involved in our modern ethical/political outlook. Taylor phrases it this way:

> A great deal of our political and moral life is focused on human ends: human welfare, human rights, human flourishing, equality between human beings. Indeed, our public life, in societies which are secular in a familiar modern sense, is exclusively concerned with human goods. … Thus one is either in this world, living by its premises, and then one cannot believe in God; or one believes, and one is in some sense living like a resident alien in modernity. (Taylor 2007: 569)

What underlies this story is the notion of ourselves as moderns having realized that certain claims of the previous moral/political dispensation in which we lived were false and considered to be "perennial truths." As a consequence, we need to liberate ourselves from them. "What this view reads out of the picture is the possibility that Western modernity might be powered by its own positive visions of the good, that is, by one constellation of such visions among available others, rather than by the only viable set left after the old myths and legends have been exploded" (Taylor 2007: 571). This approach sees the new moral/political setting not as an option but just as simply the negation of a previous order, hence the "narrative of substraction" label: the elimination of the false/oppressive order gives room for the suppressed modern ethical, political and economic ideas to "naturally" unfold in history.

---

[6] Taylor expands on his notion of "obviousness" here, in note 17.

CWS 3 is based on the rise of our modern political and moral spaces which are seen as providing the individual with "direct access" to the nation, the economy and the public sphere, in contrast with the mediated way that prevailed in the pre-modern "feudal" world, with its hierarchical relations embedded in networks marked by kinship, all of which was legitimated by religion. This meant a change in the moral imaginary in which people saw themselves as equal citizens and who enjoyed much more freedom of action. In this way, the ideas of the people as agents of collective empowerment and that of the people as nation became crucial elements of modern political self-understanding.

In light of the above, Taylor thinks, "the story of the rise of modern social spaces doesn't need to be given an anti-religious spin. But there are motivations to go this way; and like any spin, we can easily see how the wide acceptance of one such, and the relegation of religion which this involves, could harden into a 'picture' which appears obvious and unchallengeable" (Taylor 2007: 579).

Lastly, CWS4 is that of the authorization of value by the autonomous self. In this case, the story goes like this:

> Once human beings took their norms, their goods, their standards of ultimate value from an authority outside of themselves; from God, or the gods, or the nature of Being or the cosmos. But then they came to see that these higher authorities were their own fictions, and they realized that they had to establish their norms and values for themselves, on their own authority. This is a radicalization of the coming to adulthood story. … It is not just that freed from illusion, humans come to establish the true facts about the world. It is also that they come to dictate the ultimate values by which they live. (Taylor 2007: 580)

For the four CWSs described above, Taylor takes pains to show how the obviousness of their stories is not so, and how they are affected by a number of ambiguities and dilemmas.

3.2.3 Living Cross-Pressured

We have already seen above that Taylor makes the point that most people in the secularized West live within the solicitation of two poles: that of orthodox religion (mostly Christianity) and belief, on one hand, and that of secular humanism and unbelief, on the other. Most of us, then, live "cross-pressured." What this means for Taylor is that in our culture we are suspended between the above mentioned two extreme positions, each of which defines itself in opposition to the other, and by doing so they define the whole field of options. As a consequence, all possible middle positions take such poles as crucial reference points. This, as a reaction, provokes the appearance of a new host of religious positions that resist being affiliated to the extreme ones above, giving birth to the Nova Effect: a whole gamut of diverse positions, very nuanced in their specific standings, which tends to expand and multiply even more. Taylor calls this process pluralization. Besides, some people hesitate for a long time regarding their stance towards religion, being ambivalent about assuming an open or closed spin to their lives, and also moving to and from those positions (Taylor 2007: 596–99).

At the bottom of the option for one of the two previously mentioned poles is a decision of the will based on some kind of "anticipatory confidence." Both views try to answer the question about the existence of any transcendent realm. In the case of unbelief based on rejecting as immoral any premise that may not be proven through the method of science, trust is placed in the following statement: "Better risk loss of truth than chance of error." In contrast, in the case of belief, what is accepted is the epistemological view that affirms: "Certain truths open to us as a result of our commitment," as well as the claim of making our own choices before the risk of losing truth. From the perspective of the other side, each position could be seen either as closing into a self-fulfilling prophesy (unbelievers) or as that of prisoners of their own delusion (believers). This situation makes both stances a possibility for many people today. "What is more, a close attention to the debate seems to indicate that most people feel both pulls. They have to go one way, but they never fully shake from the call of the other" (Taylor 2002: 57, 2007: 555–56).[7]

As other sources of cross-pressure in contemporary societies in the West, Taylor also mentions the polemics between utilitarian ethics and Kantian morality, the instrumental approach to nature and that of the environmentalist movement, and the demands of the disciplined MMO and a Dyonisian stance towards life, inspired in Nietzsche and disseminated by Postmodern thinkers.

3.2.4 Mutual Fragilization of the Poles

Within this schema, both pole positions of belief and unbelief are mutually "fragilized." For Taylor, "fragilization" means that "greater proximity of alternatives has led to a society in which more people change their position, that is, 'convert' in their lifetimes and/or adopt a different position that their parents. Life-time and intergenerational switches become more common" (Taylor 2007: 556, note 19). This is different than the meaning Peter Berger gives to the term "fragilization"  implying a weaker position in the case of belief. Taylor sees that "faith, arising in this contemporary predicament, can be stronger, just because it has faced the alternative without distortion" (Taylor 2007: 556). Another consequence for religion is that of fragmentation of the religious landscape into a myriad of positions, as mentioned above (Taylor 2007: 594).

What is at stake in the contemporary debates between belief and unbelief in the West is ultimately, in Taylor's view, the response to the question: what does real human fulfillment (or human fullness) consist on? One way of seeing how things are like this is to consider the fact that resistance to radical positions of unbelief such as materialism in both its mechanistic and "motivational" approaches derives from an idea of human fulfillment: people feel it is difficult to do justice, from such

---

[7] The whole argument is developed in detail in Taylor 2002: 42–60.

authentic Heidegger death

views, to the fact that human beings are active, reality-shaping agents; that we have higher spiritual/ethical motivations; and that we are deeply moved by beauty (Taylor 2007: 595).

How should "fullness" be understood in this context? Taylor affirms, in this regard, that there is no escape for humans to seek some version of it, "for any liveable understanding of human life, there must be some way in which this life looks good, whole, proper, really being lived as it should. The utter absence of some such would leave us in abject, unbearable despair. So it's not that unbelief shuns Christian ideas of fullness for nothing at all; it has its own versions" (Taylor 2007: 600, 2010: 315–18).[8]

Taylor goes ahead by saying that the crucial debate is not just between rival conceptions of fullness, but between different ethical positions. Critical to the latter conversation are the answers to the following issues: (a) What are our motivations towards fullness? (b) What would cause us to take distance from a notion of fullness (seen as something illusory, as a negative belief)? (c) To what degree can fullness be achieved? (d) To what extent can the doubts casted on fullness above be eliminated? (e) If the latter is not possible, what should we do with them? What would the cost of keeping them be? (Taylor 2007: 604–5).

The polemics between belief (religion) and unbelief in the West raises dilemmas for both positions. This is extensively explored by Taylor in four realms: (a) humanism and transcendence; (b) the demand for wholeness on the part of human fulfillment; (c) that of the relationship between our drives for sex and violence, on one hand, and religious or secular commitments, on the other; and (d) achieving a sense of meaning in terms of religious or secular commitments (Taylor 2007: 618–727).

As a conclusion of his survey on these dilemmas, Taylor argues that "rather than one side clearly possessing the answers that the other one lacks, we find rather that both face the same issues, and each with some difficulty. The more one reflects, the more the easy certainties or either 'spin', transcendental or immanent, are undermined" (Taylor 2007: 726–27).

Taylor concludes that the expressivist culture in the West, with its Post-Durkhemian stance, "seems very inhospitable to belief" (Taylor 2007: 727). Part of the difficulties lays on our world's ideological fragmentation to the point of being like an exploding Nova of individual takes on reality, including belief and unbelief.

---

[8] Several authors have criticized Taylor by saying he is unduly affirming that the exclusive humanist position is less deep and fuller that that of transformative religion (McLennan 2008; Bernstein 2008) and even that the use of a sense of fullness is misleading per se (Ward 2008). Taylor's own response goes along the lines of recognizing that it is impossible for positions defending belief ("strong religion") and unbelief to apodictically prove their points and that in any of those stances there are meta-theoretical views which are also of a normative kind. (McLennan 2008, 2010). Differences between them may prove to be intractable. However, it would still be possible to phenomenologically describe (Casanova 2008) the ways in which human fullness is sought as belonging to a continuum between religion and exclusive humanism (Marty 2008).

As one would expect, other debates have occurred in connection with Taylor's use "transcendence" as part of the theoretical tools for his narrative, which I am not mentioning because they fall beyond the scope of my study.

In this context, people feel a strong motivation for not going beyond the world of the human, which causes their estrangement from important religious traditions and their inability to articulate the language of transcendence. However, the sense of something more remains, as a large number of people feel in moments of silence and reflection, contact with nature, bereavement and loss. Taylor asserts that "our age is very far from settling in to a comfortable unbelief" (Taylor 2007: 727). Even when people take safe distance from religion, they cannot help but to be touched by strong religious testimonies (Taylor 2007: 727).

3.3 Looking into the Future

At the end of *A Secular Age*, Taylor tries to provide some prognosis of the fate of the orthodox secularization theory as well as about the religious landscape (especially that of Christianity) in the future in the West. In regard to the former, he sees it declining in time, rendered more and more implausible by the events and processes taking place today in our region. He mentions that other societies will not follow the West on a substractive account of religion. On the contrary, religion will stay in non-Western realms. Many illnesses usually attributed to religion (such as intolerance, violence, etc.) will endure in the highly secularized Western societies. The heavy concentration of immanence in the West will trigger an ever stronger sense of uneasiness in many people, provoking in turn religious reactions (Taylor 2007: 770).

Religious life in the West will remain due to the intimations to transcendent reality in human life, Taylor affirms. He also makes some remarks on Christianity. He starts by saying that our contact with the divine overpasses us in a way that we are not able to grasp in its entirety. This causes us to shut out some parts of it. For different reasons, unbelievers also shut out the divine and, paradoxically, the same occurs to believers who think they have it right. Taylor wants to warn Christianity of establishing "unambiguous boundaries between the pure and the impure through the polarization of conflict, even war" (Taylor 2007: 769).

On a different topic, he sees Christians exploring their own tradition to recover elements that cannot be left out by any effort of Reform or of any other kind. Among the elements to be recovered, Taylor mentions, in a rather normative fashion, the abandonment of an excessive stress on the mind, the recovery of the passionate and of the body (including sexuality), and the abandonment of a tendency towards "homogenizing" (Taylor 2007: 770–72). In regard to the latter, he says that "the Church was rather meant to be the place in which human beings, in all their difference and disparate itineraries, come together; and, in this regard, we are obviously falling short" (Taylor 2007: 772).

When speaking specifically of Roman Catholicism, Taylor finds there is still a place for it in modern society, although it would need both a dose of humility and of what he calls good sense.

(a) On one hand, humility is needed to recognize that modernity was a needed "break" with the old order of things for the Church to liberate itself from its entanglement with a given political order and established society as manifested from the varied establishments of Christendom (Taylor 2011: 170–72).[9] "The notion is that modern culture, in breaking with the structures and beliefs of Christendom, also carried certain facets of Christian life further than ever were taken or could have been taken within Christendom" (Taylor 2011: 170). Among these facets he mentions universal human rights, seen as unconditioned by gender, culture, belonging, religious allegiance, etc. On the other hand, good sense is needed to recognize, as has been mentioned, that at the roots of modernity one find Christianity. From this perspective, however, this freedom also has a Christian meaning, "for instance, the freedom to come to God on one's own or, otherwise put, moved only by the Holy Spirit, whose barely audible voice will often be heard better when the loudspeakers of armed authority are silent" (Taylor 2011: 172). He sees this situation as a liberating one in which it is possible for us to live the Gospel in a purer manner.

(b) In modern society, however, on the side of "exclusive humanism" one finds a strong reaction against religion and against any affirmation of life by aiming at transcendence and pointing to an identity change. It is like any recovery of elements from the "old" order would entail the betrayal of all that modernity stands for. In Taylor's view, this is due to a narrowness of view: what it criticized is a view of Catholic Christianity in which human flourishing is a superstitious version reserved just for a few *spiritual virtuosi*, or the Reformed view by which what is accessible for all believers does not entail flourishing, or a mix of both. In contrast, the Christian stance of "practical *agape*," which should be lived in ordinary life and is also open to be lived in modern times, is not taken into account (Taylor 2011: 172–77). Christianity is seen, this way, as a kind of religion that goes against the modern supreme value of life and of its flourishing also through the reduction of the grip that suffering and death have on it; it is seen as the religion that prevented our ancestors from recognizing this basic fact and kept them from enjoying this value in order to obtain some supposed "higher goods" (Taylor 2011: 176).

More importantly, the "exclusive humanist" stance is not fully aware that it has nurtured what Taylor calls a "revolt from within". Lead by Friedrich Nietzsche, and developed by thinkers like Michel Foucault and Georges Bataille, the affirmation of life turns into "anti-humanism," which is characterized by the dismissal of universalism, solidarity and benevolence, and by the affirmation of chaos and destruction as a condition for life. In this sense, they go beyond life into a fascination for death and suffering (Taylor 2011: 177–81). In this light, "exclusive humanists" may find in defenders of transcendence, Roman Catholics among them, key allies for the future of their cultural project.

Another important warning Taylor makes is that the very high moral standards modernity has set up for the West are unprecedented. People are asked to outreach consistent and systematically to strangers in name of universal justice, solidarity and benevolence. However, the ethical sources made available to deal with this

---

[9] The reference is to the chapter titled *A Catholic Modernity?*

demand are not rich enough (Taylor 1989: 495–521). In his view, this is patent when, while trying to live according to such standards, people start feeling superior to others or transforming what should be ethical commitment into fashion. It is also made manifest when, while facing disappointment because of the low ethical performance of fellow human beings, people foster a sense of anger and futility, which easily transforms into contempt, hatred and even violence. It also occurs when people who have strongly taken a stance for justice generate hatred for those whom they see as evildoers. Before all these limitations, Christianity has something to offer: a faith-based spiritual commitment for love or compassion which should be seen as unconditional and based on the notion of human persons as being images of God (Taylor 2011: 185–86). "It makes a whole lot of difference whether you think this kind of love is a possibility for us humans. I think it is, but only to the extent that we open ourselves to God, which means, in fact, overstepping the limits set in theory by exclusive humanisms" (Taylor 2011: 186).

It is in the recovery of a view of "practical *agape*," of keeping a stance of humanism and of unconditional love and compassion that Taylor sees a place for Catholicism in the West in times to come. He warns about any effort to strive towards a "modern Catholicism," as if it were possible to summarize and transcend the achievements of less advantaged Catholics of past times. This he sees as an impossible chimera as well as something that goes against what he sees as Catholic principle: "No widening of the faith without an increase in the variety of devotions and spiritualities and liturgical forms and responses to Incarnation" (Taylor 2011: 168). In contrast, "the point is, taking our modern civilization for another of those great cultural forms that have come and gone in human history, to see what it means to be a Christian here" (Taylor 2011: 169). Taylor's view of Catholicism into the future is one that will recognize that the practical primacy of life, as it was stressed by secular humanism and has been described above, is a gain that should be kept and nurtured. Such gain "was unlikely to come about without some breach with established religion" (Taylor 2011: 180–81).

In conclusion, the Taylorean "revisionist" account of secularization in the West, aside from its complex and multi-layered meta-narrative, proposes itself as a view that transcends the polarization between "orthodox" and "counter-orthodox" theorists while affirming that religious motivation per se has remained operative, giving birth to new religious forms in the secular West. In his view, exclusive humanism and religiously-inspired versions of human fulfillment unavoidably fragilize each other today.

Up to now and from a sociological standpoint, it is not difficult to see that Taylor vouches for a multi-causal approach to social change in which "material" conditions—such as technology, economics, politics, demographics and stratification—as well as "non material" ones—such as religion and ideology—are potentially independent variables that may influence each other and the life course of society. Besides, one can say he mistrusts all-encompassing sociological approaches to social change due to the highly complex analysis they entail, which makes them prone either to provide generalizations which are very difficult to prove or to propose too simplistic accounts of localized phenomena. It is through sociological, historical, legal and even literary analysis that he seems to confirm what he affirms from the standpoint of social theory. Finally, Taylor seems to assess the relationship between (individual) human motivation and social change through the notion of shared "social imaginary." In so doing, he draws from Benedict Anderson and Bronislaw Baczko. Taylor sees changes in the social imaginary as happening through an elite-masses dynamic, which in turn nurtures personal motivation and triggers social change.

Four specific aspects of Taylor's philosophical project appear to be closely related to his view on social change. The first one is his hermeneutical understanding of the social sciences. The second one is his notion of human motivation, rooted in our response to demands in our effort to live fulfilled lives in a broad sense. The third one is his philosophical position some have called "falsifiable realism" (Abbey 2000: 26–31; Taylor 2013: 61–90), which gives substance to what he sees as a non-relativistic approach to the social sciences and also to the way in which he relates to Postmodern social critique. Last, but not least, the above mentioned positions are linked with an understanding of humans as "self-interpreting beings," which is at the basis of his project of a "philosophical anthropology."

The following chapters are aimed at exploring all these topics more thoroughly.

References

Abbey R (2000) Charles Taylor. Princeton University Press, Princeton

Bellah RN (1970) Beyond belief; essays on religion in a post-traditional world. Harper & Row, New York

Bellah RN (2005) What is axial about the axial age? Eur J Sociol 46:69. doi:10.1017/s0003975605000032

Berenstein R (2008) The uneasy tensions of immanence and transcendence. Int J Polit Cult Soc 21:11–16. doi:10.1007/s10767-008-9035-7

Casanova J (2008) Secular imaginaries: introduction. Int J Polit Cult Soc 21:1–4. doi:10.1007/s10767-008-9042-8

Marty ME (2008) A secular age. Church Hist 77:773–775. doi:10.1017/S0009640708001480

May C (2009) Charles Taylor, a secular age. Society 46:199–203. doi:10.1007/s12115-008-9178-1

McLennan G (2008) Among the unbelievers. New Left Review 52: 139–148

McLennan G (2010) Uplifting unbelief. New Blackfriars 91:627–645. doi:10.1111/j.1741-2005.2010.01394_1.x

Milbank J (2006) Theology and social theory: beyond secular reason. Blackwell Publishers, Oxford

Milbank J (2009) A closer walk on the wild side: some comments on Charles Taylor's a secular age. Stud Christ Ethics 22:89–104

Pickstock C (1998) After writing: on the liturgical consummation of philosophy. Blackwell Publishers, Oxford

Sheehan J (2010) Whan was disenchantment? History and the secular age. In: Warner M et al (eds) Varieties of secularism in a secular age. Harvard University Press, Cambridge, MA, pp 217–242

Taylor C (1989) Sources of the self: the making of the modern identity. Harvard University Press, Cambridge, MA

Taylor C (2002) Varieties of religion today: William James revisited. Harvard University Press, Cambridge, MA

Taylor C (2007) A secular age. Belknap Press of Harvard University Press, Cambridge, MA

Taylor C (2010) Afterword: apologia pro libro suo. In: Warner M et al (eds) Varieties of secularism in a secular age. Harvard University Press, Cambridge, MA, pp 300–321

Taylor C (2011) Dilemmas and connections: selected essays. Belknap Press of Harvard University Press, Cambridge, MA

Taylor C (2013) Retrieving realism. In: Schear JK (ed) Mind, reason, and being-in-the-world: the McDowell-Dreyfus debate. Routledge, Abingdon, pp 61–90

Ward I (2008) A secular age. J Relig 88:420–422. doi:10.1086/590032

Part II
Sources

Chapter 4
Philosophical and Classic Sociological Sources

Abstract The philosophical sources of Taylor's meta-narrative are his own works on the human person and on the hermeneutic methodology of the social sciences. In regard to the former, his views of non-metaphysical human constants as that of being self-interpretive and ethically-bounded selves, have direct impact on the way in which he developed the notion of social imaginaries. As per the latter, Taylor's views are inspired by a strong criticism of the modern model of knowledge, and by affirming that man knows only in the context of non-thematized frameworks in which he lives. As a consequence, scientific methods of universal applicability should be replaced with ad hoc criteria for interpretations localized in time and space. More concretely, this means that a social scientist, while studying any social fact, needs to take into account three levels of interpretations: that of the meaning already present in such a fact, that shared by the social agent under study with the society in which it belongs, and that due to the social scientist's own self-interpretations. In Taylor's opinion, this does not lead to subjectivism or relativism, but the formulation of theories that can defeat others by explaining a phenomenon with more depth or with a wider scope. On the other hand, his closest source among classic sociologists is Weber, with whom Taylor has several coincidences: an interpretive view of sociology, the recognition of the importance of both social and cultural factors in explaining social change, and the use of ideal-types.

Keywords Philosophical anthropology • Hermeneutics • Method • Social sciences • Self-interpretation • Subjectivism • Relativism • Classical sociology • Weber

This chapter examines the relevant philosophical and classic sociological sources of the Taylorean account of secularization. The first section focuses on Taylor's work as philosopher, giving insight into the main ideas that underpin his meta-narrative in *A Secular Age* and other secularization-related works as explained in Chaps. 2 and 3. The second section will analyze his appropriation of the thought of Weber, Durkheim and Marx, the more important representatives of classical sociology.

© Springer International Publishing AG 2017   69
Germán McKenzie, *Interpreting Charles Taylor's Social Theory on Religion and Secularization*, Sophia Studies in Cross-cultural Philosophy of Traditions and Cultures 20, DOI 10.1007/978-3-319-47700-8_4

4.1 "Philosophical Anthropology" and the Hermeneutical View of the Sciences of Man

Taylor is a philosopher who happens to have done social science,[1] particularly with his more recent books *Modern Social Imaginaries* (2004) and *A Secular Age* (2007). However, while doing the latter, he has tried to keep consistent with his understanding of the sciences of man,[2] especially that involved in the study of human agency.[3] This will become apparent in the following analysis, through which I will explain some key features of his philosophical views and how they impact on Taylor's meta-narrative (Abbey 2000; Smith 2002).[4]

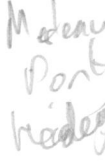 Taylor's main philosophical influences are French phenomenologist Maurice Merleau-Ponty, along with German philosophers Martin Heidegger and Ludwig Wittgenstein. German Romanticism is another important source for his thought, in particular the work of Johann Gottfried Herder. Other authors who have influenced Taylor include Aristotle, G.W.F. Hegel and J.-J. Rousseau. His philosophical work, according to Nicholas H. Smith (2002), constitutes a project, although not a systematic one. However, there is consistency in the ways in which he develops his thought. This can be seen when one compares his views on ethics, selfhood, political theory, epistemology and language. Taylor himself sees his interests in philosophical anthropology, modernity, and the place of the spiritual in human life as driving forces nurturing his academic endeavors. He also sees philosophical anthropology as crucial for the elaboration of the sciences of man.[5] While carrying on such endeavors, he has not restricted himself to the realm of philosophy as it is customarily defined at the university level, but has also explored cultural anthropology, history, sociology and psychology to produce "hybrid" discourses (Taylor 2008).

4.1.1 Humans as "Self-Interpreting" Beings

Taylor would say that human beings have always had some grasp of themselves, a self-understanding. However, concepts such as "self" and "identity" are products of modernity. They serve to denote what also has been known as person or subject. He is not interested in distinguishing the precise meanings of these different terms but

---

[1] He sees himself as an "amateur" sociologist and theologian, "albeit a very interested one," (Martin 2005: ix). The quote belongs to his Foreword to Martin's book.

[2] He uses sciences of man and social sciences as synonyms.

[3] Charles Taylor, personal communication to the author, 19 Nov 2009.

[4] These books provide overviews of Taylor's philosophical work.

[5] Taylor finds this philosophical enterprise as "terribly necessary, and also unbearably problematic. It is necessary, because the efforts to elaborate a science of human beings, in psychology, politics, sociology, anthropology (in the narrow sense), linguistics, etc., lean on certain assumptions about what human beings are like, which are often highly questionable" (Honneth and Joas 1988). The quote belongs to his Foreword to such book.

in exploring their historical and ontological features. He sees the self as changing in history. We may recall his view on the passing from the "porous" to the "buffered" self, which has been extensively explored, in the case of modernity, in his book *Sources of the Self* (Taylor 1989b).

Nevertheless, Taylor also sees some "human constants," an ontology of the self. With this he is, however, not vouching for a metaphysical or essentialist view of man. "It is simply the embeddedness of human beings in the world and their need to cope with it. Taylor does not construe this as an 'essential' feature of human subjectivity. But it is defined in a quite minimal way" (Smith 2002: 134).[6]

(a) Among these phenomenological "constants" Taylor finds in the first place that humans are "self-interpreting beings" (Taylor 1985a: 4, 45–76, 1985b: 26, 55).[7]

> I believe that what we are as human agents is profoundly interpretation-dependent, that human beings in different cultures can be radically diverse, in keeping with their fundamentally different self-understandings. But I think that a constant is to be found in the shape of the questions that all cultures must address. (Taylor 1988b: 299)

We can see that, in Taylor's view, self-interpretation is not carried on alone, but depends on the language we receive from society and culture. Our self-understanding is affected by the ways in which we relate to others and are seen by them. Self-understandings are not just extrinsic to who we are but intrinsic, so a change in the vocabulary or symbols that we use to explain ourselves entails a correspondent change in who we actually are. This "expressivist" outlook, which Taylor draws from Herder, means that "language cannot be confined to the activity of talking about things. We transform our emotions into human ones not primarily in talking about them, but in expressing them. Language also serves to express/realize ways of feeling without talking about them. We often give expression to our feelings in talking about something else" (Taylor 1985a: 233).[8]

This does not mean that our self-interpretations are impervious to delusion. Self-understandings are relevant even if they are false. Moreover, people could have different and even conflicting self-understandings. Lastly, self-interpretations are not static but change in time. This is not only because our circumstances never stay the same, but because the very fact of producing a new particular self-understanding of ourselves transforms who we are: "Or formulations about ourselves can alter what they are about" (Taylor 1985a: 101).[9]

Each human person sees this process of change in self-understanding as some kind of "progress." Taylor "proposes that the succession of self-understandings that individuals adopt is seen by them to be part of a progressive story about the unfolding or enhancing of self-knowledge" (Abbey 2000: 61). So, when someone adopts a

---

[6] Smith also mentions here other similar "constants" such as being embodied, birth, sex, death, moral valuations, narrative identities and moral sources. I will speak of some of them in this chapter.

[7] The references are to pieces *Self-Interpreting Animals* and *Interpretation and the Sciences of Man*, respectively.

[8] The quote is from the piece titled *Language and Human Nature*.

[9] The quote is from the piece titled *The Concept of a Person*.

new self-understanding, it is because it is seen by the subject as a better, clearer, more perspicuous view—in Taylor's parlance—than the previous ones. Here occurs a redefinition of the good life for each person, which links self-interpretation with morality, as will be see just below.

(b) Another constant Taylor finds in humans is that of being driven by purposes. Self-interpretations are not arbitrary but refer to purposes human beings give to themselves, which guide their actions and efforts. The same purposeful quality would be true of animals if they were able to link these goals to their own self-understandings. This is why we do not speak of them as persons, since to be one "you need to be an agent with a sense of yourself as an agent, a being which can thus make plans for your life, one who also holds values in virtue of which different such plans seem better or worse, and who is capable of choosing between them" (Taylor 1985c: 257).

As a consequence, Taylor contends that any study of human agency should take into account the implied purposes in humans. It is "teleological" in this sense, but not in the precise Aristotelian meaning of the term. Our ordinary language is filled with the assumption of the existence of our purposes and goals and the guidance they provide to our actions. The ways in which we discuss our desires, intentions, actions and responsibilities reflect this. Consequently, and in debate with behaviorists, Taylor would argue that in order to explain the behavior of ordinary people living their lives, their self-understandings matter inasmuch as they inform their agency, and therefore should be taken into consideration (Taylor 1964).

(c) Taylor also explores what he finds to be another constant dimension in humans: that of being selves-in-dialogue. This is linked in his view of the importance language has in shaping individual identity through self-interpretation.

"Man is above all the language-animal" (Taylor 1985a: 216)[10] affirms Taylor when he links the individual with a given community, since language is never "just mine" but shared. In this sense, our individual identities depend on a number of social and cultural sources, including language, which one receives as part of his life context (Taylor 1985c: 276). Other sources take symbolic forms such as religion, ritual and the various arts. The particular array of sources our culture is able to provide to us strongly conditions the kind of self-understandings we develop and, hence, our own individual identities. This allows us to grasp a key epistemological and moral insight of Taylor, namely the frameworks in which we live and the assumptions which we take for granted.

In concrete terms, what has just been said underscores the importance dialogue has for human identity. It is through conversation that we are formed as humans. This does not just denote a psychological process in individual maturation but an ontological feature of human beings: "My discovery of my own identity doesn't mean that I work it out in isolation, but that I negotiate it through dialogue, partly overt, partly internal, with others… My own identity crucially depends on my dialogical relations with others" (Taylor 1995: 231).[11]

---

[10] The quote is from the piece titled *Language and Human Nature*.

[11] The quote is from the piece titled *The Politics of Recognition*.

These conversations can occur between peoples of different cultural backgrounds, in a real or imagined fashion. In any case, they have consequences at the level of self-understanding, morality and identity.

A consequence of what has been said so far is that human beings manifest their identities and moral outlooks in narrative terms. These narratives are individually constructed in dialogue with others, society as a whole, and in the context of a given culture. Shared narratives are, in this sense, very important for our own identity-related narratives. In this regard, Taylor justifies the way in which *A Secular Age* is laid out and written:

> I have tried to give a master narrative of secularity. And one of the central ideas of the book is that one only understands what secularity is through the narrative. The aim is to criticize, and perhaps replace, a widespread understanding of secularity as the inevitable by-product of modernization, however this is understood. Generally it is seen as consisting of processes like economic growth, industrialization, social and geographical mobility, urbanization, the development of science and technology, the advance of instrumental reason and the like. Various tellings of the story of how we have become carry this sense of secularity as an inevitable consequence. To challenge this you have to tell another story. Hence the length of the book. (Taylor 2010: 301)[12]

4.1.2   Ethically-Bounded Selves

(a) For Taylor, human beings are inherently moral. This means their sense of identity will be defined by the good in their lives they consider to be higher or the most worthy. He sees humans as "strong evaluation" makers:

> These are the qualitative distinctions we make between different actions, or feelings, or modes of life, as being in some way morally higher or lower, noble or base, admirable or contemptible. It is this language of qualitative contrast that gets marginalized, or even expunged altogether, by the utilitarian or formalist [Kantian] reductions. I want to argue, in opposition to this, that they are central to our moral thinking and ineradicable from it. (Taylor 1985b: 234)[13]

These evaluations are not at play in each and every human choice, but in particular ones aimed at qualitative distinctions. They describe human moral goals, which make them also normative. However, "strong evaluations" need not to be reflexive or articulated. On the contrary, several times they are carried on in a non-reflexive way, operating as a tacit background. They "need not to be explicit or articulated in order to exercise a powerful influence on a person's actions and sense of morality

---

[12] Taylor argues that any analytical approach to secularization should not avoid history, the process by which we came to be in our present self-understanding and of our place in the world. The latter conditions the former; the very definition of what is it to live in a secular milieu entails a view of how we have overcome a previous condition. This is why he puts together a meta-narrative (2007: 28–29, 573–75).

[13] The quote is from the piece titled *The Diversity of Goods*.

and purpose. Nor do these judgments have to be part of the person's awareness to be valuable in explaining moral life" (Abbey 2000: 21).

(b) The realization of "strong evaluation" as a human constant does not mean that all human beings value the same things. On the contrary, higher goods may vary from person to person and more clearly from culture to culture. Moral pluralism exists because of this. This fact also means that individuals can change the good they value the most during their lifetime, that they are not always able to honor it in all instances, and that there are occasions in which higher goods can conflict with each other as a given individual may experience them (Taylor 1989b: 53–90). Because of this complex landscape in regard to "the good," Taylor would not vouch for universally valid moral assessments:

> We could easily decide—a view which I would defend—that the universal attribution of moral personality is valid, and lays obligations on us which we cannot ignore; but that there are also other moral ideals and goals—e.g. of less than universal solidarity, or of personal excellence—which cannot be easily coordinated with universalism, and can even enter into conflict with it. (Taylor 1985b: 233)[14]

However, even while affirming this, Taylor is not a relativist. He is not affirming that all possible goods are of the same value and that it is not possible rationally to assess which may be superior to others. On the contrary, for Taylor, to affirm that all moral orders are arbitrary is self-deceptive: "It is a form of self-delusion to think that we do not speak from a moral orientation which we take to be right. That is a condition of being a functioning self, not a metaphysical view we can put on or off" (Taylor 1989b: 99) He finds, then, that a credible moral philosophy should explain how people live their ethical commitments in their ordinary life. It should be able to do this rationally, arbitrating both between moral outlooks belonging to the same culture, and also between moral stances coming from different cultures. In this last case, a sense of the fact that certain cultural forms better promote certain moral goods is necessary, as well as performing a comparison between two different cultures in terms of gains and losses. What avoids relativism here is the fact that

> we can, in principle, understand and recognize the goods of another society as goods-for-everyone (and hence for ourselves). That they are not combinable with our own home-grown goods-for-everyone may indeed be tragic but it is not different in principle from any other dilemmas we may be in through facing incombinable goods, even within our own way of life. There is no guarantee that universally valid goods should be perfectly combinable, and certainly not in all situations. (Taylor 1989b: 61)

Taylor is not a subjectivist either. He sees that strongly valued goods command respect not because they have been chosen by individuals but because of their intrinsic worth (Taylor 1989b: 20). In this way, he rejects those views that saw the goods as projections of ourselves in a world which was, supposedly, morally neutral in itself (Taylor 1989b: 53–54). As Abbey puts it, "beginning with humans and the way they experience morality, he [Taylor] claims that the most plausible explana-

---

[14] The quote is from the piece titled *The Diversity of Goods*.

tion of morality is one that takes seriously humans' perception of the independence of the goods" (Abbey 2000: 29).

(c) Strong evaluations occur, Taylor affirms, within inescapable "moral frameworks." All humans live within them, consciously or not, since they help them to shape their own moral lives and to take positions before the crucial questions in human existence about the purpose, orientation and conduct of their lives.

> This is not meant just as a contingently true psychological fact about the human beings… Rather the claim is that living within such strongly qualified horizons is constitutive of human agency, that stepping outside these limits would be tantamount to stepping outside what we would recognize as integral, that is, undamaged human personhood. (Taylor 1989b: 27)

There is a close interaction between strong evaluations and moral frameworks. Frameworks are shaped by particular goods considered to have higher importance, while strong evaluations require a background of moral horizons to make sense at all.

(d) For what has been said, Taylor's approach to morality links the normative aspects of ethical behavior with the ontological ones: It is not just a question of how we should do the right thing (actions), but of how to be good (views, self-understanding), and what to admire or love. It is not surprising, then, that the phenomenology of the contemporary conditions of belief, described in *A Secular Age* and related works, contains a focus on the different self-understandings people have about what "human flourishing" would be, finding a gamut of positions that have at its extremes "transcendent religion" on the one hand, and "exclusive humanism" on the other.

4.1.3 Modernity and Epistemology

(a) Taylor is known for his defense of the moral achievements of modernity, which he also sees expressed, however imperfectly, in the political, economic and social realms. Whatever the difficulties such a moral ideal may be passing through at the present time (Taylor 1991),[15] he finds modern ethical claims to be keeping their strength and to be in need of being developed further. This places Taylor in a contrasting position with those, such as Alasdair MacIntyre (2007), who doubt that something genuine is at stake in the Enlightenment project and vouch for going back to an ethics of virtues, and also with those, such as Nietzsche and the Postmodern thinkers, who propose to depart from the horizon of modernity into an ethics of affirmation (Smith 2002: 201–4).

---

[15] In this work, Taylor describes the following as being the problems currently operative in modernity: atomistic individualism, the predominance of instrumental reason, and the apathy towards political participation.

In Taylor's view, the moral novelty (and greatness) of modernity consists in the "affirmation of universal human rights—to life, freedom, citizenship, self-realization—which are seen as radically unconditional" (Taylor 1992, 2011: 170)[16] the goodness of "ordinary life" (Taylor 1989b: 211ff) and the commitment towards alleviating the suffering of the whole of mankind and the establishment of a system of universal justice (Taylor 2011: 177).[17] However, as it has been mentioned, there are two sources of difficulty preventing modernity from flourishing. First, the fact that modernity in itself may not be able to provide all the necessary moral sources for it to expand and strengthen its influence (Taylor 1989b: 495–521). Second, the presence of a variant of the modern affirmation of life led by Nietzsche and thinkers such as Foucault and Bataille. This variant rejects egalitarianism within the affirmation of ordinary life, as well as benevolence, universalism and order. Instead, some of its proponents see the affirmation of life as asking for the affirmation of power and destruction, while others are very much fascinated by death and violence (Taylor 2011: 179–81).[18] Not surprisingly, Taylor does not follow in his explorations into the social sciences the kind of analysis that has become widespread in academia under the label of "Postmodern," which he finds wanting on both epistemic and moral grounds.[19]

(b) From the standpoint of knowledge, however, Taylor finds himself in a very critical position in regard to modern epistemology. He sees the modern epistemological tradition, which starts with Descartes, as kept captive within a "powerful picture of mind-in-the-world," a largely unnoticed framework, a "background understanding which provides the context for, and thus influences all our theorizing in this area" (Taylor 2013: 61; Abbey 2000: 151–93). Taylor even goes on to say:

> There is a big mistake operative in our culture, a kind of operative (mis)understanding of what it is to know, which has dire effects on both theory and practice in a host of domains. To sum it up in a pithy formula, we might say that we (mis)understand knowledge as "mediational." (Taylor 2013: 61)

He sees the "mediational model" as occurring in Descartes, linguistic philosophy, materialism and even in Kant, notwithstanding the deep differences and criticisms made between them. What they all share, Taylor says, is a fourfold bias. First, knowledge beyond the boundaries of ourselves, of our "mind/organism," is seen as the result of some features in the "mind/organism." In other words, we always grasp the outside world "only through" depictions (representations, ideas, beliefs, sentences) or categorical forms (Kant) or both. Second, what we know can always be analyzed into clearly defined and explicit elements. Third, when it comes to justifying our thought, we cannot go beyond those explicit and formulated elements.

---

[16] The last reference is to the piece titled *A Catholic Modernity?*

[17] The reference is to the piece titled *A Catholic Modernity?*

[18] The reference is to the piece titled *A Catholic Modernity?*

[19] For a critique of Postmodern epistemology by Taylor see his piece *Overcoming Epistemology* (1995: 15–19). A critique of Postmodern moral philosophy is found in *Sources of the Self* (1989b: 98–103) and in *The Politics of Recognition* (1995: 252–56). For his views on Foucault see *Foucault on Freedom and Truth* (1985b: 152–184).

Fourth, this model of knowledge presupposes in humans what Taylor calls a "dualist sorting." From this, it does not follow that the Cartesian mental/physical model is still accepted by all, because it is not, but that all the above-mentioned philosophical positions, even thoroughly materialist accounts of knowledge, in fact use the mental/physical distinction to deny the second term and explain it through the first. What underlies this approach is a notion of the material world as being devoid of teleology, of meaning, as a mechanistic realm of purely efficient causation on raw material (Taylor 2013: 68–69).

Taylor thinks the "mediational model" is neither an obvious one nor the only one possible. For example, for Plato and Aristotle, mind and body interpenetrate and knowing was not just representational but the result of the "ontological contact" of the idea with matter. Besides the mechanistic account of reality, Taylor also points out another consequence of the "mediational model": that of "disengaging" us from the bodily through objectifying it, by seeing it "as just dead, unexpressive stuff" (Taylor 2013: 70). Lastly, he also mentions the reliance of knowledge on formal rules as another outcome to be taken into account. In conclusion, "it is this dualist sorting, and the underlying disengagement from the embodied stance, which has been consecrated in the tradition as the proper 'scientific' stance to things human" (Taylor 2013: 71).

In stark contrast to the above-described model, Taylor espouses what he calls a "contact model," the one developed on criticisms proposed by Merleau-Ponty, Heidegger and Wittgenstein.

> A basic move which gives rise to this theory is a reembedding of thought and knowledge in the bodily and social-cultural contexts in which it takes place. The attempt is to articulate the framework or contact within which our explicit depictions of reality make sense, and to show how this is inseparable from our activity as the kind of embodied, social, and cultural beings we are. The contact here is not achieved at the level of Ideas [sic], but is rather something primordial, something we never escape. It is the contact of living, acting beings whose life form involves acting in and on a world which also acts on them… This original contact provides the sense-making context for all other knowledge constructions, which, however, based on mediated depictions, rely for their meaning on this primordial and indissoluble involvement in the surrounding reality. (Taylor 2013: 73–74)

This way of understanding knowledge is better than the "mediational model," according to Taylor, in that it recognizes the existence of non-thematized frameworks within which we live. Besides, it also shows how knowledge of temporal beings is not properly caught in ever-present time affirmations, but in "path-dependent" ones, usually couched in the past tense. Lastly, the "contact or immersion model" calls into question the invocation by "mediational theories" of the existence of a "good method" of universal applicability to guide knowledge; in contrast, even when recognizing the need of criteria for discerning good knowledge, these are always raised within a framework, and they are not always applicable to all situations (Taylor 2013: 74–78).

In this light, Taylor's references in *A Secular Age* to "powerful enframing assumptions," the concept of "unthought" and to Close World Structures (CWS) applied to the "orthodox" theorists find their ultimate grounding here, and should not be considered to be a mere disqualifying strategy. Taylor's following quote clarifies the matter:

> I am not urging some "post-modern" thesis that we are each imprisoned in our own outlook, and can do nothing to rationally convince each other. On the contrary, I think we can marshal arguments to induce each other to modify their judgments and (what is closely connected) to widen their sympathies. But this task is very difficult, and what is more important, it is never complete. We don't just decide once and for all when we enter sociology class to leave our "values" at the door. They continue to shape our thought at a much deeper level, and it is only a continuing open exchange with those of different standpoints which will help us to correct some of the distortions they engender. (Taylor 2007: 428)

4.1.4   Hermeneutical Nature of the Social Sciences

(a) The Taylorean view of the social sciences as hermeneutical in nature is a logical consequence of the philosophical insights I have explained so far. Taylor recognizes himself as being part of the *Verstehen* tradition developed by Wilhelm Dilthey, the already mentioned Heidegger, Paul Ricoeur, Hans-Georg Gadamer and Jurgen Habermas (Taylor 1985b: 15; Smith 2002: 120–21).[20] Generally speaking, his approach is that whereas in the natural sciences there is only one hermeneutic process at work (that of the scientist who seeks to understand the object of study, which does not produce any self-understandings), in the social sciences we have two: on the one hand, the self-interpretation human individuals give to themselves (which can be extended to sub-cultures and cultures as shared self-interpretations of particular social groups) and, on the other hand, the interpretation a scientist gives of a social fact.

In Taylor's perspective, any effort for understanding in social sciences should avoid merely accepting the particular explanation given by the social agent, or just bypassing it as irrelevant. Taylor's claim is "that the social scientist must take these interpretations [of the social agent] into account when trying to explain people and their behavior" (Abbey 2000: 154). At the basis of these convictions is the fact that humans are self-interpreting beings and that such self-understandings are part of who we are and need to be part of the object of any science of man.

Given the fact that human self-understandings vary in time, Taylor would affirm that social theories should change accordingly (Taylor 1985b: 1–3).[21] In the end, he argues that social sciences "are necessarily open-ended hermeneutical endeavors and that the sort of knowledge they yield is inevitably more uncertain and labile than the knowledge aspired to by the natural sciences" (Abbey 2000: 155). In this view, particular social theories are better than others in that they give a more comprehensive and perspicuous account of phenomena.

---

[20] The first reference is to the piece titled *Interpretation and the Sciences of Man*.

[21] The reference is to the book's *Introduction*.

(b) Taylor has developed a constant critique of an empiricist/rationalist science of man, one molded after the natural sciences, a distortion he calls "naturalism." Behaviorism, functional theories of religion, socio-biology, evolutionary psychology, among other disciplines (Abbey 2000: 152–53), have been the objects of his observations in this regard. "The basic building block of knowledge on this view is the impression, or sense-datum; a unit of information which is not the deliverance of a judgment, which has by definition no element in it of reading or interpretation" (Taylor 1985b: 19).[22] This is complemented with a model for verification that seeks to establish causal links between brute data. Knowledge thus construed, according to this view, consists of data that cannot be challenged or undermined by further reasoning. Inferences based on brute data are subject to logical and mathematical standards (Taylor 1985b: 18–21).

In contrast, Taylor sees that the notion of meaning plays a key role in the characterization of human agency at the (phenomenological) level of ordinary speech.

> There is a quite legitimate notion of meaning which we use when we speak of the meaning of a situation for an agent. And that this concept has a place is integral to our ordinary consciousness and hence speech about or actions. Our actions are ordinarily characterized by the purpose sought and explained by desires, feelings, emotions. But the language by which we describe our goals, feelings, desires is also a definition of the meaning things have for us.
>
> Moreover, our understanding of these terms moves inescapably in a hermeneutical circle. (Taylor 1985b: 23)

So there is a level in which we already experience our situation in terms of meanings (which Taylor calls "proto-interpretation"), which in turn is interpreted and 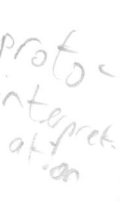 shaped by the language we use. Thirdly, the whole is interpreted as well when we give an explanation of our actions (Taylor 1985b: 27). As a consequence of this, the sciences of man cannot but move in an interpretive mode, since there are no brute data exempt from interpretations. Even more, any proposed explanation within their realm supposes a shared understanding by scientists of the language concerned. However, this does not guarantee that any colleague would agree with such proposed explanation. In order to deal with this, one could try to provide him with supplementary explanations, which would unavoidably constitute further interpretations, or one might try to awake in our interlocutor the same intuitions that had informed our explanation. In any case, "such uncertainty is an eradicable part of our epistemological predicament" (Taylor 1985b: 18). Taylor even says that calling it "uncertainty" is an "absurdly severe criterion of 'certainty,' which deprives the concept of any sensible use" (Taylor 1985b: 18).[23]

As a consequence of what has been said, the moral ideals animating human agents also need to be included in the analysis of any explanation the sciences of man may give of any process of social change (Taylor 1991: 19–20).

(c) How, according to Taylor, would an interpretive social science be possible? It is clear, for what has been said, that what is not possible is to study human agency

---

[22] The quote is from the piece titled *Interpretation and the Sciences of Man*.

[23] The quotes are from the piece titled *Interpretation and the Sciences of Man*.

as if it were brute data, since the circularity of interpretation is unavoidable. What is possible, he says, is to strive to achieve "epistemic gains," which could be determined by the application of some criteria. First, ask if the scientific hermeneutic account is superior, in terms of a more complete or profound explanation, than the pre-theoretical self-understanding of the agent. Second, inquire if a given scientific account makes more sense of the studied object than a rival one, or resolves contradictions on the latter, or brings out otherwise hidden aspects of the phenomenon. Third, ask if a proposed scientific account, when inspiring the practice of the agents, leads to a fuller or more authentic realization of the good that defines them. In this case, what is implied is Taylor's conviction that social theories' validity in regard to their contents can also be measured by the kind of practical action they are capable of fostering (Taylor 1985b: 91–115).[24]

This is social engineering

However, even when he recognizes the need of criteria and provides some, Taylor insists on the fact that they should not be seen as constituting a "formal" method[25] in the sense of one that would bracket out the "contents" of the individual's self-interpretations (culture) when studying social agency and, because of this, become universalizable.

This approach by Taylor would be particularly challenging for quantitative studies in the social and behavioral sciences. In spite of this, as one may deduce from his praise of the works of sociologists who do conduct these kinds of studies such as David Martin, Jose Casanova and Hans Joas, he is not affirming they are invalid per se for reaching knowledge in the social sciences. As I will show in the following chapter, Taylor himself makes use—in *A Secular Age* and secularization-related texts—of works by sociologists and historians who use quantitative studies to build their arguments, which are referred to phenomena narrowly framed in time (e.g., decades) and space (e.g., countries, regions) as well as in regard to culture. Assuming Taylor is being consistent with the assumptions he has stated about the sciences of man, these scholars will be found by him as apt to work with "material" variables (such as age, gender, social class, education, etc.) but, as importantly, as able to develop a "language of perspicuous contrast" which would enable them to make sense of the cultural context of the people under study in order to properly understand the motivations present in variables much more clearly filled with self-interpretations (such as self-perceptions, for example). He will find such authors to have a high degree of knowledge of themselves and of their context, an intuition of the inter-subjective language and common meanings they share with their own societies, of their own social imaginaries, and of the "social theory" prevalent in their own cultures. He will also consider them able to contrast all the elements just mentioned with the corresponding ones from the people under study, and to establish the contrasts that would allow a deeper and broader interpretation than

---

[24] The reference is to the piece titled *Social Theory as Practice*.

[25] Taylor's insistence on avoiding formalism has provoked a number of criticisms that see in his views a commitment to skepticism. However, the point he is trying to make is that knowledge in the social sciences does advance, but it does so through the comparison of interpretations (Smith 2002: 125).

the ones in vogue. I will touch on this topic again in Chap. 6, where I will claim that the social theory underpinning Taylor's meta-narrative would postulate a complementary approach between quantitative and qualitative research methodologies.

Taking these ideas into account, it is clear, nonetheless, that Taylor is conducting a critique of what he calls "mainstream sociology" and asking for an even more interpretive approach than what is in use. As a logical consequence, the kind of analysis he develops in *A Secular Age* has been described differently by several scholars because they find it unconventional.[26] In this regard, D. Stephen Long asks: "Where do we place his work? It is not quite history, social science, political philosophy, cultural studies, or theology but it draws upon all these disciplines" (Long 2009: 93). Long thinks that the difficulty of reading *A Secular Age* can be alleviated

> once we read him in the terms he himself lays down. These terms are not "categories," for this is what he explicitly avoids—the imposition of a code on some inert matter that renders it intelligible. They are "forms" (or imaginaries) found in everyday life that require a "transcendental deduction" and the articulation of the tacit background. This articulation frustrates and exceeds any immanent or designative significance of them. These forms of, or to, life are discovered by way of ad hominem practical reasoning, tracing a diachronic causation through and expressive-constitutive use of language that articulates social imaginaries, themes found in Taylor's work. They are essential for reading *A Secular Age*. (Long 2009: 96)

Whatever the appropriateness of Long's interpretation, it should be said here that the discussion on "epistemic gains" mentioned above shows how Taylor has established a set of criteria which should allow assessing the ways in which sociological knowledge is furthered. In this sense, however unusual his approach might be, it is not a mere relativistic position.

(d) An application of what has been said in a concrete case of social scientific research helps to make more sense of what has been described.[27] If we were studying secularization by correlating variables such as attendance at religious services (external behavior) and obedience to religious authority (internal behavior), we might put together a survey by which we would ask, among other things, about the frequency of attendance at religious ceremonies and about the levels of inner obedience to religious leaders. To measure the latter, we might come up with a number of propositions to which the interviewee would be asked to answer if he agrees or not. Of course, a number of methodological steps would be taken in order to avoid biasing the information collected, which includes the proper use of language, the order of the questions, the protocol for the survey, etc. Implied in this data gathering process would be a particular research design, which would include a conceptualization

---

[26] Martin E. Marty (2008) thinks that *A Secular Age* is an exercise of philosophy of history, whereas Daniel Ross (2009) finds it to be a work of history, phenomenology and sociology. Martin Jay (2009) finds it to be an exercise of Catholic apologetics. All of them find the book's argumentation as complex, nuanced and non-linear, fact that only is interpreted negatively by Jay.

[27] This is an adaptation of a different example given by Taylor in *Interpretation and the Sciences of Man* (1985b: 28–32).

of the variables at stake, of their measurement and about the operationalization of the latter.

We would like to find out if the two mentioned variables are related, and, if so, in what way. Among other options, it could be the case that less frequent attendance would be the effect of inner dissent or, vice versa, that less frequent attendance would cause dissent. Other scenarios could be that both variables really consequences of a third one, or that people still attend even when they are not completely willing to obey their religious leaders, or that no correlation was to be found. To find this out, the social scientist would take the information collected through the above-mentioned survey and make use of statistical methods.

Even when "hard" data collected this way is usually interpreted by "mainline" sociology, Taylor would affirm that even very specific information which might be considered as "hard" (such as the subject of study's gender, age, etc. and particularly his external behavior, such as "attendance to religious services") may be in need of interpretation in itself. Consequently, information related to the subject's motivations for internal behavior (such as "obedience to religious authority") more clearly requires a hermeneutical assessment.

In Taylor's view, if a process of interpretation as described is not performed, the risks social science faces here are various. In the first place, there are considerations about the mindset of those who phrased the survey questions, of those who chose what propositions to include in the semi-structured questions. It reflects the scientist's understandings of what "attendance to a religious service" and "obedience to religious authority" are, which in turn means it is an interpretation that can be challenged by a "more perspicuous one." This takes us also into an analysis of the language the scientist has at hand to express himself (what Taylor calls "field" of meanings).

However, this is not the most relevant criticism Taylor makes. A second and greater risk is to think it is possible to coach the propositions of the survey in a way that they would not be subject to interpretive dispute. It is true there is information that can be gathered through a set of given propositions in a questionnaire to choose from, but anything related to the interviewee's self-understanding (as his inner disposition to obey a given religious authority) would not be properly assessed this way. What it is implied here, that the meaning "obedience" has for him can be assessed by recording the interviewee's assent of dissent to a set of propositions and that these truly represent his beliefs, affective reactions and values, is not true. In a sense, it is through these propositions that we want to reflect in a way the inner world of the interviewee into the brute data coming out from the survey. However, according to Taylor, this is not completely so, because the meaning of religious obedience here is dependent on a field of inter-subjective meanings the interviewee shares with his family, friends and community. These inter-subjective meanings are not just in the mind of the interviewee but are also embodied in practices themselves (in this case, those of "attending to a religious service" and "obeying a religious authority"). "The meanings and norms implicit in these practices are not just in the minds of the actors but are out there in the practices themselves, practices which cannot be conceived as a set of individual actions, but which are essentially modes of social relation, of mutual action" (Taylor 1985b: 36).[28] Inter-subjective meanings give people a common language to talk about social reality and a common understanding of norms (Taylor 1985b: 39). As a result, the social scientist of our example should explore this common language, which includes both ideas and practices, prior to the elaboration of the survey, and complement the findings of the latter with further exploration into this shared universe of meaning. While doing all this, the scientist could not avoid entering into thoroughly hermeneutic territory.[29]

(e) Taylor conceives the social sciences as founded not on brute data but on readings of meanings. Its object (that is, meanings) should fulfill these characteristics: "The meanings are for a subject in a field or fields; they are moreover meanings which are partially constituted by self-definitions, which are in this sense already interpretations" (Taylor 1985b: 52).[30] The latter can be re-expressed or uncovered by this particular science.

In order to assess its object of study, the social sciences should be considered to be hermeneutical, that is proceeding in an interpretative circle, as mentioned. Because of this, a certain measure of insight is required from the scientist, and it could be the case that a "gap in intuitions" occurs between colleagues, this meaning that one of them "cannot understand the kind of self-definition which others are proposing as underlying a certain society or set of institutions" (Taylor 1985b: 52). This, however, reflects a "limiting case." As Smith puts it, "in the normal case of social scientific enquiry, according to Taylor, interpreters share enough common background for testing to take place on the basis of evidence" (Smith 2002: 125).

"Gaps in intuitions" could entail not only the existence of different theoretical approaches, but also diverse options in life. "This puts an end to any aspiration to a value-free or 'ideology-free' science of man. A study of the science of man is inseparable from an examination of the options between which men must choose" (Smith 2002: 125). Lastly, the human sciences such conceived are largely *post eventu* affaires. Prognosis is difficult because conceptual innovation in turn alters human reality. Complete predictability, for the social sciences would imply "to have explicited so clearly the human condition that one would already have pre-empted all cultural innovation and transformation. This is hardly in the bounds of the possible" (Taylor 1985b: 57).[31] This criticism in particularly aimed by Taylor at social theory that uses a "closed system" approaches to social phenomena.

All this notwithstanding, prediction is not impossible in Taylor's view of the social sciences (as we have seen in the last section of Chap. 3). One logically concludes from the latter that prediction could be done inasmuch the self-interpretations held by the people under study remain constant or just undergo small changes, and if the researcher is able to keep an adequate "empathic" approach to the group under

---

[28] The quote is from the piece titled *Interpretation and the Sciences of Man.*

[29] Ruth Abbey expresses this in a concise formula: "So, in order to understand the person, we need not just empirical information about his race, class occupation, age, background and so on, but also some sense of how he sees himself" (Abbey 2000: 59).

[30] The quote is from the piece titled *Interpretation and the Sciences of Man.*

[31] The quote is from the piece titled *Interpretation and the Sciences of Man.*

study. Taylor himself takes this step in *A Secular Age* when he explores the possible scenarios of openness or closedness towards transcendence in the immediate future of Western countries (Taylor 2007: 769–772). Not surprisingly, he affirms that "of course, this cannot be foretold in any detail; and moreover, things will almost certainly work out differently in different societies" (Taylor 2007: 769–770).

In this perspective, when considering Taylor's meta-narrative on secularization in the West, it is hardly surprising that he gives "social imaginaries" a key role in the process. The previously mentioned inter-subjective meanings—which furnish a common language to talk about society and norms, and should be taken into consideration, in the first place, by a hermeneutic science of man—make possible the existence of "common meanings." These are more than basic vocabularies, but they constitute a common reference world: significant beliefs, actions, celebrations, and feelings that a community shares and which give it consistency (Taylor 1985b: 38–39).[32] These too are the primary objects of a hermeneutic social science. Both, inter-subjective and common meanings, are included in the notion of social imaginary Taylor uses as an interpretive devise in *A Secular Age* and other secularization-related works.

(f) "Interpretative social theory, as Taylor conceives it, thus has an intrinsically critical bent: it takes the spontaneously generated self-interpretations of a culture as the point of departure, and advances new, more perspicuous and more explanatory interpretations in their place" (Smith 2002: 128). This asks social science to free itself from ethnocentrism, a general demand that turns more critical when doing comparative and cross-cultural studies.

Taylor explains how this could be possible by saying:

> Because we take languages of understanding seriously in regard to their value/ontological commitments, we don't need automatically to assume that ours is correct in its commitments and that foreign languages are wrong. We can, on the contrary, start with the assumption that we may learn something more about ourselves as well in coming to understand another society. (Taylor 1981: 205; 1985a: 116–33)[33]

Following this insight, he affirms that the adequate language to understand another society/culture is not just "ours" or "theirs," but "what one would call a language of perspicuous contrast" (Taylor 1981: 206).[34] This is a language in which one could express our way of life[35] and that of the society/culture studied in relation to a number of human constants (as defined above) at work in both. In this clarifying

---

[32] The quote is from the piece titled *Interpretation and the Sciences of Man*.

[33] The last reference is to the piece titled *Understanding and Etnocentricity*.

[34] The quote is from the piece titled *Understanding and Explanation in the Geisteswissenschaften*.

[35] This concept is taken from Wittgenstein's *Lebenform*. By this, Taylor understands the existential "background" in regard to which our words and utterances could make sense. This view is opposed to that of modern rationalism, which sees the human agent as disengaged and considers him as having incorporated into the very structure of his mind the proper procedures for rational thought. In contrast, Taylor believes that human agents are always embedded in a culture, a form of life, that is, are always embodied. These constitute the very conditions of human understanding, in contrast to with which our utterances make sense. He expands on this in a piece called *Lichtung or Lebensform: Parallels between Heidegger and Wittgenstein* (Taylor 1995: 61–78).

language the possible human variations would be so formulated that both our form of life and that of people of a different culture could be perspicuously described. In this way, in regard to a specific matter, one form of life could be superior or inferior in relation to the other, or both could be found equally wanting (Taylor 1981: 206).[36] This entails that the other's self-interpretation should be understood in their terms, and also that the self-interpretations operative in the scientist's life should be readily available to him. As a result, it could be that either their understanding or ours may prove to be inappropriate or distorted in some respects. Or it could be that both understandings are. What is pursued here is to strive for a "third language" in which both the "home" and "alien" languages could be put in contrast to each other in regard to specific constants. Taylor finds inspiration for this perspective in Gadamer's notion of the "fusion of horizons" (Gadamer 2003: 336–84; Taylor 1995: 252–53).[37]

The superiority of one account over the other should not be regarded as such in general, but also in respect to the specific aspect in consideration in our study. Social/cultural self-interpretive schemes are incommensurable for Taylor. However, this fact, instead of preventing him from making cross-cultural judgments or according them no rational basis, leads him to believe that they contain rival claims over domains of life that make them competitors that should be contrasted.

It is important to make note that in this form of study in the social sciences a successful understanding of the other's society/culture brings with it an alteration of the self-understanding of the scientist.

> It will be frequently the case that we cannot understand another society until we have understood ourselves better as well. This will be so wherever the language of perspicuous contrast which is adequate to the case forces us to redescribe what we are doing… We are always in danger of seeing our ways of acting and thinking as the only conceivable ones. That is exactly what ethnocentricity is. (Taylor 1985b: 129)[38]

In this way, Taylor moves away from radical cultural relativist positions.[39] These views propose, in the first place, that the social sciences should include at least the language of the people being studied in its explanation, or frame social explanations in terms of such language. Second, they require from scientists to recognize that self-interpretations by people are incorrigible (that is, not to be challenged). Taylor's "language of perspicuous contrast" would avoid the great burden the first condition puts on the sciences of man and the risk of endless relativism implied in the second condition.

---

[36] The quote is from the piece titled *Understanding and Explanation in the Geisteswissenschaften*.

[37] The last reference is to a piece titled *The Politics of Recognition*. Taylor has also answered to criticisms against his proposal of convergence in a piece called *Comparison, History, Truth* (Taylor 1995: 146–64).

[38] The quote is from the piece titled *Understanding and Ethnocentricity*.

[39] Taylor particularly comments on the classical work by Peter Winch by name *The Idea of a Social Science* (1958).

He also takes distance from "neutralism," this is, the belief that one could adopt a neutral stance towards the self-descriptions one studies, particularly their evaluative components.

> The supposedly neutral terms in which other people's actions are identified—the function of a functional theory, or the maximization-descriptions of various consequentialist accounts of individual action—these all reflect the stress on instrumental reason in our civilization since the seventeenth century. To see them everywhere is really to distort the action, beliefs, etc. of alien societies in an ethnocentric way. (Taylor 1981: 206)[40]

Taylor believes the stance described above projects our own views and practices on the agents we are studying and does not allow them to express a set of views and practices that in no way correspond our own (Taylor 1981: 209).

Lastly, he also criticizes a "simple realist" stance by which one sees the need of grasping the self-understandings of the people under study both when the scientist shares such self-interpretations or finds them misleading. "To the extent that we see people's behavior as minimally rational, in one common sense of this word 'rational', viz. as responding appropriately to what surrounds them as they understand it, identifying the shape of their erroneous views is obviously essential to the task of explanation" (Taylor 1981: 199). The problem Taylor finds here is not that this position is politically incorrect nor—concerning "strong evaluations"—that there is no truth of the matter. He would not agree with these propositions. The fault Taylor finds is that the final account the scientist would give will be couched in terms of his own value/ontological commitments. Doing this fails to see that "the evaluations of a given language must be seen in the context of a form of life. And forms of life are not candidates for affirmation or denial; they are just how people in fact live" (Taylor 1981: 202). With this, Taylor is stressing the point that assertions done by the people under study make sense within the context of their form of life, and the way in  which words are related in such a context is not usually the same as the way they are in the scientist's cultural form of life. To express this with an example, the terms used in the formula "I am close to God," uttered by the people who are the subject of study, are not related in the same way as those that the scientist's mind finds in the formula "I am in bed" (Taylor 1981: 202–203).

The account of secularization in the West contained in *A Secular Age* and other secularization-related works reflects the hermeneutical view on the social sciences thus far described, or at least tries to do so.[41] I will now illustrate this through some general remarks.

In regard to its form and method, Taylor provides a meta-narrative that focuses on secularization as change in the "condition of belief" for people, exploring both the variations in their self-understanding and in socio-cultural structures through the last 500 years.

In this way, he reaches the phenomenological descriptions contained in the notions of immanent frame, living cross-pressured in regard to secular/religious

---

[40] This quote and the following references are from the piece titled *Understanding and Explanation in the Geisteswissenschaften.*

[41] Charles Taylor, personal communication to the author, 19 Nov 2009.

allegiances, Nova and Supernova Effects. Taylor does this within a very precisely defined span of time and focused on the United Kingdom and France, both countries in which he could enter more easily into a *Verstehen*-inspired engagement, seemly because he is a French-Canadian—whose home received a French background on his mother's side and a British one on his father's side—and because of his studies at Oxford and La Sorbonne. I believe he purposely takes advantage of his awareness of his own background to carry out a social scientific approach in which facts pertaining to the process of Western secularization are interpreted by taking into account the meanings given to them by social agents, as well as by their shared self-interpretations. It is in this way that Taylor elaborates his own explanatory meta-narrative.

He builds a series of interconnected stories that give support to each other: one of Ancien Régime-Mobilization-Authenticity dispensations in regard to society's structure and religious forms, one of Paleo-, Neo- and Post-Durkhemian schemes for the relationship between religion and political system, one that goes from Scientific Revolution-Providential Deism-Modern Moral Order- Romanticism-Exclusive Humanism in the realm of the history of ideas, the Reform narrative in regards to Christian theology and pastoral practice, etc. Last but not least, there is the story of the passing from a "Porous" to a "Buffered Self," which in one sense summarizes the most relevant change in human self-interpretation in the West, which in turn is linked with ethically bounded purposes aimed at human flourishing.

While telling these different stories, Taylor tries to make patent how social imaginaries were constituted in the countries he studies, explaining not only theoretical issues but also changes in social practices (Taylor 2007: 159–218). Besides, he is also aware of the existence of strong meta-narratives with which he is competing, which tell a quite different story of secularization (which he calls "substraction theory"). Taylor makes references to them, particularly to their weaknesses and to the ways in which his own meta-narrative gives a better account of the process of secularization and even puts at stake uncovered issues. He is particularly insistent in pointing out the unacknowledged frameworks operative within his rival's accounts in the form of "unthoughts" and Close World Structures (CWS) (Taylor 2007: 428–37, 550–93).

Lastly, it is not surprising how Taylor carefully chooses his sociological sources from those which are very much historically and culturally focused—as we will see below—and are more susceptible to a hermeneutic interpretation. It seems that the more closely bounded the sources are to take into account particular cultural self-understandings into their analysis, the better (Taylor 2007: 426). Also, Taylor's (normative) commitment to the moral ideals and achievements of modernity explains his choice of theological sources and his view on the future of religion in the West.

4.2   Taylor and Classical Sociology

Taylor's meta-narrative of secularization, and in general his philosophical work, refers in different ways and with diverse attitudes to the so-called "founding fathers" of sociology: Weber, Durkheim and Marx. This section situates Taylor's thought in relation to them, starting with Max Weber, the classical figure most influential on it.

4.2.1   Taylor and Weber

(a) Taylor offers a generally positive evaluation of Max Weber's work as a social scientist, considering him as a representative of the *Verstehen* school, which contrasts with that of empirical sociology (Taylor 1985a: 122).[42] There is, then, in the first place, a common point in affirming an interpretive understanding of the social sciences.

Second, both Taylor and Weber seek an explanation of social processes with a focus on structural causes for social behavior as well as on the ideas and moral ideals that inform the underlying motivation of the human agents (Taylor 1991: 19–20). In this regard, Taylor explicitly says:

> All historiography (and social science as well) relies on (largely implicit) understanding of human motivation: how people respond, what they generally aspire to, the relative importance of given ends and the like. This is the truth behind Weber's celebrated affirmation that any explanation in sociology has to be "adequate as to meaning." (Taylor 1989b: 203)[43]

As a consequence, religious motivation is not to be understood merely as a by-product of other factors, but with life of its own (Taylor 2004: 63–65).

Third, Taylor borrows from Weber the methodology of using "ideal-types" as means of finding the most appropriate cause-effect relationships to explain the object of study. This is carried out, in the Weberian view, against the backdrop of *ad hoc* ideal-types, which allow us to compare the possible cause-effect relationships. Such comparisons are useful in determining the deviations between the sets of cause-effect units with which we may be working in regard to the ideal-type. By asking ourselves what gives place to such deviations, we refine our hypothesis. In a similar way, by asking why an expected effect didn't occur (counter-factual analysis), we also refine our set of hypothetical causes (Ringer 2004: 77–104). In Taylor's case, his Ancien Régime-Age of Mobilization-Age of Authenticity schema; the Paleo-, Post- and Neo-Durkhemian dispensations; and the four different types of Closed World Structures, are explicitly ideal-types (Taylor 2007: 437, 461, 557).[44]

Other points of contact between Taylor and Weber's thought are: the focus on specific, localized and verifiable phenomenon; a multi-causal approach to social

---

[42] The reference is to the piece titled *Peaceful Coexistence in Psychology.*

[43] Weber's quote is from *Economy and Society* (1978: 11).

[44] These are just three passages where this borrowing is explicit.

change; the understanding of social phenomena as caused not by only one but by a set of various causal agents, which are contingent to particular historical moments, and a substantive understanding of religion (Taylor 2004: 72–73).[45]

(b) However, in spite of all the ways in which both thinkers coincide, there are important differences that need to be mentioned. First, both of them see the "herme-neutical" tasks of the social sciences differently. Max Weber's understanding of the social sciences, in a very schematic summary, stresses the need of starting from a singular empirical phenomenon which must be explained. The next step asks for the determination of the significant elements appearing there and their interconnec-tions. Lastly, the social scientist should search the most appropriate cause-effect relationships to explain the object of study.

Weber thinks that the social sciences should be hermeneutical for a number of epistemological reasons. First, from the very beginning, the historian or sociologist decides which elements present in the phenomenon are to be taken into account to offer a scientific explanation of it. This he calls "value relevance" (*Wertbeziehung*), and has its place before social research starts. In this sense, in the particular case of the focus of the *Archiv fur Sozialwissenschaft und Sozialpolitik* he worked for as an editor, Weber says: "The quality of an event as a 'social-economic' event is not something which it possesses 'objectively.' It is rather conditioned by the orienta-tion of our cognitive interest, as it arises from the specific cultural significance which we attribute to the particular event in a given case" (Weber 2011: 64).[46] However, during the research process, the social scientist should act just on the evidence of empirical facts and abstain from "value judgments" (*Werturteil*).

A second epistemological reason must be added: In order to propose a probable cause-effect hypothesis, certain knowledge of "rules of adequate causation," under-stood as rules derived from experience, is needed. These "rules," in turn, are cultur-ally conditioned. Third, the social sciences entail interpretation because the study of social behavior—either that of individuals or groups—should include the (rational) motivation the agent(s) give to it: "A correct causal interpretation of a concrete course of behavior is achieved when such overt behavior and its motives have both been correctly ascertained and if, at the same time, their relationship has become intelligible in a meaningful way" (Weber 1993: 81). This request for addressing the rational motivations of human agents is also related with anthropological concerns, specifically with Weber's view that humans are creative sense-giving beings. We all

> are *cultural beings*, endowed with the capacity and the will to take a deliberate attitude towards the world and to lend it *significance*. Whatever this significance may be, it will lead us to judge certain phenomena of human existence in its light and to respond to them as being (positively or negatively) meaningful. Whatever may be the content of this attitude— these phenomena have cultural significance for us and on this significance alone rests its scientific interest.(Weber 2011: 81)

---

[45] Here Taylor endorses the Weberian approach to the rise of Capitalism while compared with that provided by Marxism.

[46] The reference is to the piece titled *'Objectivity' in Social Science and Social Policy.*

human first

In contrast, for Taylor, the need for a hermeneutical social science is anthropological in the first place: we are constituted as human beings in part by our self-understandings (Taylor 1985a: 3).[47] Furthermore, and quite differently from Weber, he distances himself from the belief that, in order to secure knowledge, what is necessary is to follow the proper general method. On the contrary, he affirms the need, for any "disengaged" (modern scientific) science, of an "engaged" human scientist, who carries out a hermeneutical approach to social studies, which includes the self-realization of existing within "inescapable frames" by living as an embodied being, who performs intentional actions, and whose knowledge of things always takes place within a tacit background about reality (Taylor 1995: 73).[48] Because of these conditions, there would not be a generalizable method for the social sciences, but just some principles and guidelines to be applied ad casum, as it was mentioned earlier in this chapter.

Second, Weber asks for a "value-free" social science, in spite of his interpretive approach to it. He defines "value-judgments" (*Werturteil*) as "practical evaluations of the unsatisfactory or satisfactory character of phenomena subject to our influence" (Weber 2011: 1),[49] and finds they have no place in the sciences of man, which focus on statements of facts. "The investigator and teacher should keep unconditionally separate the establishment of empirical facts (including the "value-oriented" conduct of the empirical individual whom he is investigating) and *his* own practical evaluations, i.e., his evaluation of these facts as satisfactory or unsatisfactory" (Weber 2011: 11; 20–21).[50] For Taylor, this ideal is simply an impossible condition to meet, as we have already explained.

re-expl

Third, Weber's view of rationalization as an overarching process is contested by Taylor. As we may recall, Weber affirms a process of rationalization of action as proper to modernity, which entails that each realm of society is understood and organized into systems, each based on its own immanent laws. Another consequence is the exclusion of forces from outside the world: what he calls "disenchantment" (*Entzauberung*). In this view, a mystery is not something to enter into but something to conquer through reason. Secularization is the consequence of these changes on religion. It encompasses both rationalization and disenchantment.[51]

Furthermore, Weber emphasizes the role of three modes of rationality in social life. By "practical rationality" he understands "the methodological attainment of a definitely given and practical end by means of an increasingly precise calculation of

---

[47] The reference is from the book's *Introduction*.

[48] This reference is to a piece called *Lichtung or Lebensform: Parallels between Heidegger and Wittgenstein*.

[49] This quote is from a piece called *The Meaning of 'Ethical Neutrality' in Sociology and Economics*.

[50] Scholars have noted that Weber himself did not comply with his value-free requirement for carrying out sociological research (e. g., Abraham 1992).

[51] The most important text for the understanding of this process due to tensions between salvation religion and its ethics of fraternity on the one hand, and the economic, political, aesthetic, erotic and intellectual realms on the other, is *Religious Rejections of the World and Their Directions* (Weber 1958: 323–59).

adequate means" (Weber 1958: 293).[52] In contrast, "theoretical rationality" is that through which "the systematic thinker performs on the image of the world: an increasing theoretical mastery of reality by means of increasingly precise and abstract concepts" (Weber 1958: 293). Lastly, "substantive rationality" involves a choice of means to ends in the realm of a given system of values. Although the three types of rationality had existed in different cultures through history, the subtype of "practical rationality" that involves universal rules, laws and institutions, is proper of the modern West, particularly of the economy, legal system and science. The rationalization of the conduct of everyday life is proper of modernity and because of this pervasive presence it gained such importance. The best example of this is Calvinist ethic, which was

> a significant promoter of modern capitalism and its instrumental rationality. Even more than that, modern science, individualism, liberalism and modern democratic elements were also promoted by the Protestant ethic and its connection to Cartesian philosophy and utilitarianism, its individual freedom for God (inner-world individualism) and its foundations of free associations. (Reckling 2001: 163)

It can be said, then, that for Weber rationalization and its consequences are the hallmark of modernity. However, the greater freedom gained and individualistic outlook enjoyed by Westerners seems to be overpowered in the end by a drive towards uniformity: "standardization, stricture and orientation of consciousness, action and destiny of actors: schematization of leading a life" (Weber 1978: 956). The strength of these impersonal forces is such that any non-rational reaction to the process (e.g., Romanticism, anarchism, some forms of socialism) is doomed to failure. Weber seems to have been looking for different ways of individualist escape strategies (through charismatic authority, autonomy, individual responsibility and the like), but his view of the future was gloomy. In the end, "Weber scientific concept of rationalization banishes his anthropological concept of the sense-giving subject, his original starting point" (Reckling 2001: 165).

Taylor disagrees with the Weberian understanding of rationalization as a universal process which is integral to modernity (Weber 1958: 138–39).[53] It is not that he is not aware of the revolutionary effects that modern science had in the West, but Taylor's point is that such a process cannot be seen as general nor steady, it is not a "set of transformations which any and every culture can go through—and which all will probably be forced to undergo" (Taylor 1999b: 154). In contrast, he sees rationalization as something that occurred in the West that is dependent on a particular constellation of understandings of person, nature, society and the good. The process, instead of being defined by its point or arrival (growth of scientific consciousness, a secular outlook or instrumental rationality) should be seen as defined by its point of departure: a particular culture (Taylor 1999b: 154).

Another point of discrepancy comes to the fore when one considers Taylor's view on rationality. Although there is no direct critique by him on Weber's diverse

---

[52] The quote is from the piece titled *The Social Psychology of the World Religions*.

[53] The quote is from the piece titled *Science and Vocation*.

types of rationality, it is possible to gain some insight from Taylor's critique of Habermas. The German philosopher speaks—inspired by Weber—of scientific, moral and aesthetic reason, this last one aimed at self-realization. Each mode would entail a diversity of specific procedures within its domain. The bottom line here is that each social sub-system would have its own set of rules and procedures which correspond to a particular kind of rationality. Taylor sees here that rationality "ceases to mean a single thing, and to have a similar shape in the different domains" (Taylor 2009). He will say in this regard that

> it is obvious that modernity has led to a relative differentiation of the three areas. Sciences, or at least the natural sciences, now exist which are value-free; questions of personal realization have, as mentioned, been accorded a separate status. Yet some theorists have gone still further and asserted that modernity has separated three independent domains of rationality off from one another, that is, three areas in which questions are resolved on the basis of respectively different justifying reasons and criteria. (Taylor 2002: 133)

Taylor calls into question this approach in two ways. First, it is not clear that questions about truth, morality and authenticity should only be answered in a logically independent sphere of their own. In fact, our practical (moral) reason does not just proceed formally without referring to substantive moral goods. Even Kant, who initiated in Western philosophy a formal approach in ethics, would base his system on a substantial claim: that we are rational beings, and we should act accordingly, since it is our nature. Hence, moral reason is inextricably linked to theoretical rationality. The same is true the other way round. Moreover, "an overselective singling out of that third dimension [aesthetic rationality] would just be distorting in the picture it would give. If questions of personal realization are severed from considerations of truth and morality, then this opens up a realm of pure subjectivism" (Taylor 2002: 133).

Second, Taylor thinks we should not take for granted that the distinction of three kinds of rationality governing corresponding social sub-systems would lead to better answers to the questions and problems that may rise in each differentiated domain. He recalls here his strong criticism against the kind of procedural ethics which Habermas proposes in his "theory of communicative action" (Taylor 2002: 130–32). As a consequence of the preceding considerations, Taylor's account of secularization in the West would not make use of the Weberian ideal-type distinctions between modes of rationality. Instead, while recognizing the relative differentiation of the three kinds of rationality, he would strongly affirm their interdependence. This view underlies his meta-narrative.

Touching on a different topic, it could also be said that Taylor does a better job than Weber in integrating the development of reason (what he calls "naturalism") with that of the non-rational "expressivist" trend in the West. The former is referred to the development of science and neutral observation as well as to a cluster of moral aspirations and motivations of modern man, which include certain practices, institutions and life forms. The latter argues that "the crucial moral source lies in the deep inwardness of human feelings and emotions, which become 'expressed' through language, gestures or art, and thereby fulfill the individual and common nature" (Reckling 2001:167). For Taylor, the expressivist movement is not anti-modern per se but, on the contrary, it has a great cultural influence in modernity. "The idea of an expressive and authentic fulfillment of personal and collective life is nowadays a common landmark in western societies. It concerns the culture of adventures in leisure time, sports, sex, fashion or local and regional political movements, etc." (Reckling 2001:168).

All this notwithstanding, Taylor would agree with Weber's view of disenchantment up to a point. It is true that with modernity we no longer need to ask the help of magic to master or implore the spirits, since we now master through science and technology (Weber 1958: 139).[54] However, the process started earlier as when Axial religion (and in this case Christianity) marshaled against the magical practices of Pre-Axial religion (Taylor 2011: 288–92, 2007: 34–35, 551–54).[55] Taylor sees, as Weber does, that there is a decline in the belief in the world as being filled with spirits and moral forces that give meaning to things. He finds that people start to see that meanings were in the minds of individuals, who imposed them on things. In spite of this, the process has not taken us into a world deprived of meaning, with no place for wonder, as Weber would suggest. Science itself gives space for wonder as, for example, evolution theory shows:

> Clearly, the simple fact that we understand better how different species evolved, however 'mechanistic' the process identified, cannot take away from our wonder at the scope and intricacy of the resultant system. We are faced, however we understand it, with the fact that we can thus respond with wonder; we might want to add that anyone with sufficient knowledge, training, and consciousness cannot but feel this wonder. (Taylor 2011: 299–300)

Before this wonder, one could take an agnostic or atheistic stance, but also a religious and even an enchanted one, to some degree (Taylor 2007: 426).

An important consequence of this discussion about rationalization as integral to secularization is that Taylor does not see the differentiation thesis as a good enough explanation for the latter (Taylor 2007: 2, note 3). The rationally-driven autonomization of sub-spheres of the social life, in spite of its intentions, does not eliminate religious motivations from being operative in sub-systems of human social life different than the religious one. "The fact that activity in a given sphere follows its own inherent rationality and doesn't permit of the older kind of faith-based norming doesn't mean that it cannot still be very much shaped by faith" (Taylor 2007: 425). Second, it does not draw clear-cut boundaries between the sub-systems, particularly between the religious and the public spheres (those deemed non-religious) (Taylor 2007: 426). It is not just that religious marginalization in society did not completely occur, but also that rationalization did not eliminate the intimations of religion.

---

[54] The quote is from the piece titled *Science and Vocation*.

[55] The first reference is to a piece titled *Disenchantment-Reenchantment*.

4.2.2 *Taylor and Durkheim*

(a) In spite of the fact that Taylor uses terms such as Paleo-, Neo- and Post-Durkhemian dispensations as referring to a sequence of stages that—among others—characterize the process of secularization, there is little coincidence between his and Durkheim's thought. Even when using these terms by which he describes the relationship between religion and society, Taylor sometimes means precisely the opposite of what Durkheim did. For example, in a passage that has already been mentioned, while characterizing the Ancien Regime as Paleo-Durkhemian, he explains the following:

> Societies organized by such a church are in this (loose) meaning "Durkhemian," in the sense that church and social sacred are one—although the relation of primary and secondary focus is reversed, since for Durkheim the social is the principal focus, reflected in the divine, while the opposite is true for ultramontane Catholicism. (Taylor 2007: 442)

In short, then, these dispensations should be understood as expressing just the ways (if any) in which religion and society are related, particularly the manner in which religion still performs a shaping role within the political system.

There are several other places where Taylor acknowledges the fact that religion performs functional roles in society. For instance, he mentions, as Weber does, the role of Calvinism in the appearance of Capitalism (Taylor 2004: 72–74, 2007: 178–79); that of the logic of reform in the Catholic and Protestant spiritual lives during the Age of Mobilization, which reinforced the persuasion process of people by governments so that they would become active participants of the Modern Moral Order (Taylor 2007: 468–70); or the role religion played in establishing political identities of groups in the United States and the United Kingdom, where Evangelicals linked themselves to the nation, and where Irish and Polish Catholic minorities in those countries struggled to keep their own identities, which were in contrast to that of the majority (Taylor 2007: 470). However, for Taylor, these instances should not make us consider religion a priori as an epiphenomenon of social functions (Taylor 2007: 433). Besides the capacity religion has to furnish a universe of language and symbols on which people construct their self-interpretations and, hence, their identity and moral outlook, there is still room for religious motivations as such in modernity (Taylor 2007: 437).

(b) It is fair to say that Taylor is very critical of Durkheim's thought and generally, of all functionalist approaches in sociology. In his work of 1989, *Understanding and explanation in the Geisteswissenshaften*, he takes issue with this kind of theory by saying that it succumbs to the temptation of oversimplifying the object of study and of not taking seriously the human agents' self-understanding. What is needed, Taylor says, is a *Verstehen* comprehension of the world of the people we are studying. "We have no way of knowing that we have managed to penetrate this world in this way short of finding that we are able to use their key words in the same way they do, and that means that we grasp their desirability characterizations" (Taylor 1981: 194). By "desirability characterizations" we should understand the people's aspirations, emotions, and sense of the admirable or contemptible, using their language in the way they use it. A study like this is necessarily interpretive and deals with "value-filled" desirability characterizations (Taylor 1981: 192–93).

When commenting explicitly on functionalist theories in the social sciences, Taylor gives an example that recalls the Durkhemian view:

> Let us say there is some truth in the claim that religions generally contribute to social integration; and that we can establish this. The question still arises of the significance of this finding. How much can we explain of the actual shape of religious practice by this functional theory?
>
> Even though we may show our theory to be true, in some senses, we may be challenged to show that it is significant. Does it explain something substantive about the religious forms of the society, or is it rather in the nature of a banal observation about the poor long-term prospects of disruptive religions? (Taylor 1981: 195–96)

The point this example makes, according to Taylor, is that functionalist approaches in the sciences of man are insufficient, that by not taking into account the self-interpretation of the object of study, they remain at a too general level, like self-fulfilling prophecies that demonstrate what is already part of their presuppositions, and do not give an account of explanatory significance for the case at hand (Taylor 1981: 196).

(c) Another strong point of divergence between Taylor and Durkheim is the quite different way in which both understand the methodology of the social sciences. In *The Rules of the Sociological Method*, Durkheim takes pains in offering a clear, concise and empirical explanation of how the then recently-born sociology should proceed to ensure real scientific knowledge. It seeks to ensure the proper status of science to sociology and how sociology is different from philosophy and psychology. Without entering into the details of this work, it is clear for Durkheim that sociology occupies itself with social facts (Durkheim 1965: 1–13), which are to be seen as "things," "objectively" (Durkheim 1965: 143–44):

> Things include all objects of knowledge that cannot be conceived by purely mental activity, those that require for their conception data from outside the mind, from observations and experiments, those which are built up from the more external and immediately accessible characteristics to the less visible and more profound. (Durkheim 1965: xliii)[56]

This kind of study includes the recognition of social phenomena as external to individuals, their classification, and the establishment of causal relationships between them, studying each of them in both their causal and functional roles, using the method of correlation as the instrument of research par excellence (Durkheim 1965). In the process, researchers are required to put aside their preconceptions (Durkheim 1965: 144) and the intimations of common sense (Durkheim 1965: xxxvii–xxxix),[57] and to conduct themselves with a scientific outlook as "in the state of mind as the physicist, chemist, or physiologist when he probes into a still unexplored region of the scientific domain" (Durkheim 1965: xlv).[58] In sum, there is a very close parallel here with the methodology of the natural sciences.

---

[56] This quote is from the *Preface* to the Second Edition.

[57] This quote is from the *Preface* to the First Edition.

[58] This quote is from the *Preface* to the Second Edition.

In contrast, as we have seen, Taylor sees the sciences of man as hermeneutic and including in their dealings the human agent's self-interpretations. He also strongly criticizes the empiricist paradigm.[59]

4.2.3   Taylor and Marx

Taylor's commitment to socialism, which dates from the 50s and the 60s, lead him first to become one of the founders of the British New Left (Caldwell 2009: 348–55). In those years, "Taylor articulates a distinctive conception of the tasks and priorities of social criticism" (Smith 2002: 172).[60] In the 60s, he became an activist of the New Democratic Party, which represented Canadian socialism. At the time, his approach to Marxism was ambivalent, turning into a highly critical stance later (Smith 2002: 180–83; Taylor 1989a). Ian Fraser would interpret this event as a shift in Taylor's personal framework for pursuing the good: from Marxism to Catholicism (Fraser 2003: 760). *A Secular Age* reflects this last development and in what follows I will relate Taylor's late thought with that of Marx.

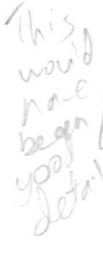

(a) There are a number of points of accord between Taylor and Marx. In the first place I would mention their shared critique of capitalism. For Taylor, as for Marx, modern capitalism has produced oppression, exploitation and domination.

> When we come to the full development of human power over Nature, as we see with mature capitalism, this awesome power turns out to be in no one's control. Rather, it exercise follows blind laws of endless accumulation which capitalist society inexorably obeys, even though the cost to its members is terrible. The global process of capitalist society is willed and desired by no one. Rather, it controls the lives of all the individuals who make it up. (Magee 1978: 46; Taylor 1975: 548–551)

However, Taylor would later add that there is a need of seeking ways through which conflicting demands could be reconciled, which asks for the laborious creation of a rational society where individuals look after their goals on their own and as part of a community. He would understand the feminist and LGTBQ movements, as well as environmentalism and cultural/ethnic minorities, as reflecting today the ethical dilemmas (which underlie social conflicts) raised by the modern understanding of increased freedom, respect for human rights and acceptance of diversity. "The too quick belief in a specious solution can wreak terrible destruction, as the sad story of Bolshevism shows beyond question" (Taylor 1994: 214).[61]

---

[59] Other differences between Taylor and Durkheim are related to their views on language (Taylor 1985a: 244–45) and the Taylorean critique of the theory of the passing from "mechanical" to "organic solidarity" (Taylor 1999b: 155).

[60] Taylor's assessment of Capitalism in the United Kingdom by that time is highly critical (Taylor 1960).

[61] Taylor has also explored the epistemological difficulties in affirming a general, trans-cultural, theory of conflict, as Marxism does, in a piece called *The Hermeneutics of Conflict* (Taylor 1988a: 218–228).

Another convergence occurs when they consider the importance of "ordinary life" (Fraser 2003: 763–65). Taylor understands this as "the belief that the central point of human experience and human fulfillment is to be found in the life of production and reproduction, of work and family, or labour and sexual love. In various forms, this has been one of the great revolutionary forces in modern culture" (Taylor 1988a: 227, 1989b: 211–302). He finds this ideal expressed in the bourgeois ideal of life, and also in "the most influential revolutionary ideology of our [20th] century, Marxism, with its apotheosis of man the producer" (Taylor 1989b: 14).

A third point of contact is that of considering the human self as concrete, situated within a given society, and seeking for self-realization. Besides, Taylor would here consider Marx—particulary in his early writings—as an exponent of expressivist Enlightenment, aiming at human integrity and wholeness, which does not accept divisions between body and soul, inclination and will. The Marxist notion of "alienation," in his view, "belongs intrinsically to a expressivist structure of thought. Man's work and its product, the man-made environment, is his expression, and hence its loss is not just deprivation but self-diremption; and its recovery is not just the means to happiness but regaining wholeness and freedom" (Taylor 1975: 548). As in several other places in his writings, this can be seen when Marx criticizes Adam Smith by affirming that labor is not just self-sacrifice, but "a positive, creative activity" (Marx 1971: 126, 1975: 272–82).

(b) Taylor's early differences with Marx himself are difficult to document since there are just a few Taylorean sources on the topic. In contrast, his criticisms of Marxism grew in time and reached its apex in the contribution of an article called "Marxism and Socialist Humanism,"[62] he wrote in 1989 for an edited book. In what follows, I will draw from Taylor's thought on Marxism from the materials available, pointing out eventual references to specifically Marxian positions.

Taylor's coincidence with Marxism (and with Marx) in his view of class struggles as reflecting the existence of objective economic oppression fades when Taylor also sees them as expressing political and social factors as such, and not only as a by-product of the economic conditions. This is very important in his meta-narrative of secularization in the West in which economic factors are as important as political and social ones in regard to social change. This can be perceived, for instance, in the analysis of the estrangement of the Christian churches, during the Age of Mobilization, from the working class because of the churches support of the (economic) elites (Taylor 2007: 442–44, 467) or, previously in time, in Taylor's view of the support of the Catholic Church of the political (and economic) system during the Ancien Regime with its oppressive consequences on the peasantry and rising bourgeoisie (Taylor 2007: 438).

Of similar importance for Taylor's analysis of secularization is his critique of the Marxist (and Marxian) view of social change as the consequence, in the end, of mere economic forces and its dismissal of non-economic ones as "idealism" (Taylor 1989b: 199–207).

---

[62] "By humanism I mean some kind of doctrine about human potentialities which can command our moral admiration," defines Taylor (1989a: 61).

I think this kind of objection is based on a false dichotomy, that between ideas and material factors as rival causal agencies. In fact, what we see in human history is ranges of human practices that are both at once, that is, material practices carried on by human beings in space and time, and very often coercively maintained, and at the same time, self-conceptions, modes of understanding. These are often inseparable. (Taylor 2004: 31: 2007: 212)

This Taylorean view on the relationship between ideal and material causes is systematically intertwined with his historical accounts in *A Secular Age*.

(c) Taylor's criticisms of Marxism also include a number of other topics (Caldwell 2009: 355–59). The first to be mentioned is that what he would call "mainstream" Marxism, following the "late" Marx, does not pay enough attention to the self. "It has nothing to say about the personal level—and I wonder if that is entirely true. It's true of the historical record up till now" (Magee 1978: 52), says Taylor. Ian Fraser recognizes this criticism of Marx when he affirms that Taylor "indeed has a point in suggesting that Marx needed to say more about the personal level of the individual" (Fraser 2003: 761). The works by Neo-Marxists thinkers such as Walter Benjamin and Ernst Bloch seem to Taylor as trying to overcome this absence by paying attention to art, philosophy and even transcendence, but they do not represent the main trend in Marxist tradition at all (Taylor 1989a: 69).

Second, Taylor sees Marx's and the Marxist notion of freedom as devoid of real meaning. This view inherits the Rousseaunian understanding of freedom as not being dependant on others, but determining the conditions of our own existence. "Marx then transposes it into a social form, in which the self-creating subject is no longer an individual but a social subject: the 'species being.' That is a very important change" (Taylor 1989a: 65). As a result, freedom ends stripped from its consequences for individuals and its relationship with any external source of guidance other than the mere will of the individual.

Third, and as a consequence of the previous point, Taylor sees Marx and Marxism as having an authoritarian and anti-democratic bent. These orientations project an erroneous idea of political rule: "It gives us an unanimist depiction of democracy: democracy and self-rule are attained when people achieve unanimous common will. Somewhere there is a real will that will unite all of us round it together" (Taylor 1989a: 65–66). As a result of this, what occurs in practice is that such anonymous common will is not agreed to by the masses but by the revolutionary elites. Besides, a centralizing policy is put in place in order to avoid regional diversity. In spite of the fact that Marx's desires may have been different (Marx 1968: 56–59), in the end, Taylor thinks, when Marxist revolutions were carried out, they produced a totalitarian system (Magee 1978: 56–57).

In contrast with such model, Taylor proposes a "civic humanist democracy" in which there will be continuous conflict, opposition and rivalry. However, "this [last] model makes us look at society as a participatory community in which the common institutions, the common rules and laws that give structure to the form of participatory life, are seen as the common repository of the human dignity of all participants" (Magee 1978: 64).

Fourth, and as a consequence of his previously explained view of the sciences of man as hermeneutic, Taylor would not accept Marx's approach as a "scientific" understanding of social facts if it, in any sense, parallels that of the natural sciences with its notion of "neutrality" or "disengagement" on the part of the researcher. The scientific character of Marxist methodology is aimed at the analysis of empirical information—largely determined by economic factors—in order to uncover the social trends which would help explain and predict social, political, and other "material" and even "non-material" phenomena. In contrast, Taylor's view of the social sciences would not only recognize the importance of both "material" and "non-material" causes, but will also affirm that the relative strength of each of them is contingent upon particular historical circumstances. Besides, as has been said several times before, to really grasp social facts attention should be paid to the motivation of the social actors and, hence, their self-interpretations and moral outlooks. Also, as it has been mentioned before, Taylor would strongly qualify the way in which the human sciences could predict social behavior.

Lastly, Taylor criticizes Marxism's lack of transcendence. Because of its "militant atheist materialism… when it comes to voicing a humanist doctrine, to defining the human potentialities that we hope socialist society may liberate, Marxism has too narrow a range. Beyond the potentialities for greater production and the domination of nature, what are they?" (Taylor 1989a: 67). He answers that Marxism does not offer a substantial content to what human self-fulfillment might be. Even when he recognizes that Marx seems to point to a situation in which human beings would become "artistic creators" (Taylor 1989a: 68), Taylor affirms that the Marxian interpretation of such creative action is one of self-expression (through production) rather than one of expressing something beyond ourselves. In this regard, he illustrates his point by saying that Modernist literature and art "which have gone to the self-expressive end of the spectrum have always become the more trivialized, shallower, less interesting." In contrast, art works which have gone "towards the exploration or expression of something beyond us have been the deepest and most memorable" (Taylor 1989a: 69).

More specifically, and in contrast with Marxism, which belongs to a group of positions that eliminates the transcendent beyond life, Taylor would affirm the need of recognizing that "the point of things isn't exhausted by life, the fullness of life, even the goodness of life…Then acknowledging the transcendent means seeing a point beyond that" (Taylor 2011: 173).[63] This position, he thinks, should be seen at least as plausible. However, he insists on the fact that for him "transcendence" means both a notion of human flourishing, on the one hand, and an emphasis on spiritual transcendence on the other (Taylor 1999a: 109–110).

In regard to Neo-Marxist thinkers, besides Benjamin and Block, there are just a few mentions to them in Taylor's later reflections on political philosophy.[64] In *A Secular Age*, he cites Theodor Adorno and Walter Benjamin as a variety of expressivist thinkers (Taylor 2007: 760). Benjamin's is cited again in relation with his

---

[63] The quote is from the piece titled *A Catholic Modernity?*

[64] Earlier references by Taylor would include the Yugoslavian group *Praxis*, which explored a version of socialist humanism in the form of a Marxist libertarian theory, and "world systems theory" (Magee 1978: 57–58).

notion of "homogeneous time" (Taylor 2007: 54, 58 and 798, note 45) and other minor topics (Taylor 2007: 419, 483 and 722). Marcuse's influence is noted in the advent of the Age of Authenticity (Taylor 2007: 476–77). However, in all these cases, such mentions do not denote significant influences on Taylor's main argument. The work by Neo-Marxist thinkers such as Antonio Gramsci, Max Horkheimer, Ernst Bloch, George Lukacs, Karl Korsch, Ralf Dahrendorf or Immanuel Wallerstein is not cited. Taylor's interaction with Jurgen Habermas' thought will be discussed in the following chapter.

4.2.4 Classical Sociology as "Acultural Theory"

Broadly speaking, Taylor would disagree with the general approach the founding fathers of sociology take towards the social processes involved in the coming of modernity, excepting part of Weber's thought. He sees such a standpoint as proper to what he calls "acultural theories," which are characterized by explaining the transformation brought about by modernity as a "culture-neutral operation," one through which any culture could go and "which all will probably be forced to undergo" (Taylor 1999b: 154). The operations are usually couched either in terms of a growth in reason (e.g., science, technology, instrumental reason) or in terms of social changes (e. g,. industrialization, mobilization, urbanization). This process "is not seen as supposing or reflecting an option for one specific set of human values or understandings among others" (Taylor 1999b: 154). Social factors are usually seen as impacting on values and not that much as reflecting them.

"Acultural" views of the coming of modernity are predominant, Taylor thinks, for several reasons. Among them is the fact that a view that sees our culture as one among others is a relatively recent acquisition in the West. Besides, we fear that "a cultural theory might make value judgments impossible" (Taylor 1999b: 158) because any such theory would entail the recognition of cultural pluralism and the risk of making impossible an affirmation of the supremacy of the West. This ethnocentric understanding, Taylor thinks, has been present in modernity since its origins up until relatively recent times, when it presented itself as the liberation of falsehood and oppression, while seeing other peoples as inferior (barbarians, infidels or savages). Another factor to be considered is the vogue for materialistic explanations in the social sciences and history, which are seen as more empirically credible causes.

However, Taylor asserts that theories of this nature include a number of mistakes. First, the advent of modernity in the West cannot bracket out the original moral outlook that made modernity possible. To ignore this is to miss things in two ways: on the one hand, "we misclassify changes that reflect the culture peculiar to the modern West as the product of unproblematic discovery, or the ineluctable consequence of a social change"; on the other hand, we narrow the focus of our analysis and fail to see how these changes are due to changes at the level of culture, of the social imaginary, of the understanding of human agency (Taylor 1999b: 160). In this regard, we take as perennial what in reality is contingent to Western history.

Second, "acultural theories" implicitly affirm that "the dissipation of certain unsupported religious and metaphysical beliefs" (Taylor 1999b: 161) is a direct consequence of changes in the ways humans use reason, and that the process (which includes mankind as a whole) suggests a point of convergence: that of the (Western-like) modernization of all cultures. This is not the case at all, according to Taylor, because a successful transition into modernity "involves people finding resources in their traditional culture, which, modified and transposed, will enable them to take on the new practices" (Taylor 1999b: 162).

Third, in contrast to the "acultural" view of false religious and metaphysical beliefs as falling down due to the advancement of scientific rationality, Taylor affirms that by the time of the dawn of modernity, our ancestors' beliefs just made sense against a tacit background of their time. Such a situation is very different than the one we live in at the present, in which our tacit background in not the same (Taylor 1999b: 165–68).

Summarizing, we see how Taylor's sociological thought heavily leans towards Weber's and takes marked distance from that of Durkheim and Marx. However, this is qualified by virtue of some reservations about the Weberian notion of rationalization as an all-encompassing global process. It is the task in the next chapter to elucidate Taylor's contemporary sociological sources.

References

Abbey R (2000) Charles Taylor. Princeton University Press, Princeton

Abraham G (1992) Max Weber and the Jewish question: a study of the social outlook of his sociology. University of Illinois Press, Urbana

Caldwell M (2009) Charles Taylor and the pre-history of British cultural studies. Crit Arts 23:342–373. doi:10.1080/02560040903251134

Durkheim E (1965) The rules of sociological method. Free Press, New York

Fraser I (2003) Charles Taylor, Marx and Marxism. Polit Stud 51:759–774. doi:10.1111/j.0032-3217.2003.00457.x

Gadamer HG (2003) Truth and method. Continuum, New York

Honneth A, Joas H (1988) Social action and human nature. Cambridge University Press, Cambridge

Jay M (2009) Faith-based history. Hist Theory 48:76–84. doi:10.1111/j.1468-2303.2009.00486.x

Long DS (2009) How to read Charles Taylor: the theological significance of a secular age. Pro Ecclesia 43:93–107

MacIntyre A (2007) After virtue. A study in moral theory. University of Notre Dame Press, Notre Dame

Magee B (1978) Marxist philosophy. Dialogue with Charles Taylor. In: Magee B (ed) Men of ideas. The Viking Press, New York, pp 44–58

Martin D (2005) On secularization: towards a revised general theory. Ashgate, Aldershot

Marty ME (2008) Review of a secular age. Church Hist 77:773–775. doi:10.1017/s0009640708001480

Marx K (1968) Address of the general Council of the International Working Men's Association on the civil war in France, 1871. In: Lenin VI, Marx K (eds) The civil war in France: the Paris commune. International Publishers, New York, pp 36–85

Marx K (1971) Labour as sacrifice or self-realization. In: McLellan D (ed) Marx's Grundrisse. Macmillan, London, pp 123–127

Marx K (1975) Economic and philosophic manuscripts of 1844. In: Marx K, Engels F Marx and Engels collected works: 1843–1844. Vol. 3. International Publishers, New York, pp 231–246

Reckling F (2001) Interpreted modernity: Weber and Taylor on values and modernity. Eur J Soc Theory 4:153–176. doi:10.1177/13684310122225055

Ringer FK (2004) Max Weber: an intellectual biography. University of Chicago Press, Chicago

Ross D (2009) Review essay: a secular age. Thesis Eleven 99:112–121. doi:10.1177/0725513609345380

Smith NH (2002) Charles Taylor: meaning, morals, and modernity. Polity Press, Cambridge

Taylor C (1960) What's wrong with capitalism? New Left Rev 2:5–11

Taylor C (1964) The explanation of behaviour. Routledge & Kegan Paul, London

Taylor C (1975) Hegel. Cambridge University Press, Cambridge

Taylor C (1981) Understanding and explanation in the Geisteswissenschaften. In: Leich CM, Holtzman SH (eds) Wittgenstein: to follow a rule. Routledge & Kegan Paul, London, pp 191–210

Taylor C (1985a) Human agency and language. Philosophical papers. Vol. 1. University Press, Cambridge

Taylor C (1985b) Philosophy and the human sciences. Philosophical papers. Vol. 2. University Press, Cambridge

Taylor C (1985c) The person. In: Carrithers M, Collins S, Lukes S (eds) The category of the person: anthropology, philosophy, history. Cambridge University Press, Cambridge, pp 257–281

Taylor C (1988a) The hermeneutics of conflict. In: Tully J (ed) Meaning and context: Quentin Skinner and his critics. Princeton University Press, Princeton, pp 218–228

Taylor C (1988b) The moral topography of the self. In: Messer SB et al (eds) Hermeneutics and psychological theory: interpretive perspectives on personality, psychotherapy, and psychopathology. Rutgers University Press, New Brunswick, pp 298–320

Taylor C (1989a) Marxist and socialist humanism. In: Archer R (ed) Out of apathy: voices of the new left thirty years on. Verso, London, pp 61–78

Taylor C (1989b) Sources of the self: the making of the modern identity. Harvard University Press, Cambridge, MA

Taylor C (1991) The malaise of modernity. Concord, Toronto

Taylor C (1992) Inwardness and the culture of modernity. In: Honneth A (ed) Philosophical interventions in the unfinished project of enlightenment. MIT Press, Cambridge, MA, pp 88–110

Taylor C (1994) Charles Taylor replies. In: Tully J, Weinstock DM (eds) Philosophy in an age of pluralism: the philosophy of Charles Taylor in question. Cambridge University Press, Cambridge, pp 213–257

Taylor C (1995) Philosophical arguments. Harvard University Press, Cambridge, MA

Taylor C (1999a) Concluding reflections and comments. In: Heft J (ed) A Catholic modernity?: Charles Taylor's Marianist Award lecture, with responses by William M. Shea, Rosemary Luling Haughton, George Marsden, and Jean Bethke Elshtain. Oxford University Press, New York, pp 105–125

Taylor C (1999b) Two theories of modernity. Public Cult 11:153–174. doi:10.1215/08992363-11-1-153

Taylor C (2002) Language and society. In: Rasmussen DM, Swindal J (eds) Sage masters of modern social thought. Vol. 4: Jurgen Habermas. Sage, London, pp 123–135

Taylor C (2004) Modern social imaginaries. Duke University Press, Durham

Taylor C (2007) A secular age. Belknap Press of Harvard University Press, Cambridge, MA

Taylor C (2008) What drove me to philosophy? In: The 2008 Laureates. http://www.inamori-f.or.jp/laureates/k24_c_charles/lct_e.html. Accessed 28 June 2015

Taylor C (2009) The philosopher-citizen. In: The immanent frame. http://blogs.ssrc.org/tif/2009/10/19/philosopher-citizen. Accessed 28 June 2015

Taylor C (2010) Afterword: apologia pro libro suo. In: Warner M et al (eds) Varieties of secularism in a secular age. Harvard University Press, Cambridge, MA, pp 300–321

Taylor C (2011) Dilemmas and connections: selected essays. Belknap Press of Harvard University Press, Cambridge, MA

Taylor C (2013) Retrieving realism. In: Schear JK (ed) Mind, reason, and being-in-the-world: the McDowell-Dreyfus debate. Routledge, Abingdon, pp 61–90

Weber M (1958) From Max Weber: essays in sociology. Oxford University Press, New York

Weber M (1978) Economy and society: an outline of interpretive sociology. University of California Press, Berkeley

Weber M (1993) Basic concepts in sociology. Carol Publishing Group, New York

Weber M (2011) The methodology of the social sciences. Transaction Publishers, New Brunswick

Winch P (1958) The idea of a social science. Routledge & Kegan Paul, London

Chapter 5
Contemporary Sociological Sources

Abstract Taylor's criticisms of what he calls "mainstream sociology" have led him to choose among contemporary sociological thinkers those who have more culturally- and hermeneutically-sensitive approaches, and those who he can reinterpret in such terms. The more important scholars in this regard are David Martin, Jose Casanova, Hans Joas and, in a lesser degree, Robert Bellah, particularly in the ways in which they see secularization as having multiple trajectories, which are affected by social and cultural factors, a process which is in no way linear. Another point of contact is the way in which they consider the secular/religious divide to be porous, unstable and subject to different legal arrangements. Ideas such as deprivatization of religion, Axial Religion, civil religion, and religious fragilization have also been assimilated from them by Taylor. A second tier of influences refers to work of sociologists Taylor uses for elaborating more specific topics. He cites Benedict Anderson and Bronislaw Baczko when developing what social imaginaries are; he refers to thinkers such as Jurgen Habermas, Stephen Werner and Pierre Rosanvallon when studying modern social imaginaries. Lastly, in his characterization of contemporary religion Taylor seeks support in the work of Robert Wuthnow, Danièlle Hervieu-Lèger, Grace Davie and Wade Clark Roof.

Keywords Sociology • Sociological sources • Secularization • Hermeneutics • Social sciences • Culturally sensitive • Deprivatization • Fragilization • Social imaginaries • Contemporary religion

Taylor makes use of a significant number of contemporary sociological sources in *A Secular Age* and in other secularization-related works. Sometimes these references are made to substantiate some of his claims. This usually happens in two ways: either by showing where his ideas are coming from (denoting theoretical influences), or by pointing out concrete cases that prove what he is affirming (providing evidence of particular cases). In other instances, references are made to point out significant differences or to show how some author's opinions coincide on a particular topic despite the fact that they are reached through different approaches. Taylor's sociological sources mainly appear in *A Secular Age* in Chap. 2, which focuses on the development of what he calls "Disciplinary Society"; Chap. 3, which focuses on the shifts that occurred in modernity at the level of social imaginaries; and Chaps.

© Springer International Publishing AG 2017   105
Germán McKenzie, *Interpreting Charles Taylor's Social Theory on Religion and Secularization*, Sophia Studies in Cross-cultural Philosophy of Traditions and Cultures 20, DOI 10.1007/978-3-319-47700-8_5

12 and 13, which contain his narrative on the changes in religion and its place in society since the end of the Ancien Régime, through the Ages of Mobilization and Authenticity, to the present times.

When receiving the 2007 Templeton Prize, Taylor explicitly spoke of the authors who exercised a deeper influence on his meta-narrative of secularization:

> Breaking out of the old intellectual mould opens up a whole new field of great importance: what are the new forms of religion which are developing in the West? And what relation do they have to those which are growing elsewhere, in Asia, Africa, Latin America? This is part of what I am trying to study in my work [on secularization], drawing on the pioneering analysis of David Martin, on the writings of Robert Bellah, and on the recent work of younger sociologists, like Jose Casanova and Hans Joas. (Taylor 2007c)[1]

In what follows, I will present Taylor's major contemporary sociological sources by locating them in his meta-narrative, as outlined earlier in Chaps. 2 and 3. The first section will focus on his definition of the problem; the second one will deal with the socio-historical development of secularization; the third one will be concerned with what Taylor calls "History of Reform"; the fourth and last one will delve into contemporary religion and today's conditions of belief. While exploring Taylor's sources at all these levels, special attention will be given to David Martin, Robert Bellah, Jose Casanova and Hans Joas. However, in a narrative as broad as that of Taylor, it is natural to expect additional sources of influence. In a few instances it will be pertinent to mention particular debates held by Taylor with authors with positions different than his, or significant coincidences on a specific key concept. In this regard other sociologists will be mentioned for specific topics in which they are relevant.

5.1 Sources for the Redefinition of the Problem

5.1.1 New Hermeneutics and a Non-universal Uneven Trajectory

Taylor draws from David Martin's views on how to approach the phenomenon of secularization in the West. In a foreword he wrote for the English edition of Martin's book *On Secularization: Towards a Revised General Theory* (2005), which I identified in Chap. 1, he mentions three points in particular. The first is what he calls a "hermeneutical turn" by which, instead of considering how modernity (in the singular) causes a number of global changes (rationalization, privatization, differentiation, etc.), Martin shows that it takes variegated national and regional trajectories (Taylor 2007a: 426, note 11 and 429, note 18).[2] This variety of paths is also affected

---

[1] In the "Preface" to *A Secular Age*, Taylor explicitly talks about the positive effect of his conversations with Casanova and Joas during the last stage of the writing process of his book (2007a: ix).

[2] Here Taylor mentions Martin's misgivings about the term "secularization" and that he has continued using it in a nuanced way.

by the cultural-religious milieux in which the process occurs: Anglo-Protestant, on the one hand, and Catholic, on the other (Taylor 2007a: 449, note 54; Martin 1990). "In other words, he [Martin] let history, culture, different theologies and ecclesial structures back into the subject, and made it possible to face some of the awkward facts on the ground that mainstream sociology too effortlessly ignored" (Martin 2005: ix).[3]

Second, as a consequence of the previous point, Taylor thinks that Martin's approach "made us recognize different dynamics of 'secularization', where the original theories assumed a single one" (Martin 2005: ix; Taylor 2007a: 461, note 65). Underlying this latter view, one could find a kind of secular-liberal triumphalism.

Third, there is a deeper connection here between Taylor and Martin in regard to why a new hermeneutic approach to secularization should be needed. The latter finds sociology as "ideologically inflected, and even infected, especially by enlightened assumptions" (Martin 2005: 11). His response to this is a call for an interpretive approach to the discipline, and particularly to secularization theory. In his mind, there is a need for a theory which would also propose its own assumptions for debate, and which would take into account not only physical and biological factors but also social and cultural elements in explaining social change (Martin 2005: 9).

It is not difficult to see how these views coincide with those espoused by Taylor on the importance of a hermeneutic and culturally-sensitive social science. His own insistence in criticizing the "orthodox" account of secularization because it turns religion into an epiphenomenal reality, and subject to a "story of substraction," shows this, the same as his reflections on Close World Structures as epistemic unnoticed biases.

5.1.2   Some Misunderstandings

Taylor draws from different authors specific criticisms against "orthodox" and "counter-orthodox" positions on secularization, particularly those against identifying the latter with differentiation, privatization, and those who do not see it as a necessary consequence of urbanization, immigration or religious pluralism.

(a) Casanova's comments on the "differentiation thesis" have been positively assessed by Taylor, who sees them helping the clarification of the meaning of the decline of religious beliefs and practices at the societal level (what, as we already know, he calls "secularity 2"). Taylor adds that the differentiation of the religious sphere does not exclude "religious saturation," meaning a situation in which there are still references to God and the spirits in relation to ordinary activities. Differentiation appears to be conducive to the retreat of religion only when our notion of religion is bound exclusively to institutional arrangements, which is not necessarily the case.

---

[3] The quote if from Taylor's *Foreword* to Martin's book.

It is worth noting that after his scholarly exchange with Taylor, who finds the "differentiation thesis" good but incomplete, Casanova has also called this thesis into question, at least in part:

> One should ask whether it is appropriate to subsume the multiple and very diverse historical patterns of differentiation and fusion of the various institutional spheres (that is, church and state, state and economy, economy and science) that one finds throughout the history of modern Western societies into a single, teleological process of modern functional differentiation. (Casanova 1994: 103)[4]

(b) Jose Casanova's views on the "deprivatization" of religion are also amply accepted by Taylor (Taylor 2007a: 426, note 7; Casanova 1994: 5, 20, 211). The latter says that even when different spheres (as the state, economy, science) have separated and freed themselves from religion, this doesn't mean that the latter is only lived at the margins of society. On the contrary, religious traditions so react against such localization (Taylor 2007a: 426). Taylor also states, as it has been mentioned earlier, that religion *de facto* plays the role within the secular public sphere of legitimating, at the level of the particular individuals and minorities, their particular political identities, which in theory are supposed to become disengaged from confessional allegiances and be supportive of the general political identity of the country through a Rawlsian "overlapping consensus" (Taylor 2004: 193–94). In light of this, Taylor in regard to democracy insists not on the general application of the principle of separation between church and state (which he sees as just one of the possible institutional settings than can be proposed), but on a previous topic, namely that of "principled distance" on the part of the government from particular religious allegiances and even from secular systems of belief (Taylor 2011a: 303–325).[5]

(c) Taylor has endorsed Casanova's comments on immigration as having ambiguous effects on secularization—sometimes producing it, and sometimes fostering religiosity, as in the case of the United States (Taylor 2007a: 523, note 37; Casanova 2007). In this sense, equating social mobilization with secularization would be wrong.

(d) Taylor has also criticized those who see urbanization as a necessary cause of secularization by citing the work by Hugh McLeod and Roger Finke. He takes from the former his discussion about how urbanization in the United Kingdom accentuated the decline of religious belief and practice, whereas the opposite can be said of the United States. The generalization may not even hold for the United Kingdom in the nineteenth century. Taylor recalls Finke's work showing greater religious vitality in competitive urban environments to further stress this point (Taylor 2007a: 426, notes 8 and 9; McLeod 1995, 2000; Finke 1992).

---

[4] In support of his insights Casanova cites Charles Tilly's work (Tilly 1984: 43–60).
[5] The reference is to a piece titled *What Does Secularism Mean?*

(e) Hans Joas develops a critique of the ways in which Peter Berger—in spite of having recently espoused the "desecularization" thesis—still sees religious pluralism as eroding religious vitality (Berger 1994). Taylor supports this criticism of Berger (Taylor 2007a: 556 and 833, note 19; Joas 2008: 21–35). The problems are historical, sociological and philosophical. First, Joas thinks that pluralism has been a constant feature of European Christianity. Judaism and Islam for him are also part of the European heritage, along with pre-monotheistic religions, which persisted and influenced the way in which Christianity was lived in the area. He sees Berger as exaggerating the novelty of modern pluralism.

Second, Joas considers Berger's position wrongly to assume the following as true: "The less room for individual reflection within an institution, the stronger the institution is." On the contrary, when institutions open themselves up for discussion, hence pluralism, the chances for learning and controlled change are greater. This is also true for religious institutions, which can adapt themselves to novel situations. Besides, pluralism should be seen not just as an empirical fact, as Berger says, but also as a value that can be embraced by individuals and institutions (Joas 2008: 24–26).

Third, Joas criticizes the "counter-orthodox" (RCT) theorists by saying that, while at a first glance they contradict Berger's views, they nevertheless share with them a similar assumption: "that faith is somewhat based on acts of choice" (Joas 2008: 28). He thinks that cost/benefit calculations are not strong enough to produce religious motivations. Although part of the process of defining a particular religious allegiance, they are not the most important element that comes into play in them. "Religious faith is based either on traditions internalized in the process of self-formation—or on experiences of self-transcendence" (Joas 2008: 29) The latter are marked by a certain passivity, as when one is seized by someone or something, by which we surrender ourselves to such a reality. More importantly, these kinds of experiences are recognized as such a posteriori, and they require interpretation but are not already part of our cultural/religious interpretive frameworks. When the will acts, it is to surrender, which is clearly different than the act of choosing between several preferences (Joas 2008: 29). Taylor would agree with these views.

(f) For the sake of thoroughness, it should be reiterated here that Taylor takes from Roy Wallis and Steve Bruce the working definition of religion he uses in reference to understanding what secularization is:

> Religion for us consists of actions, beliefs and institutions predicated upon the assumption of the existence of either supernatural entities with powers of agency, or impersonal powers or processes possessed of moral purpose, which have the capacity to set the conditions of, or to intervene in, human affairs. (Wallis and Bruce 1992: 10–11; Taylor 2007a: 429, note 20)

Taylor affirms that this definition prevents a too broad notion of religion by recognizing the role of "impersonal powers," while noting that there are spiritual agents that are not "supernatural," and that religion in the West is linked to a certain idea of human flourishing.

5.1.3   Conditions of Belief

From an experiential standpoint, a religious or non-religious stance is felt in different ways by different people. This is also related with the particular ways a given human being is "enframed" socially, culturally and ethically. Taylor wants to focus on this level to see how the conditions of belief have changed due to secularization. He sees the mentioned stances as "alternative ways of living our moral/spiritual life, in the broadest sense" (Taylor 2007a: 5). At one pole of the continuum, Taylor mentions "places of fullness": "the presence of God, or the voice of nature, or the force which flows through everything, or the alignment in us of desire and the drive to form." (Taylor 2007a: 6). At the other pole there is "exile," the sense of having lost our place. "What is terrible in this latter condition is that we lose a sense of where the place of fullness is, even of what would it look like, or cannot believe in it any more" (Taylor 2007a: 6).

Here, Taylor supports his own claims by referring to Joas' view of potential religious experiences and their articulations (Taylor 2007a: 6, note 9; Joas 2008). Joas speaks of experiences of self-transcendence as those which "are not yet experiences of the divine, but without which we cannot understand what faith, what religion, is" (Taylor 2007a: 7). They are situations in which a person is pulled beyond the limits of himself. In these situations, I am "being captivated by something outside myself, a relaxation or liberation from one's fixation on oneself" (Taylor 2007a: 7). Experiences of this kind are those of ecstatic communion with nature; some interpersonal interactions; when one falls in love, which may also include sexual experiences; some experiences of giving and receiving help; and collective ecstasy. However, there are other experiences of self-transcendence that are not "rousing" but "shaken by suffering": (uncommon) horror of nature, loss of trust and betrayal, the loss of a loved one due to death. Joas also mentions, citing Paul Tillich, the experience of anxiety at the existential realization of our own finitude (Joas 2008: 7–11).

Although all people, at some point, have these experiences, they are articulated differently by religious and non-religious persons. While for the former, and as interpreted through the lens of a particular religious tradition, they may signify "the experience of an unconditional and unavailable [sic] other" (Joas 2008: 11), for the latter they are seen as nothing more than psychological phenomena. Joas thinks, in a similar fashion as Taylor does in *Varieties of Religion Today* (2002b, 2007a: 555–56), that "just as the believer cannot compel the nonbeliever to accept his religious interpretation on the basis of logic, the nonbeliever cannot advocate his nonreligious interpretation as the only rationally defensible one" (Joas 2008: 12).

5.2 Sources for the Socio-historical Analysis of Secularization

Taylor's meta-narrative of the process of secularization in the West, as we may recall, is divided in three stages: Ancien Régime, Age of Mobilization and Age of Authenticity. Generally speaking, he sees (a) such a social process as depending also on (b) cultural and historical contexts:

> Situations are so various and sui generis, and recognizable repeatable factors may be understood and lived so differently in these situations, that in the end we can be surer of certain particular causal attributions than we ever can of what appear to be the generalizations based on them. (Taylor 2007a: 426)

The relationship, in Taylor's view, can be reversed as well, and (b) cultural and historical processes could also depend on (a) sociological ones. In this way, the whole discussion goes back and forth between these two factors. However, I think it is useful to bear in mind Taylor's aim in *A Secular Age*, which is to produce a meta-narrative that finds a leading thread in the changing of social imaginaries in the West. His goal is not to offer an account providing a sociological/historical explanation of all causal factors that caused secularization to occur.[6] In contrast,

> What I have tried to do in *A Secular Age* was sketch the changeover, the process in which the modern theory of moral order gradually infiltrated and transformed the social imaginary. In this process, what is originally just an idealization grows into a complex imaginary by being taken up and associated with social practices, in part traditional ones, though it is often transformed by the contact. This is crucial to what I called above the extension of the understanding of moral order. It couldn't have become the dominant view in our culture without this penetration/transformation of our imaginary. (Taylor 2010: 312)

This study is akin to that of the "history of mentalities" and focuses on social imaginaries (Taylor 2010: 314). As a consequence, I will concentrate first on Taylor's contemporary sociological sources for his understanding of such imaginaries. I will then focus on Taylor's use of the notion of civil religion (which he takes from Bellah) and to his view of the relationship between elites and masses and its impact on social imaginaries (as influenced by Casanova).

In this section I will not include authors who, as historians who pay particular attention to sociology, are also sources for Taylor's socio-historical account of secularization in the West, specifically in his analysis of the Ancien Régime, the Age of Mobilization and part of the Age of Authenticity. In reference to these authors, he explicitly says: "I owe a lot to the interesting discussions in the works of McLeod, Brown, Blatschke, Raeidts, van Rooden, Wolffe and others" (Taylor 2007a: 437, note 37). Generally speaking, the most important are John Wolffe (1994) and Hugh

---

[6] This could be somewhat paralleled by Taylor's method in *Sources of the Self*, where the thread of the narrative is the exploration of what attracted people to the moral ideal embodied by modernity. "This can, up to a point, be explored independently of the question of diachronic causation" (1989: 203).

McLeod (1992, 1995, 1997, 2000) for their studies on England, and Philippe Boutry (1996) for his work on France.

Taylor's sociological influences on his view of the most recent developments occurred in the Age of Authenticity, those which we are living today, will be studied in a separate section at the end of this chapter.

5.2.1 Social Imaginaries in General

Taylor explicitly says that, when developing his theory of social imaginaries, he drew "heavily" from the thought of Benedict Anderson, Jurgen Habermas, Steven Warner and Pierre Rosanvallon (Taylor 2007a: 159, note 1). In a different place, he also mentions a work by Polish thinker Bronislaw Baczko, *Les Imaginaires Sociaux: Mémoires st Espoirs Collectifs* (1984), one from which Taylor has drawn "a great deal" (Taylor 2004: 176, note 1). He also mentions, in earlier versions of his theory, partial coincidences with the concept of "habitus" by Pierre Bourdieu (Taylor 1999: 166–68) and that of "imaginaries" by Cornelius Castoriadis (Taylor 2007b: 29). Taylor also acknowledges other influences, without explicitly enumerating them (Taylor 2007a: 159, note 1). What sources impact his general understanding of social imaginaries?

(a) Benedict Anderson's *Imagined Communities* contains the notion of "imagined community" that Taylor seeks to develop (Taylor 2007a: 195, 208–209, 713, 2007b: 29; Anderson 2006: 9–36). Anderson's point here is to carry out a study on the structure of nationalism. He defines "nation" as "an imagined political community—and imagined as both inherently limited and sovereign" (Anderson 2006: 6). In this context, "imagined" means that "all communities larger than primordial villages of face-to-face contact (and perhaps even these) are imagined" (Anderson 2006: 6). Anderson goes on by saying that national communities were not formed in the first place by structures and institutions but by three kinds of antecedent cultural factors. First, the religious community as gathering a vast number of people who may not find themselves related to each other except in the religious realm, and in a very real and powerful way indeed. Second, the dynastic realms implied that pre-modern states were defined by centers and not through a clearly defined piece of territory. Lastly, there is a change in the understanding of time, a view that has also been taken by Taylor and explained before (Anderson 2006: 19–26). In pre-modern times, ordinary time received its order and meaning from a "higher time," which would include eternity. The latter even introduces what seem to be inconsistencies in ordinary (secular) time. However, they are not so and receive their meaning from the "higher" vantage point which has linked together. "Higher time" is more real than secular time. With modernity, this distinction falls apart and time is seen as entirely secular, homogeneous and empty. Links between events of the same kind are expressed in terms of causality when they stand at close distance in time.

After the initial influence of Anderson's idea of "imagined communities," Taylor has developed a structured discourse on "social imaginaries" on his own. In his view, it comes to include "background understandings," which are tacit and pre-reflective, embedded in all kinds of paradigmatic stories, images and ideologies, forming a kind of tradition or communal memory (Taylor 2007b: 30). This common understanding (which is not a social theory), that helps us to make sense of ourselves, our role in society and society as a whole, is also expressed in practices. Vice versa, practices contribute to reinforce the imaginary (Taylor 2004: 23–30, 2007a: 171–76, 2007b: 30–31).

(b) For its part, Bronislaw Baczko's book *Les Imaginaires Sociaux* (Taylor 2004: 176, note 1, 2007a: 175, note 15) (not available in English) carries with it a view of social imaginaries as referring to "la production de representations globales de la société et de tout ce qui se rapport à elle, par example, de l' 'ordre social', des acteurs sociaux et de leurs rapports réciproques (hiérarchie, domination, conflit, etc.), des institutions socials, et notamment des institution politiques, etc" (Baczko 1984: 31–32).[7] Conversely, and in addition to being about social life, social imaginaries exist within large numbers of people:

> Au travers de ces imaginaires sociaux, une collectivité désigne son identité en élaborant una représentation de soi; marque la distribution des rôles et positions sociales; exprime et impose certaines croyances communes en plantant notamment des modèles formateurs tells que le "chef", le "bon sujet", le "vaillant guerrier", le "citoyen", le "militant", etc. Ainsi es notamment produite una representation totalisante de la societé comme un "ordre" où chaque élément trouve sa place, son identité at sa raison d'être. (Baczko 1984: 32)[8]

This view by Baczko is clearly coincident with aspects of Taylor's view on social imaginaries, particularly with his understanding of social imaginaries as non-thematized shared self-understandings. Other coincidences should be added: The fact that, for both authors, social imaginaries are also normative by establishing an understanding of how society should work; that the modern social imaginary, even when inspiring a similar set of institutions in different countries, is lived differently in them; and that the notion of time occupies a very important role in the particular shaping of imaginaries (Abbey 2006: 355–57).

(c) While developing his concept of "social imaginary," Taylor has linked it more clearly to his hermeneutical view of the social sciences in his article "Two Theories of Modernity." There he explains that, in order to understand the development of

---

[7] "The production of global representations of society and about everything that is related to it. For example, the social order, social actors and their reciprocal relationships, social institutions (hierarchy, domination, conflict, etc.), notably political institutions, etc." (Translation by the author).

[8] "Through its social imaginaries, a collectivity defines its identity while elaborating a representation of itself; it marks the distribution of roles and social positions; explains and imposes certain common beliefs by identifying formative models such as 'the boss,' the 'good guy,' the 'brave warrior,' the 'citizen,' the 'activist,' etc. In this way, a totalizing representation of society as an 'order' is produced, where each element has its place, its identity and its rationale." (Translation by the author).

modernity in the West, three levels of (self-) understanding should be differentiated. The most explicit one (a kind of upper level) is that of explicit doctrine about society, the divine, the cosmos (including a certain social theory). The next level (the middle one) would be that of the symbols, rituals and works of art. Then, there is "what I called, following Bourdieu, the habitus or embodied understanding" (Taylor 1999: 167) (the lower level). It is the last two elements of this triple division which constitute the Taylorean social imaginary:

> As well as the doctrinal understanding of society, there is the one incorporated in habitus, and a level of images as yet unformulated in doctrine, for which we might borrow a term frequently used by contemporary French writers: *l' imaginaire social*—what we can call the social imaginary. (Taylor 1999: 168)

So there is a coincidence with Bourdieu in regard to "habitus" as an aspect of social imaginaries: the ways we are taught to behave, which become unreflective, second nature to us. Taylor would even cite the former to show this:

> One could endlessly enumerate the values given body, made body, by the hidden persuasion of an implicit pedagogy which can instill a whole cosmology, through injunctions as insignificant as "sit up straight" or "don't hold your knife in your left hand", and inscribe the most fundamental principles of the arbitrary content of a culture in seemingly innocuous details of bearing or physical and verbal manners. (Bourdieu 1990: 69; Taylor 1999: 166)[9]

One of the reasons for Taylor to cherish Bourdieu's concept of "habitus" is that he sees it as fostering a view of the social sciences that takes distance from "intellectualist epistemology" and makes room for an understanding expressed in "the scientific consequences of embodied understanding" (Taylor 1995: 174).[10] This means, for Taylor, that while knowing the world, a human being does not behave primarily as a locus of representations but as someone who acts in and on the world through practices. Since this contact with the world happens in and through the body, "our bodily know-how, and the way we act and move, can encode components of our understanding of self and world" (Taylor 1995: 170).

(d) I will close this section on the sources for the Taylorean notion of social imaginary in general saying that between Castoriadis and Taylor there merely seems to be a coincidence in aspects of this concept as opposed to an influence of the former on the latter. "[In Castoriadis view] the social imaginary occurs at the moment when we reimagine moments of freedom, autonomy, change—when we innovate by reinterpreting. I am trying to suggest that it is not just at the moment of innovation that the social imaginary operates, but all the time" (Taylor 2007b: 29; Castoriadis 1987).

---

[9] Taylor uses the French edition of the book. Further evidence of a coincidence in this point can be found in short references from two works by Taylor. The first one is the piece *Social Theory as Practice*, where he affirms that "there are important points of convergence" (Taylor 1985: 91) between the article's views and those by Bourdieu in *Outline of a Theory of Practice* (1977). The second one is Charles Taylor's piece *To Follow a Rule* (1995: 165–80).

[10] The quote is from Taylor's piece *To Follow a Rule*.

5.2.2   Modern Social Imaginaries

As I mentioned before, other important sociological sources for Taylor, particularly in the way he describes modern social imaginaries, are Jurgen Habermas, Steve Warner and Pierre Rossanvallon. Modern social imaginaries, in Taylor's view, express themselves in a cluster of important practices: those of the market economy, the public sphere and the common agency as sovereign people.

(a) In regard to the public sphere, there is a strong influence by Habermas, specifically through his work *The Structural Transformation of the Public Sphere* (1962, published in English in 1989), and by Michael Warner's work *The Letters of the Republic* (1990) (Taylor 2007a: 186).

On the one hand, Habermas' influence can be seen particularly as a source of ideas for the appearance and development of what we now know as the public sphere (Taylor 2004: 83–107).[11] Although there is coincidence in the fact that such a milieu was born in the late seventeenth century, due to the rise of the bourgeoisie and the development of capitalism, and through trade and circulation of information, the account by Habermas is much more extensive. Its focus is on France, the United Kingdom and Germany. It includes the basic blue print of the social structures that belong to the bourgeois public sphere (public authorities distinct from the private realm, and the latter, in turn, split in two: the world of family and economics, on one side, and that of clubs, press and towns, on the other) (Habermas 1989: 27–30). It also delves into the political functions of the public sphere, its conceptualization as such, as well as the ways in which Habermas sees it as having transformed itself and its political role to the point of advancing its own extinction (Habermas 1989).

The frame for this discourse is Habermas' intent to rehabilitate Marxism. This can be seen especially in the second half of the book, where he describes the transition from the liberal bourgeois public sphere to modern mass media society and the social welfare state. Inspired by the Frankfurt School approach, Habermas analyses the negative impact of commercialization and consumerism on the public sphere, the role of political parties in undermining parliamentarian politics, as well as numerous factors impeding rational-critical debate. His thesis is that these corroding traits are the dialectical fire-back of the very same forces that created the public sphere.

In contrast, Taylor's short account is much more focused on developing the notion of the public sphere in relation to social imaginaries. He underscores its independence from the political order and its character for becoming the benchmark of legitimacy for it. For Taylor, the public sphere welcomes potentially anyone as a participant, and is the place where society can come to a common mind on matters linked to the common good. In this way, the public sphere is an entity outside the sphere of political power, which, nonetheless, is normative for it. Its newness is due

---

[11] Habermas' mentioned book is cited several times in this section, which corresponds to Chaps. 6 and 7, named Public Sphere, and Public and Private, respectively (Taylor 2007a: 185–196).

to the fact that it is constituted by nothing (God, the Great Chain of Being or "the law of the people") outside the common action that is being performed (Taylor 2004: 83–107). This view makes use of some of Habermas' ideas within a very different line of argumentation.

(b) Michael Warner's piece (1990), on the other hand, provides Taylor with an approach to the constitution of the public sphere in the United States in the eighteenth century. One of the main ideas Warner develops is that the nature of impersonal writing embodied in the printing medium, which is per se susceptible of limitless dissemination, helped to build the notion of the public sphere as composed by (imagined) fellow citizens. Taylor gives particular attention to Warner's "principle of supervision," by which political authorities should make their proceedings available to public scrutiny. He also points out the "principle of negativity," which demands that the discourse in the public sphere be carried on as abstractly and universally as possible, making no mention to the personal lives of individuals (Taylor 2004: 89, note 6 and 90, note 7; Warner 1990: 41–42).

(c) On a different topic, that of the people as sovereign, Pierre Rosanvallon's work influenced Taylor on how such self-understanding developed in France and entered its social imaginary (Taylor 2007a: 205, note 65; 199, note 47). Rosanvallon's book *La démocratie inachevée* (not available in English) contains a social history of how the notion of the people as sovereign developed in theory and practice in the time immediately before the French Revolution and afterwards (2000). In his view, the advent of representative democracy in general is marked by misunderstandings and tensions. Particularly in France, there coexisted different views on representation (as a technical device for government or as a philosophy of life), on the meaning of popular sovereignty (as residing in the nation or in the people in action), on the times for exercising it (extraordinarily or on a regular basis), on the changing meaning of particular concepts (the difficulty of language). To these elements, the uncertainty of the ways in which representative government should be implemented and lived by the people caused uneasiness among the poor and impatient (Rosanvallon 2000: 9–28). "Le double spectre de l'aristocratie et l'anarchie pèse ainsi en permanence sur les hommes de 1789. La simple evocation du possible avènement d'une 'novelle aristocratie' suffit par exemple à render suspect à certains le processus représentatif" (Rosanvallon 2000: 26).[12]

This description serves Taylor's purpose of underlying how the appearance of the self-understanding of the people as sovereign in the social imaginary faced, in the case of France, not only a difficulty in regard to its theoretical explanation, but also a lack of points of reference on how to live it. In contrast, says Taylor, the same process in the United States as a consequence of the American Revolution had the advantage that, at the level of practice, assembly-based representative government

---

[12] "In this way, the double specter of aristocracy and anarchy constantly burdened the men of 1879. For example, the simple reference to the potential rise of a 'new aristocracy' was enough to clothe with certain suspicion the representative process." (Translation by the author).

was a custom with of long history, so (at least some of) the new American citizens had an idea of its practice (Taylor 2004: 109–141; 2007a: 109–25 and 196–207). In this way, Taylor is able to find two ideal-types for the transformation of social imaginaries: one by which new self-understandings appropriate and reinterpret practices already in existence (the American case), and another where such practices need to be created (the French case). In the latter case, post-revolutionary instability lasts longer (Taylor 2004: 109–110). Over time, France reached the proper practices for government legitimation, "but the forms that took hold in France turned out to be interestingly different from the Anglo-American mode" (Taylor 2004: 141, 2007a: 207). Taylor cites Rosanvallon again (1992) to refer to how universal suffrage was achieved in France and entered into its social imaginary (Taylor 2004: 141, note 38, 2007a: 207, note 65).

5.2.3   Civil Religion

As key to his analysis of the secularization process, Taylor focuses on the relationship between religion and political system and proposes three ideal-types: those of Pre-Durkhemian, Neo-Durkhemian and Post-Durkhemian dispensations. As I have mentioned before, these should not be considered as progressing in time but as modes in which religion and the political system could relate to each other in a given country. It is frequently the case that one of these modes predominates while the others have little influence, which takes Taylor to associate them with the historical stages he calls Ancien Régime, Age of Mobilization and Age of Authenticity.

In order to give support to his view of a Neo-Durkhemian dispensation in the United States, Taylor relies on Robert Bellah's notion of "civil religion" which he finds a "tremendously fertile idea" (Taylor 2007a: 447–48; Bellah 1970).[13] This notion relates the political system with religion in a way in which the latter has greater sovereignty than the former, providing to it with an ultimate point of reference and justification. However, this "civil religion" is formal (infrequent and abstract) and marginal (with no official support in the legal order). Bellah does not imply here any kind of idolatrous worship of the state nor confusion between the political and religious realms.

Taylor extends the use of the concept to refer to any situation where the modern political system and religion still kept a particular relationship of mutual support, either formally through social structures or informally through a given culture. Exemplary cases of the latter would be Ireland and Poland.

---

[13] Taylor makes reference to Chap. 9, *Civil Religion in America*.

5.2.4   Elite-Masses Relationships

To complete the view of Taylor's utilization of sociological sources in this section, I should mention a last topic: that of the influx elites may have in the social imaginaries, which does not operate the same in the United States as in Europe. This, Taylor believes, is important to explaining the "American exception" in regard to secularization. Although academia seems to be equally secular in the United States as in Western Europe, the effect this has on large segments of society at large in the former is less significant. In contrast, in Europe, and following an insight by Jose Casanova, Taylor thinks that "perhaps the sense that religion is declining, and that this is a sign of 'modernity', not only makes people downplay their religious beliefs and involvements, but acts as a damper on these as well. A belief in secularization theory would be acting here in part as a 'self-fulfilling prophesy'" (Taylor 2007a: 525, note 40).

5.3   Sources for a History of Reform

In following the outline of my presentation of Taylor's meta-narrative in Chap. 3, this section will include both his account of the rise of exclusive humanism and what he calls "History of Reform." However, since the former is mostly a history of ideas just indirectly connected with sociological changes, I will focus primarily on his sources for the latter.

Taylor has relied, in his account of secularization in the West, on a narrative of the genealogy of the relationship between religion on the one hand, and culture/society on the other. This links two processes as well: (a) that of the passing from "early" (Pre-Axial) religion, to Axial and Post-Axial religion, and (b) that named as History of Reform. This denotes a process in which religious practice becomes gradually more and more disembedded. This means that people in the West pass from a situation in which religion is considered inseparable from social life, in which we see the world as inhabited by spiritual forces, and human flourishing as concerned primarily with every-day goods, into a scenario in which the world is seen as composed of individuals, whose goal is to reorder human society in a way that may embody the Gospel demands in a stable and rational manner.

5.3.1   Axial Religion

Taylor gives foundation to his History of Reform far away into the past, for which he relies on the work by Robert Bellah. He proposes his categories of "early religion" and Axial religion as inspired in Bellah's work (1970, 2005; Taylor 2007a:

147, note 1, 149, note 4).[14] With this distinction, Taylor wants to stress the embed-ded character of humans living in the "early religion" stage, which means they could not but understand themselves as belonging to a given society and cosmic order. In this phase, human flourishing is seen as happening in the ways ordinary things do. In contrast to this, in Axial religions, there is a drive toward radically questioning this because humans come to see they, in some way, should transcend the given order so they can flourish (Taylor 2007a: 147–58). Besides cognitive and ethical changes in religion, the appearance of greater urban conglomerates also aided this process (Taylor 2007a: 153–54, note 16). From this seed, in time, the movement toward reform mentioned above takes life.

Curiously, Taylor also recalls Bellah near the end of *A Secular Age*, where he does a balance of the History of Reform and explores its future. "The point is, once more, that we need to leaven Christianity with a dose of paganism, but that our Christian life itself has suffered a mutilation to the extent that it imposes this kind of homogenization" (Taylor 2007a: 772). He normatively promotes, in the face of what has occurred, an open Christian community that may welcome all peoples in their diversity and varied life paths. Also, he asks to keep a realistic view about the history of Christianity in which all higher realizations of the Christian ideal are not without ambiguities. No unproblematic breaks with the past should be carried out, but, on the contrary, one should keep in mind the shortcomings of Christianity in past times. In this, he tries to follow Bellah's insight that inspired his *Religion in Human Evolution*: "Nothing is ever lost" (Taylor 2007a: 772; Bellah 2011),[15] by which the former means that religion has been closely bound with human evolution, both biologically and historically, and still is. For such reason, it never stops chang-ing and, at the same time, its present condition always builds on the past. Moreover, Bellah thinks that religion at the same time that plays a role in selection, playing in this way a role in the evolutionary process, is also partially protected from it and can trigger creativity and create unprecedented paths to follow (Schneider 2011).

5.3.2   History of Reform

(a) Taylor substantiates his view on this topic by drawing from David Martin's socio-theological analysis of the relationship between faith and nature. As men-tioned before, Martin affirms there is a dialectical relationship between them (or, in sociological terms, between religion and the secular) already imbued in the very essence of Christianity due to its incarnational nature and the fact that the announced Kingdom is to be present hic et nunc, even though in a way that is an "already-but-not-yet." The Gospel aims to enter into the world and change it, but while doing so

---

[14] The first reference is to Chap. 2 titled *Religious Evolution*.

[15] Taylor mentions this idea as the motto of the work by Bellah that by then was about to be pub-lished (Bellah 2011).

it is affected by the world as well. Each entrance implies a risk and a cost. Each entrance also affects the language Christianity uses both in ways that favor or disfavor secularization (Martin 2005: 171–99).[16]

Within this framework, Martin finds four waves of secularization processes in the West, each of them as a response corresponding to a particular missionary drive. (a) The first one comes after the Catholic Christianization due to the conversion of the masses through the conversion of the monarchs and the assimilation of the faith to power, hierarchy, compulsion, war and violence. (b) Then, the reaction to the Catholic Christianization follows due to the conversion of the urban masses through the apostolate of the mendicant orders in the thirteenth century in the form of the division between a group of spiritual *virtuosi* and the masses, the focus on the natural world in the Renaissance, the development of rationality and what he calls "proto-science", and the naked recognition of political facts as in Macchiavelli. (c) The third wave of secularization comes after the sixteenth century Protestant Christianization which fosters city governments ruled by "the elect", a naturalistic and rationalistic moralism, the assimilation of the church into the state, the transformation of ministry into a profession, and the focus on empirical reality through individual reason. Lastly, Martin mentions the secularizing wave that is a consequence of (d) Protestant Christianization in the way of evangelical and Pentecostal sub-cultures. The bottom line is that, after each of these movements described above, one finds that a sort of "watering down" of Christianity takes place, either through massive conversions or the "opening" of the life of holiness to the laity, or through the identification of Christianity with a specific socio-political order (Martin 2005: 3–7).

Martin explains the dynamics that have led to the current state of affairs regarding secularization in the West. In the first place, he finds the emergence of the autonomy of nature, which entails the rejection of the operation of spiritual/divine forces in nature. A natural religiosity becomes, then, not a necessity but an option. Second, the autonomy of the nation signifies the invention, on its part, of its own mythic self-presentation. There is a shift into contractual notions of membership, departing from sacred and integral bonds. Third, the autonomy of religion is represented, for Martin, by Evangelicalism (which includes Pentecostalism), because of its focus on the inward feelings of individuals and its success in establishing denominational sub-cultures which, while keeping a strong identity, are also vehicles for modernization, particularly in Latin America, Africa and the Pacific rim. Religion becomes a matter of choice, the end of a long trend of individualization, pragmatism and engagement with society in Christianity.

Taylor finds the four-staged socio-theological explanation above as supportive of his narrative of a History of Reform (Taylor 2007a: 90–145): "I believe that one should see the secular modern West as the product of one such large-scale 'incursion', that of Latin Christendom, which in the later Middle Ages embarked on a

---

[16] He also praises this feature of Martin's thought in his *Foreword* to the same book (Martin 2005: x), and by citing another work by the latter (Taylor 2007a: 281–82, note 18, 291–92, note 26; Martin 2002a).

long series of reforms (including but not confined to the Reformation) that ended up creating the disciplined, productive, pacified, rights-affirming world we live in" (Martin 2005: x)[17]

(b) Norbert Elias is another important sociological source for Taylor in his History of Reform (Elias 1978a, b).[18] A somewhat recently rediscovered thinker, Elias developed a critique of the mainstream sociology of his time (first, the mainly functionalist grand theories and, later, the fracture of the sociological field in a vast array of competing paradigms), reviewed the basic concepts of sociology, and created his own under the rubric of what he called "figurational sociology." In regard to methodology, he vouched for a theory strongly rooted in empirical facts, embedded in history and developed *post factum*. He also thought that sociological facts were made of inter-dependent relationships (between persons, groups, or persons and groups), which were always in the process of changing. Because of this, he resisted the reification of concepts such as society or groups (for this purpose, Elias used the term "figurations" to refer to such relationships). Consequently, he privileged a diachronic approach. Within these inter-dependent links, Elias developed a theory of power that he saw to be polymorphous, one by which the terms linked, in different ways, ask for each other (Dunning and Hughes 2013: 17–75). Within this approach, he studied several topics, among them that of civilization in the West.

For Elias, the "process of civilization" is not unilinear, but multi-paced and multi-causal. Nor does it have a positive connotation. It is ambiguous. Civilization, in his parlance, is the idea by which French, British and Germans, and all Western Europe by extension, see themselves reflecting a higher ideal of human life, an ideal that nurtures the sense of superiority that was very much apparent during the colonial expansion of the nineteenth century. It consists in the gradual increase of social constraint and self-constraint—particularly in the areas of sex and anger—by which elites, and later the masses, came to be "civilized" in the way we know it to be at the present in the West (Elias 1978b: 229–333).

In connection to Elias' thought, as expressed in the above-referred work, *The Civilizing Process*, it is only fair to say that there are close parallels between it and the narrative of Reform. As a matter of fact, Taylor considers it a "masterful book" (Taylor 2007a: 137).[19] He values Elias's findings of the change in the West due to the appearance of stricter rules for living together because of the growth of the courts, and due to denser and more inter-related societies. "But I think the developments he describes can also be understood in two other, related contexts. I want to see them as reflecting the way in which the disengaged, disciplined stance first restricts intimacy, and then makes us take a distance from our powerful emotions and our bodily functions" (Taylor 2007a: 139).

---

[17] The quote is from Taylor's *Foreword* to the book.

[18] This work was published in two volumes, here cited: Vol. 1 is subtitled *A History of Manners*, and Vol. 2 goes under *Power & Civilty*.

[19] Taylor cites lengthy sections of Elias work (1978a, b) in Chap. 2, *The Rise of the Disciplinary Society* (Taylor 2007a: 90–145).

Taylor thinks this leads to a human self-understanding as disembodied beings, as agents of disengaged discipline capable of dispassionate control (Taylor 2007a: 141). These elements, along with others, give rise to what he calls the "buffered self" (Taylor 2007a: 300).

There is also a strong coincidence between Taylor and Elias in the sequence of the changes in "habitus" (in Elias words)[20] or "social imaginary" (in Taylor's) already described. For the former, the stages go from courtesy, to civility, to civilization; for the latter, the process of configuring the Modern Moral Order goes simply from courtesy to civility (Taylor 2004: 33–48, 2007a: 214–18). The outcome of the process also includes a sense of fastidiousness in regard with the previous stage of indiscriminate (and often promiscuous) contact and a preference for selecting those with which one would share in the sphere of intimacy. This idea is one in which Taylor also follows Elias (Taylor 2007a: 540).

5.4   Sources for Contemporary Religion and the Secular/Religious Divide

5.4.1   Religion Today

(a) In regard to his view of contemporary religion, Taylor cites the sociological works by Robert Wuthnow (1998a, b), Danièlle Hervieu-Lèger (1999), Grace Davie (1994, 2000), Wade Clark Roof (1999) and Paul Heelas and Linda Woodhead (2005). These authors focus on events occurring in the United States, England and, in the case of Hervieu-Lèger, Western Europe and the United States.

While referring to the work of these sociologists, Taylor points to issues such as the contemporary stress on unity, self-fulfillment, integrity, holism and authenticity as integral components of the religious quest (Taylor 2007a: 505–535). The latter also has consequences in concrete practices (diets, meditation, etc.) and emphasizes feelings and experiences (Wuthnow, Heelas and Woodhead). The dominant image is that of the spiritual seeker, living the proper existence in a "journey mode" in which changes of paths or "conversions" are not unusual (Hervieu-Lèger).

In the "seeker" instance, the imposition of any external religious authority on the individual's private or subjective life is strongly resisted. However, according to Wuthnow, there is also an alternative stance, that of the "dwellers," located in a

---

[20]Elias' concept predates and is related to that of Pierre Bourdieu. With this term, he refers to the psychological make-up, the mentality and the behavioral and affective make-up of a given society (Elias 1978b: 232, 234–35). It can also be understood to be an "embodied social learning" of which we are not generally aware and that we take as given, but is nonetheless not fixed but in change (Elias 1996: ix, 19). The first reference is to the *Preface* written by Eric Dunning and Stephen Mennell.

For the relationship between Elias and Bourdieu see the work of Eric Dunning and Jason Hughes (2013: 188–200).

defined religious tradition, although not impervious to some of the characteristics of
religion in our times. Wuthnow's work, which is focused on the United States in the
last 60 years, specifically in spirituality, finds that, within a predominantly scenario
of dwelling, a seeking alternative has risen and gained strength.

> A spirituality of dwelling emphasizes *habitation*: God occupies a definite place in the uni-
> verse and creates a sacred space in which humans too can dwell; to inhabit sacred space is
> to know its territory and to feel secure. A spirituality of seeking emphasizes *negotiation*:
> individuals search for sacred moments that reinforce their conviction that the divine exists,
> but these moments are fleeting; rather than knowing the territory, people explore new spiri-
> tual vistas, and they may have to negotiate among complex and confusing meanings of
> spirituality. (Wuthnow 1998a: 3–4)

Taylor takes Wuthnow's view and applies it to all North Atlantic countries.
Similarly than the latter, he sees a third middle way as a better one, one of kenotic
and holistic spirituality. In Taylor's understanding, "much of today's spiritual/reli-
gious life is to be found in this middle ground" (Taylor 2007a: 512).[21]

The seeker mode, which could also be called as a "spiritual but not religious"
stance is also characterized by the "découplage de la croyance et de la pratique"
(unleashing of belief and practice) and "désemboîtement de la croyance, de
l'appartenance et de la référence identitaire" (lack of interlocking between faith,
belonging and identity references), as expressed by Hervieu-Léger. It could also be
summarized by Davie's phrase "believing without belonging." The risk of reducing
religion/spirituality to the search of mere (immanent) self-development is increasingly present in this scenario. Taylor would share what Wade Clark Roof has said
about spirituality in the United States in this regard and apply his insights to the
West as a whole. Roof is concerned, among other things, with showing how contemporary forms of spiritual quest, even when they may contain elements aimed at
addressing psychological health and personal well-being, are truly committed with
de-centered experiences of the self that are ethically challenging (Roof 1999:
39–41).[22]

All the above described dynamics have impacted on Christianity in the West, and
will continue to do so, Taylor thinks.

Taylor uses the sociological sources mentioned above to describe our contemporary landscape in order to substantiate his own position with some empirical data,
without necessarily assuming each scholar's interpretations. For example, Taylor
insists that, even in the scenario described for contemporary religion, the calling for
authenticity does not necessarily mean the rejection neither of the transcendent nor
of personal transformation. Contrasting his work with the above-cited book by
Heelas and Woodhead, he says that *A Secular Age*

> Is an attempt to study the fate in the modern West of religious faith in a strong sense. This
> strong sense I define, to repeat, by a double criterion: the belief in transcendent reality, on

---

[21] Wuthnow would advocate for what he calls a "practice-oriented spirituality" (1998a: 15–18).
[22] Taylor would similarly criticize what he sees as "flattened forms" of the drive towards authenticity (2007a: 508–509).

one hand, and the connected aspiration to a transformation which goes beyond ordinary human flourishing, on the other. (Taylor 2007a: 510)

More specifically, Taylor criticizes Heelas and Woodhead's view as one which, based on the subjective turn as defining contemporary Western culture, too simply opposes spirituality to religion by way of the opposition between inner and outer sources of significance and authority to cultivate individual lives (Heelas and Woodhead 2005: 6). For Taylor, this contrast is not exhaustive:

> The first term could be seen as a definition of contemporary ethics of authenticity; the second invokes one view of what is supremely important in life. The question set in the first can initiate a quest, and this *can* end in the second as an answer. Nothing guarantees this, but nothing ensures its opposite either. (Taylor 2007a: 509)

In his view, many seekers in our times are looking for transcendence and transformation at a non-ordinary level, which is a religious one. Taylor does not espouse a view in which the future of religion in the West is the eclipse of religion by spirituality, as defined by Heelas and Woodhead. Instead, as I have mentioned before, he sees between two minority poles composed by exclusive humanists on the one hand and followers of transcendent religion on the other hand, a vast host of intermediate positions that could be and de facto are taken.

(b) Three other particular characteristics of religion today are to be mentioned, features of which Taylor looks for the support in the thought of Martin, Casanova and Joas.

The influence David Martin has on important Taylorean theses has already been noted. However, Taylor also quotes Martin's studies on the expansion of Evangelical and Pentecostal Christianity, particularly in Latin America, as a fact that shows how religion is relocating itself in human life and society at present (Taylor 2007a: 493, note 38, 495, note 40; Martin 2002b: 14–15). Coming from Martin's work on the dilemmas of contemporary religion, another quote focuses on the fact that, at present, urban Westerners have a diminished sense of personal guilt (Taylor 2007a: 618, note 1; Martin 1978: 94), given the fact that urban mentality is very much interested in hedonism and technology, and that evil actions have been translated, through a "therapeutic turn," into signals of sickness. As a consequence of turning this view into an absolute, the importance of ethical choices is diminished as is the depth of our inner lives. This is taken by Taylor to introduce the ambiguity of today's polemics between religion and secular humanism: is human fulfillment hampered by religious notions of sin or ethical failure or, on the contrary, it is secured? Conversely, is a secular stance one which prevents the self-stultification of human beings due to the notion of sin and evil? Taylor unfolds his arguments in this regard in Chaps. 17 and 18 of *A Secular Age*.

Another characteristic of the contemporary ways in which people seek to live Christianity (particularly Catholicism) is described when Taylor proposes the following ideas by Casanova. Traditional spiritual practices can be pursued with original and contemporary motivations and languages (Taylor 2007a: 518, note 28).[23]

---

[23] This is a private communication from Casanova to Taylor.

This can occur because people can choose to engage with all or some of the following dimensions of religious life: that of the church as a whole (proper to the Ancien Régime); that of the parish life, within a network of inter-personal relationships; and that of the private devotional life. In the end, these ideas give support to Taylor's argument about secularization as religious change, one in which some old religious forms may keep existing and new spiritual forms appear in our contemporary scenario in the West.

The Taylorean view on "fragilization" receives support from that by Joas (Taylor 2007a: 556 and 833, note 19; Joas 2008: 21–35). In Taylor's opinion, both polar positions of belief and unbelief are mutually "fragilized," which means that easier access to alternatives has lead to a society in which more people change their position, that is, convert, in their lifetimes or adopt a different position from that of their parents. This is different than the meaning Peter Berger gives to the term "fragilization" implying a weaker position in our times for the case of belief (Berger 1994). This is criticized by Joas in his previously cited essay "Religion in the Age of Contingency." As a matter of fact, within this polarized continuum, faith can be stronger just because, since the accesses to non-religious stances before life are easier to choose, any standing religious option would have be in need of facing disbelief without distortion, as both Taylor and Joas affirm. However, in their view, our modern situation prevents this kind of strong faith from caricaturizing and bashing non-believers or people from other religious traditions because it stems from the fact that the religious option must be rooted in its own sources instead than in easy criticism of others.

5.4.2 Varieties of the Secular/Religious Divide

Another area of analysis of religion today is its place in relationship to the public sphere. Taylor sees this divide as often blurry, varied and taking different shapes in the West.

(a) It is not just that religion has not kept itself on the fringes of society, says Taylor, but also that it actually plays a role within the secular public sphere: that of legitimating, at the level of the particular individuals and minorities, their peculiar political identities. In democracy, these should be supportive of the general political identity of the country through an "overlapping consensus" (Taylor 2004: 193–94). Taylor thinks that the key principle here is one that asks the government to keep a "principled distance" from particular religious allegiances and even from secular systems of belief (Taylor 2011a: 303–25).[24] Church-state separation, in this light, would just be one of various possible institutional arrangements for the above-mentioned principle.

---

[24] The reference is to a piece titled *What Does Secularism Mean?*

In this regard, Taylor cites Casanova to show how "democracy requires that each citizen or group of citizens speak the language in public debate that is most meaningful to them. Prudence may urge us to put things in terms which others relate to, but to require this would be an intolerable imposition on citizen speech" (Taylor 2007a: 532, note 51; Casanova 1994). As a consequence, public discourses, in some cases, could be expressed in religious language.

Moreover, Taylor also seeks support in arguments by Casanova when he observes how the visibility in public life by churches and religious bodies is unlikely to disappear and is actually desirable if it takes place within a Post-Durkhemian dispensation (Taylor 2007a: 488, note 29; Casanova 1994). For these reasons, a variety of drawings for the secular/religious divide has occurred even within the West, a variety that is still open (Taylor 2002c: 36–37), which fits with the Taylorean affirmation of the existence of "multiple modernities" around the world.

(b) As a consequence of what has been said, Taylor enters into contention with Jurgen Habermas when the latter insists on stressing the difference between the nature of "secular reason" and "religious thought" (Habermas 1984: 143–271).[25] In Habermas' early view, secular reason is enough to reach the normative conclusions we need to establish our democratic state or define political ethics, because it is a "neutral" language that everybody can use to build consensus. In contrast, religious languages are problematic for this purpose since all would not necessarily agree on them. In the end, they would either reach the same conclusions of secular reason, or affirm things contrary to secular reason, or even point out superfluous matters. However, although Habermas has shifted into a more positive understanding of the role religion may play in the political arena, he still holds that there is a distinction between secular reason as "neutral" and religious thought as "non-neutral" (Habermas 2011).

Taylor would agree that the political language in a democratic state should be secular, but only when expressing legislation, administrative decrees and court judgments. In these instances it is "official language." Such a requirement neither includes citizen deliberation nor deliberation in the legislature, where religious language, along with non-religious language could be used. "The state can be neither Christian nor Muslim nor Jewish; but by the same token it should also be neither Marxist, nor Kantian, nor Utilitarian. (…) The decisions [by the state] can't be framed in a way which gives special recognition to one of these views. This is not easy to do; the lines are hard to draw; and they must always be drawn anew" (Taylor 2008, 2011b).

Taylor goes on to affirm that the problem is that the view of the democratic state as having a neutral stance towards diversity (this being religious or non-religious) is problematic for secular Westerners because of what he calls an "odd fixation on religion." This attitude is fed by the past and current conflicts between liberal states

---

[25] Here, Habermas recalls Weber's view of modernization as trans-cultural and universal rationalization and follows his distinction between scientific, moral and aesthetic reason, which entails a diversity of procedures in each of them. For the evolution on Habermas' view of religion, see the work by Eduardo Mendieta (2013).

and religion, as well as by an epistemic view by which "religiously informed thought
is somehow less *rational* than purely 'secular' reasoning. The attitude has a political
ground (religion as threat), but also an epistemological one (religion as a faulty
mode of reason)" (Taylor 2008).[26]

5.5   A Balance of Taylor's Sociological Sources

(a) To make a balance of Taylor's sociological sources, we should recall the last
chapter, where we saw how his own philosophical views play a decisive role in the
meta-narrative of secularization. The fact that he has criticized the "mainstream"
way of carrying on the work of social science, and that he has argued for more cul-
turally- and hermeneutically-sensitive human sciences, provides a framework for an
analysis of *A Secular Age* and related works. Besides, in connection with classical
sociology, it seems clear that Taylor is closer to the Weberian tradition, his criticisms notwithstanding.

(b) Among contemporary sociologists, those who have more clearly influenced
his meta-narrative as a whole are Martin, Casanova, Joas and Bellah. This is particularly true since these authors have been trying to think on the issue of secularization
in different ways than "orthodox" and "counter-orthodox" theorists—as has Taylor.
By doing this, they have provided Taylor with additional insights on the hermeneutical problems at stake and on the difficulties related to specific reductive explanations of the phenomenon.

Bellah's reflections on religious evolution and Axial Religion, and Martin's
views on the dialectic between faith and nature in Christianity, have both given support for the general outline of Taylor's History of Reform. Besides, Casanova (with
his view on public religions) and Joas (with his insights on the meaning of fragilization) have also inspired Taylor's account of contemporary religion.

(c) There is, however, a second tier of influences, which are important in reference to more specific topics. In this context and in relation to the notion of social
imaginaries, which is crucial for Taylor's hermeneutic, new names appear. These
sociologists who have been in Taylor's own words important for the way in which
he unfolded the topic include Anderson, Baczko, Habermas, Werner and Rosanvallon.
The last three are particularly relevant for the way in which Taylor specifically
explains the modern social imaginaries.

Another issue in which Taylor heavily relies on contemporary sociological work
is that of the status of contemporary religion. Although in no way as decisive as the
previous group of scholars, these authors provide Taylor with the basic elements of
analysis for his own characterization of our present religious situation. The more
important of these thinkers are Wuthnow, Hervieu-Lèger, Davie, Roof, Heelas and

---

[26] For a longer explanation on this, see Taylor's piece *Why We Need a Radical Redefinition of
Secularism* (Taylor 2011c). For a wider Taylorean critique of Habermas' thought see *Language
and Society* (2002a).

Woodhead. Taylor situates the insights of these authors within that of the immanent frame which holds that we live cross-pressured somewhere between two poles that mutually fragilize each other. It is in this particular situation that we witness the current vast multiplication (Supernova Effect) of positions in regard to religion/spirituality.

(d) Although Taylor has not explicitly mentioned him as a strong influence, I would argue that Elias' approach is in several aspects very close to that implicit in Taylor's view: it is largely a *post eventu* analysis, focused on social changes which result from contingent causes, and which, for the most part, are unplanned and a result from both human agency and structural constraints. Lastly, I believe we should see the relationship between Taylor's view on social imaginaries and that of Pierre Bourdieu's "habitus" and Cornelius Castoriadis "imaginaries" as coincidences that deserve further study.

These findings in regard to Taylor's sources present a number of points of reference characteristic of the social theory discourse underlying his meta-narrative of secularization. I will carry out the task of articulating the latter in the next chapter.

In summary, the core sociological influences on Taylor's thought about secularization are Weber, among the classical figures of sociology, and Martin, Bellah, Casanova and Joas among contemporary sociologists.

References

Abbey R (2006) Book review: back to Baczko. Eur J Polit Theo 5:355–364. doi:10.1177/1474885106064666

Anderson B (2006) Imagined communities: reflections on the origin and spread of nationalism. Verso, London

Baczko B (1984) Les imaginaires sociaux. Mémoires et espoires colletifs. Payot, Paris

Bellah RN (1970) Beyond belief; essays on religion in a post-traditional world. Harper & Row, New York

Bellah RN (2005) What is axial about the axial age? Eur J Sociol 46:69–89. doi:10.1017/s0003975605000032

Bellah RN (2011) Religion in human evolution: from the Paleolithic to the axial age. Belknap Press of Harvard University Press, Cambridge, MA

Berger PL (1994) A far glory: the quest for faith in an age of credulity. Free Press, New York

Bourdieu P (1977) Outline of a theory of practice. Cambridge University Press, Cambridge

Bourdieu P (1990) The logic of practice. Stanford University Press, Stanford

Boutry P (1996) Prêtres et paroisses au pays du Curé d'Ars. Cerf, Paris

Castoriadis C (1987) The imaginary institution of society. The MIT Press, Cambridge, MA

Casanova J (1994) Public religions in the modern world. University of Chicago Press, Chicago

Casanova J (2007) Immigration and religious pluralism: an EU/US comparison. In: Banchoff TF (ed) Democracy and the new religious pluralism. Oxford University Press, Oxford

Davie G (1994) Religion in Britain since 1945: believing without belonging. Blackwell, Oxford

Davie G (2000) Religion in modern Europe: a memory mutates. Oxford University Press, Oxford

Dunning E, Hughes J (2013) Norbert Elias and modern sociology: knowledge, interdependence, power, process. Bloomsbury Academic, London

Elias N (1978a) The civilizing process. 1: A history of manners. Urizen Books, New York

Elias N (1978b) The civilizing process. 2: Power & civilty. Urizen Books, New York

Elias N (1996) The Germans: power struggles and the development of habitus in the nineteenth and twentieth centuries. Columbia University Press, New York

Finke R (1992) An unsecular America. In: Bruce S (ed) Religion and modernization: sociologists and historians debate the secularization thesis. Clarendon, Oxford, pp 145–169

Habermas J (1984) The theory of communicative action, vol 1, Reason and the rationalization of society. Beacon, Boston

Habermas J (1989) The structural transformation of the public sphere: an inquiry into a category of bourgeois society. MIT Press, Cambridge, MA

Habermas J (2011) 'The political'. The rational meaning of a questionable inheritance of political theology. In: Mendieta E, VanAntwerpen J (eds) The power of religion in the public sphere. Columbia University Press, New York, pp 15–33

Heelas P, Woodhead L (2005) The spiritual revolution: why religion is giving way to spirituality. Blackwell, Oxford

Hervieu-Léger D (1999) Le pèlerin at le converti. La religion en movement. Flammarion, Paris

Joas H (2008) Do we need religion? On the experience of self-transcendence. Paradigm Publishers, Boulder

Martin D (1978) The dilemmas of contemporary religion. St. Martin's Press, New York

Martin D (1990) Tongues of fire: the explosion of Protestantism in Latin America. B. Blackwell, Oxford

Martin D (2002a) Christian language and its mutations: essays in sociological understanding. Ashgate Pub, Aldershot

Martin D (2002b) Pentecostalism: the world their parish. Blackwell, Oxford

Martin D (2005) On secularization: towards a revised general theory. Ashgate, Aldershot

McLeod H (1992) Secular cities? Berlin, London, and New York in the later nineteenth and early twentieth centuries. In: Bruce S (ed) Religion and modernization: sociologists and historians debate the secularization thesis. Clarendon, Oxford, pp 59–89

McLeod H (1995) European religion in the age of the great cities, 1830–1930. Routledge, London

McLeod H (1997) Religion and the people of Western Europe, 1789–1989. Oxford University Press, Oxford

McLeod H (2000) Secularisation in Western Europe, 1848–1914. St. Martin's Press, New York

Mendieta E (2013) Religion in Habermas's work. In: Calhoun CJ et al (eds) Habermas and religion. Polity, Cambridge, pp 341–407

Roof WC (1999) Spiritual marketplace: baby boomers and the remaking of American religion. Princeton University Press, Princeton

Rosanvallon P (1992) Le sacre du citoyen histoire du suffrage universel en France. Gallimard, Paris

Rosanvallon P (2000) La démocratie inachivée. Histoire de la souveraineté du peuple en France. Gallimard, Paris

Schneider N (2011) Nothing is ever lost: an interview with Robert Bellah. In: The immanent frame. http://blogs.ssrc.org/tif/2011/09/14/nothing-is-ever-lost. Accessed 27 June 2015

Taylor C (1985) Philosophy and the human sciences, vol 2, Philosophical papers. University Press, Cambridge

Taylor C (1989) Sources of the self: the making of the modern identity. Harvard University Press, Cambridge, MA

Taylor C (1995) Philosophical arguments. Harvard University Press, Cambridge, MA

Taylor C (1999) Two theories of modernity. Public Cult 11:153–174. doi:10.1215/08992363-11-1-153

Taylor C (2002a) Language and society. In: Rasmussen DM, Swindal J (eds) Sage masters of modern social thought, vol 4, Jurgen Habermas. Sage, London, pp 123–135

Taylor C (2002b) Varieties of religion today: William James revisited. Harvard University Press, Cambridge, MA

Taylor C (2002c) What It means to be secular. A conversation with philosopher Charles Taylor. Interview by Bruce Ellis Benson. Books & Culture 36–37

Taylor C (2004) Modern social imaginaries. Duke University Press, Durham

Taylor C (2007a) A secular age. Belknap Press of Harvard University Press, Cambridge, MA

Taylor C (2007b) On social imaginaries. In: Gratton P, Manoussakis JP (eds) Traversing the imaginary: Richard Kearney and the postmodern challenge. Northwestern University Press, Evanston, pp 29–47

Taylor C (2007c) Statement by Charles Taylor at the Templeton Prize News Conference. In: Templeton Prize. http://www.templetonprize.org/pdfs/Templeton_Prize_Chronicle_2007.pdf Accessed 24 Feb 2014

Taylor C (2008) Secularism and critique. In: The immanent frame. http://blogs.ssrc.org/tif/2008/04/24/secularism-and-critique. Accessed 28 June 2015

Taylor C (2010) Afterword: Apologia pro libro suo. In: Warner M et al (eds) Varieties of secularism in a secular age. Harvard University Press, Cambridge, MA, pp 300–321

Taylor C (2011a) Dilemmas and connections: selected essays. Belknap Press of Harvard University Press, Cambridge, MA

Taylor C (2011b) Dialogue: Charles Taylor and Jurgen Habermas. In: Mendieta E, VanAntwerpen J (eds) The power of religion in the public sphere. Columbia University Press, New York, pp 60–69

Taylor C (2011c) Why we need a radical redefinition of secularism. In: Mendieta E, VanAntwerpen J (eds) The power of religion in the public sphere. Columbia University Press, New York, pp 34–59

Wallis R, Bruce S (1992) Secularization: the orthodox model. In: Bruce S (ed) Religion and modernization: sociologists and historians debate the secularization thesis. Clarendon, Oxford, pp 8–30

Warner M (1990) The letters of the Republic: publication and the public sphere in eighteenth-century America. Harvard University Press, Cambridge, MA

Wolffe J (1994) God and greater Britain: religion and national life in Britain and Ireland, 1843–1945. Routledge, London

Wuthnow R (1998a) After heaven: spirituality in America since the 1950s. University of California Press, Berkeley

Wuthnow R (1998b) Loose connections: joining together in America's fragmented communities. Harvard University Press, Cambridge, MA

Part III
Taylorean Social Theory

Chapter 6
Interpreting a Social Theory

Abstract Taylorean social theory is a particular interpretation of Taylor's meta-narrative on secularization. It is "social theory" in the sense that it offers a theoretical understanding of the social processes and social agents involved in secularization as social change. This understanding requires a greater hermeneutical work than that by mainstream sociology. Its analysis makes particular use of the ideas of social imaginaries and elite-masses dynamics. Its sources include those coming from Taylor philosophical anthropology and his views on the method of the social sciences. They also include the sociological sources for his meta-narrative, as well as the work by Margaret Archer and other sociologists and thinkers. Taylorean social theory can be characterized by seeing the interaction between structure and human agency as circular, by the recognition of the ability of human agency (particularly that organized as social movements) to change structures, by insisting on an equally important role of social and cultural factors when explaining social change, by considering social system always open (and social processes leading both to either stability or change), by studying social change always in its historical development and by proposing a necessarily complementary use of quantitative and qualitative studies on the same phenomenon. Taylorean social theory uses a set of general basic concepts and practical criteria and guidelines for an interpretive ad casum study, expresses its results in the form of narratives and acquires its validating strength from "transcendental arguments." In its current formulation it is about Western secularization, although it seems it could be generalizable to other macro-social processes.

Keywords Social theory • Secularization • Theories of secularization • Hermeneutics • Social imaginaries • Elite-masses dynamics • Problem of human agency • Social structures • Human agency • Open social systems • Narratives • Transcendental arguments

After exploring Taylor's meta-narrative of Western secularization and his philosophical and sociological sources, I will now make use of them, along with the work of Margaret Archer, to propose a social theory that provides with a coherent view of social change in that context. This, of course, is the result of my own interpretation

© Springer International Publishing AG 2017   133
Germán McKenzie, *Interpreting Charles Taylor's Social Theory on Religion and Secularization*, Sophia Studies in Cross-cultural Philosophy of Traditions and Cultures 20, DOI 10.1007/978-3-319-47700-8_6

of Taylor's narrative, one that also draws from his views on humans as self-interpreting and ethically-bound beings, and on hermeneutic methodology of the social sciences.[1] In doing this, I am trying to take the most of such views to make my own interpretation richer so that the engagement with "orthodox" and "counter-orthodox" theories may yield more interesting results. So, whenever I cite Taylor's ideas in this and the following chapters, it is important to bear in mind that I am using them to substantiate my own views, and not to express aspects of his thought as such.

By social theory I do not mean here the kind of theoretical thinking that, in sociology, guides empirical research, usually validated through statistical methods, and constitutes the framework of its interpretation. I do mean, as I have mentioned at the beginning of the book, an understanding of the social processes and social agents involved in secularization inspired by Taylor's philosophical views. This also differentiates my "social theory" from the meaning widely associated with the term today, which refers to those theoretical endeavors aimed at criticizing modernity in general and, in particular, of the oppression and inequalities present in capitalism, an enterprise which finds in Marx its first proponent and continues through the work of people such as Foucault, Derrida, Habermas and Judith Butler (Lemert 2010). While Taylor himself recognizes such oppressions and inequalities, and is himself a Socialist, he still values the moral achievements of modernity—which he finds expressed, although imperfectly, in modern political, economic and social institutions—and sees them as valid (Taylor 1991). My interpretation would agree with this. If the study of structures (social, linguistic or other), and their coercive role is important, it is also relevant the role of human agents in their transformation, as well as of the cultural factors in the creation and maintenance of such structures. If the oppressive action of hidden forces is to be recognized, they are never disembodied from groups of persons who guide them (consciously or not), groups that can be countered in different ways through existing or new mechanisms (Taylor 2004). To affirm this is not to become less critical, but being so while taking into account a broader range of facts.

Taylorean social theory does not refer to a theory that is, in a subsequent stage, applied to the study of a given social fact, but to a set of concepts, guidelines and criteria that, reflecting the non-metaphysical human constants explained in Chap. 4, allow a hermeneutic understanding of such a fact in a very particularized manner, one which pays particular attention to the meanings that social facts always carry (and given to it by the human agent), to the self-understandings shared by social agents with their society at large, and those under which the social scientist abides.

Two clarifications seem to be in order here. First, Taylorean social theory, as an interpretive enterprise, stresses the recognition of the importance of the agent's self-understanding in social research, which should lead social scientists to pay close attention to the cultural context of the people under study, particularly their language, symbols, as well as shared understandings and practices, and to develop a "language of perspicuous contrast" in which it is possible to make sense of them and of their

---

[1] Charles Taylor, personal communication to the author, 19 Nov 2009.

social context. In order to develop such a language, Taylor's interpretive approach requires from the social scientist an awareness and skills that are not always stressed in mainstream sociology: a high degree of knowledge of himself and his context, an intuition of the inter-subjective language and common meanings he shares with his own society, a clear notion of his own social imaginary and of the social theory predominant in his own culture. Social scientists should be able to contrast these elements with the corresponding ones from the people under study and to establish the contrasts that would allow a deeper and broader interpretation than the ones in vogue.

These views can be illustrated, for instance, in Taylor's meta-narrative, in the frequency with which his analyses are carried out by comparing the United Kingdom and France in regard to the same topic. In these instances, it is not unusual to have Taylor contrasting the two countries in regard to linguistic uses, self-understandings, shared practices, the dominant ideas of the time, popular culture and the like, which he seeks to connect with the place of religion in society, its relations with the political system, the ways in which it is lived by concrete individuals and groups, etc. This is also complemented with mainstream sociological findings by scholars akin, at least in Taylor's opinion and in different degrees, to the views just described. Not only qualitative sociological studies but also quantitative ones could be used if those who conducted them were appropriately attuned with the "field of meanings" of the groups under study and were able to contrast them from those of their own. The results of these quantitative studies would remain valid during the time in which the shared self-interpretations of the group under study would remain constant or just change slightly. Because of the above mentioned requirements, Taylor's sociological method tends to be highly particularized in reference to the object of study.

Second, Taylorean social theory does not develop a formal method nor a universal theory that is then applied to a given phenomenon under study. In contrast, it proposes a certain understanding of the sciences of man that guides such study in a way that contributes to makes sense of a socio/cultural phenomenon that is happening or has occurred. "We could say that social theory arises when we try to formulate explicitly what we are doing, describe the activity which is central to a practice, and articulate norms which are essential to it" (Taylor 1985: 93).[2] Taylor will expand this and mention that social theory is the study of society seen, among other things, as institutions, practices and self-understandings (Taylor 1985: 93), which, in the case of his Western secularization, is done through the study of changing social imaginaries.

In what follows, I will explain what Taylorean social theory is. However, I will first localize it in the landscape of past and contemporary sociological theory. In order to achieve this goal, I will use the following points of reference: the problem of the relationship between structure and human agency (with a digression on social imaginaries), the dilemma between focusing on social change or social stability, the relationship between sociology and history, and the use of qualitative and quantitative analysis for verification.

---

[2] The quote is from a piece titled *Social Theory as Practice*.

6.1   Mapping Taylorean Social Theory

6.1.1   *Structure and Human Agency*

(a) The relationship between these two elements is, on the one hand, key for the making of any social theory and, on the other hand, has been the object of systematic study and clarification relatively recently. The problem at hand can be expressed succinctly like this: "Basically it concerns how to develop an adequate theoretical account which deals simultaneously with people constituting society and the social formation of human agents" (Archer 1985: 58).

Taylorean social theory situates itself somewhere in the middle of the two poles: neither giving social structures the whole weight in defining social change, nor assuming that human agency has it all. Holding the first position one finds functionalism, close-ended social system theory, varieties of Marxism and Neo-Marxism, structuralism, and several Postmodern thinkers. Espousing the second one, we may find versions of individualism, symbolic-interactionism, psychology and phenomenology. By doing this, Taylor gets closer to the positions on this issue held, among others, by Amitai Etzioni (1968), Alain Touraine (1977, 1985), Norbert Elias (Dunning and Hughes: 2013), and more comprehensively by Anthony Giddens (1979, 1984),[3] Margaret Archer (1988; 1995),[4] Pierre Bourdieu (1984: 1990)[5] and Jurgen Habermas (1987).[6]

Social structures are described as sets of processes detached from any agential perspective (Taylor 2004: 163); systems, in the sense of inter-connected processes (Taylor 2004: 163); institutional forms and social practices (Taylor 2004: 1); norms (Taylor 2004: 3); and patterns (Taylor 1989: 204–207). In what follows, I will refer to structures in the social realm (encompassing the political, economic, religious polity, etc.) and to those in the cultural realm (including athematic self-understandings, systems of belief, and their ethical consequences).

Common sense explanations of social phenomena based solely on purposive human agency are sometimes inadequate and even illusory (Taylor 1985: 92).[7] However, the complete attribution of social change to mere non-purposive structural factors seems equally inadequate. For example, in Taylor's critique of Foucault's notion of "strategy" as the logic of self-perpetuation of the impersonal system of power in which we live in the West and that keeps us under check (as "power without subject"), he finds it difficult to accept that there is no need of further explanation of the matter.

---

[3] His proposal is called "structuration theory."

[4] Her approach is called "morphogenetic."

[5] His position, also called "structuralist constructivism," tries to go beyond the antinomy of objectivism and subjectivism through a focus on practice (Bourdieu and Wacquant Loïc 1992: 7–26).

[6] He speaks of the need of overcoming the uncoupling of system and lifeworld (Habermas 1987: 153–197).

[7] This reference is to a piece titled *Social Theory as Practice*.

Where there are patterns in this action which are not on purpose, we have to explain why action done under one description on purpose also bears this other, undersigned description... It is certainly not the case that all patterns *issue* from conscious action, but all patterns have to be made *intelligible* in relation to conscious action. (Taylor 1985: 171)[8]

In the case at hand, Taylor explores possible explanations in considering the (largely unacknowledged) purposes of a given group (Taylor 1985: 171–72).[9] This shows that he considers that human agency cannot be ruled out completely from social structural conditioning. He even suggests, making use of an analogy with the links between language and speech acts, that structure and human agency maintain a "circular" or dialectical relationship between them (Taylor 1985: 173). In this light, Taylorean social theory accepts a view by which social agents are both conditioned by social structures, but also independent from them to a certain degree. For their part, structures emerge from agents but also embrace agents. In both cases, structures and human agency have a "life of their own," but at the same time structures emerge from and are kept in place by inter-personal networks, and human agency receives its possibilities, resources and constraints for action from the structural conditions (Taylor 2004: 163–73; 2002: 124–27; Sztompka 1994: 213–16).[10]

(b) The structure/agency problem also appears in the discussion about determinism and voluntarism in sociology. In this regard, Taylorean social theory leans towards a middle solution which, can be seen in his reluctance to accept social change as being driven entirely by forces that operate "from behind the backs of the agents" (Taylor 2004: 164) on the one hand, and also in his already mentioned acceptance of the existence of non-purposive effects of human agents that can and do have structural consequences, on the other (Taylor 2004: 163–67).

However, it is worth mentioning that, even when maintaining both poles in tension, Taylor's description of structural constrains is cast in terms of agency, which may have intended and unintended structural consequences. This goes along with the fact that he sees elite-mass dynamics (which are social movement dynamics) as crucial for the transformation of social imaginaries, which in turn are key to explaining social change (as in the case of secularization in the West). Along these lines, Taylorean social theory middle solution leans further towards voluntary human agency.

(c) Another important point appears when we relate the structure/agency problem with that of macro-/micro-dynamics. It is clear that there is not a perfect parallelism between the two. Agency and structure can refer to either the micro- or macro-levels: agency can refer either to individuals or social groups, whereas structure can refer to micro-structures (such as the family) or to large-scale macro structures. Even more, the micro-level may not necessarily point to conscious and

---

[8] This quotation is from a piece titled *Foucault on Freedom and Truth*.

[9] Here, he also accepts other kinds of structural conditioning such as "invisible hand" theories, in which "the situation is so constituted that individual decisions are bound to concatenate in a certain systematic way" (1985: 170) and models of "mass mobilization," which go beyond the combination of individual actions (1985: 170–71).

[10] The first reference is to a chapter titled *Agency and Objectification*.

[handwritten: cultural = spiritual]

creative actors or to a more "mindless" agent such as that of RCT. On the other hand, the macro-level could be linked to the culture of the whole of society or to some specific sub-cultures within it.

In the context of Taylor's meta-narrative, the macro-level would denote structures, whereas the micro-level would refer to conscious and creative individuals and groups. In Taylorean social theory there is interplay between the both the macro- and micro-levels, which are considered as really representing different things (as opposed to be mere analytical devices). Social macro-dynamics do condition (individual and grouped) social agents, as when societal secularization in the West impacts how such agents actualize their religious lives. Conversely, social micro-dynamics also affect and change the structural tendencies as can be seen, for instance, in the resistance of religious organizations to becoming marginalized and sidelined from the public space, or in the appearance of new forms of religious life and religious organization. In this context, another expression of the importance of social micro-dynamics for Taylor is the relevance he gives to the elite-mass relationship in the transformation of shared social imaginaries. This, in the end, makes his position closer to that of social movement and social network theories.

6.1.2   Social Imaginaries as Linking the Social and the Cultural

It should be added in relation to the previous point, that Taylor's theoretical choice of social imaginaries, which our own interpretation assumes, is somewhat unusual to contemporary sociology in that it blends the social and cultural realms into a single dynamic in which each element has a similar weight. In the same way that social factors can produce cultural changes, cultural factors have the potential to achieve social changes. In his view, opposing, in principle, both elements as rival causal agencies constitutes a false dichotomy:

> In fact, what we see in human history is ranges of human practices which are both at once, that is, "material" practices carried out by human beings in space and time, and very often coercively maintained, and at the same time, self-conceptions, modes of understanding. These are often quite inseparable… Just because human practices are the kind of thing which make sense, certain "ideas" are internal to them; one cannot distinguish the two in order to ask the question, which causes which. (Taylor 2007: 212; 1989: 204)

One may even say that, in the case of secularization in the West, the huge changes in human self-understanding this implies brings Taylor to affirm the cultural realm as having greater weight than the social: "The [modern] social imaginary I talk about did as a matter of fact originate in theory. This is something exceptional in history. The earlier social imaginaries weren't like this… This feature is distinctive of the modern idea of moral order" (Taylor 2010: 314; 2007: 212).

The very definition of social imaginary links cultural and social elements together. On the one hand, the cultural realm (to the right of Fig. 6.1) comprises the self-understanding shared by the people about how they fit together, which assumes the existence of a given universe of language and symbols; narratives and myths; categories; forms of experience; and ways of living (Taylor 2004: 1).

On the other hand, the social realm (to the left of Fig. 6.1), includes the common social practices through which individuals interact with other individuals, groups and society as a whole. These practices are embedded in social structures and functions, institutions, roles, norms, social classes, bureaucracy, along with more dynamic realities such as socialization processes, deviance and social control, social mobility, etc. Among such practices, one could mention the democratic rule, the market and the public sphere as peculiar to modernity. Figure 6.1 shows how both shared self-understanding and social practices maintain a circular relationship: shared self-interpretations make sense, regulate and legitimate social practices (Taylor 2004: 3, 24); shared social practices reinforce, gloss and enhance the culturally-rooted self-interpretations (Taylor 2004: 25–27, 30). In such a figure, we see how this circular relationship that takes place in social imaginaries at the same time links the cultural and social realms (in green and pink, respectively) as inescapable frameworks. The social framework has a negative and positive relationship with individual and group action: it situates (constrains) human agency within a field of possibilities; it also enables human agency to make sense of all its possible courses of action at a given time. The same can be said of the cultural realm.

As a consequence, it is difficult to speak of Taylorean social theory as exclusively related to social phenomena. Figure 6.2 (next page) shows how it must be spoken of as always referred to social and cultural phenomena. It is in each of these realms that human agency operates in the way it has already been described.

Fig. 6.1 Social imaginaries and social agency

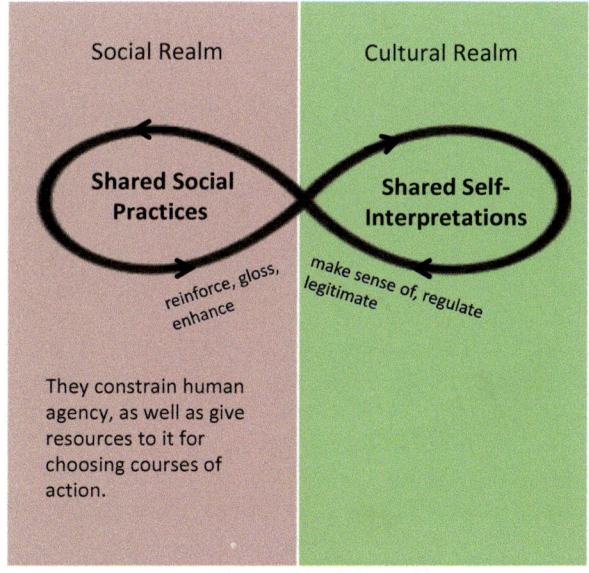

Fig. 6.2 Social imaginaries and socio-cultural agency

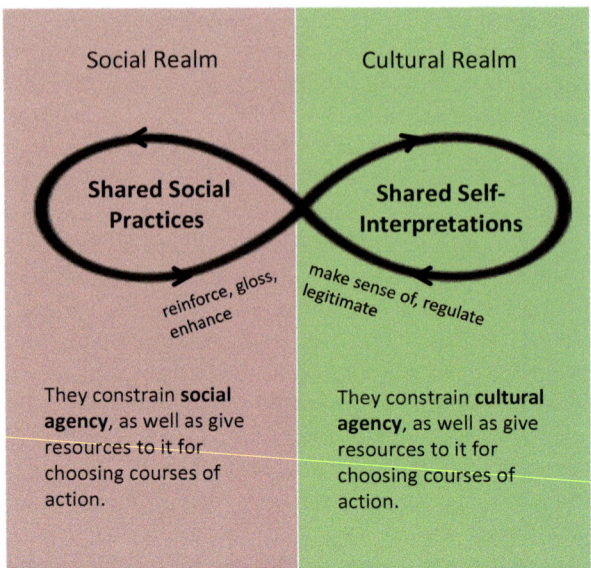

In connection to this, Taylor speaks of a relationship between the social and the cultural in a way in which, at a given concrete event, each of them always necessitates the presence of the other (Taylor 1989: 205):

> The relationship [between the cultural and the social] is much more intimate and reciprocal. Certain moral self-understandings are embedded in certain practices, which can mean both that they are promoted by the spread of these practices and that they shape the practices and help them establish. It is equally absurd to believe that the practices always come first, or to adopt the opposite view, that ideas somehow drive history. (Taylor 2004: 63)

6.1.3   Social Change vs. Social Stability

Taylor's account of secularization includes an analysis of social structures (Ancien Régime, Age of Mobilization, Age of Authenticity), religio-political arrangements (Paleo-, Neo- and Post-Durkhemian), and types of religious life in each. Through an analysis of the descriptions Taylor gives of each of the above-mentioned structures, Taylorean social theory would espouses a notion of social structure as giving integration to diverse elements in social life, as well as an awareness that such structures change. Similarly, it sees cultural structures as integrating culture, and at the same time amenable of change. In this light, one can say that the process of Western secularization is one of socio-cultural change through the transformation of social imaginaries through an elite-mass dynamic. Such a transformation can occur both due to the appearance of new self-understandings that modify/replace specific social practices, and to the changes in social practices which in time modify/replace previously existing self-interpretations.

In this light, Taylorean social theory is closer to those perspectives that focus on social change (versions of Neo-Marxism, social movements theory) than to those centered on the study of society as a closed system in continuous search of equilibrium (as in functionalism and exchange theory as proposed by Talcott Parsons and George C. Homans, respectively) (Buckley 1967: 23–36). Even functionalist perspectives that offer models of system self-modification (such as feedback and "purposive" systems) are difficult to harmonize with Taylor's views.

However, highly deterministic theories of social change such as social evolutionism and Neo-Evolutionism, theories of modernization (such as convergence theory), historical cycles and Marxist historical materialism (Sztompka 1994: 97–117) rank even farther away from our perspective. In this regard, it is enlightening to recall how Taylor points out that the kind of prediction involved here is unachievable, since this would demand that social sciences "have explicited so clearly the human condition that one would already have pre-empted all cultural innovation and transformation. This is hardly in the bounds of the possible" (1985: 57).[11]

6.1.4 Sociology and History

The sciences of man, in our view, are not amenable to offering general laws that may be applicable to (interpretation-free) particular occurrences because they are constitutively hermeneutic. This means such sciences need also to focus in the specific cultural conditions of the subjects under study to make sense of the social dynamic in which they are inserted and vice versa. This makes Taylorean social theory very much attuned to the conditioning effects of place and time. In connection with this Taylor would affirm that "sociology without history can't really get to the really important issues" (Taylor 2008; 1989: 199–207).

As a consequence, Taylorean social theory becomes close to those views that seek to integrate both sociology and history (Sztompka 1994: 202–212). This has occurred, in the case of sociology, in the work of Weber and partly in the work of Marx, and in the thinking of other authors such as Norbert Elias (1978a, b), Robert Bellah (1985), Neil J. Smelser (1973), Schmuel Eisenstadt (1963), Seymour M. Lipset (1967), Charles Tilly (1976) and others (Burke 1980: 27–30). Taylor's views are similar to those by Philip Abrams who affirms that sociology is historical per se, that the relationships between structure and agency must be assessed in time. "This shaping of action by structure and transforming of structure by action both occur as processes in time" (Abrams 1982: 3). As a consequence, sociology needs to focus on society's history to pursue any study of it.

Taylor's openly admitted admiration for Elias' already cited book, *The Civilizing Process*, allows the assumption that he is somewhat attuned with at least the basic principles of Elias' "figurational sociology" as they appear in that work. As we may recall, Elias proposed a theory that should be rooted in empirical facts, embedded in

---

[11] The quote is from a piece titled *Interpretation and the Sciences of Man*.

history and developed *post factum*. More importantly, sociological facts in general should be seen as made out of inter-dependent relationships (between persons, groups, or persons and groups) that are always in the process of changing. In this light, he argues against the reification of concepts such as society or groups (for this purpose Elias used the term "figurations" to refer to them). Both Elias and Taylor view structural changes as driven by changes in practices at the level of the social imaginary. Structures (Taylor 1989: 204–207),[12] in last analysis, appear to be constituted of patterns kept alive within inter-individual and inter-group networks. Taylorean social theory shares these same views.

6.1.5   Qualitative and Quantitative Verification

Taylorean social theory seeks to verify its affirmations and does so through quantitative and qualitative approaches. The following cases, taken from Taylor narrative, illustrate ways in which this can be done.

Taylor does not conduct quantitative research himself. Instead, he strongly relies, as mentioned in the last chapter, on the works by sociologists and religious historians who have studied specific areas in the United Kingdom and France during the span of time covered by his meta-narrative of secularization. He does not disregard quantitative empirical studies per se but ask them to recognize the need of taking into account the meanings that social facts always carry (and given to it by the human agent), to the self-understandings shared by social agents with their society at large, and those under which the social scientist abides. This hermeneutic sensitivity should thoroughly inform the method of study in all its phases, from the phase of research design, through conceptualization, measurement and operationalization, all the way down to sampling and analysis of data. The results of these studies, as it has been said at the beginning of this chapter, would only remain valid during the time in which the shared self-interpretations of the group under study would remain constant or just change slightly. An illustration of this has already been given in Chap. 3 when it deals with the method of the social sciences.

Taylor's use of quantitative and qualitative approaches seeks to complement each other. In the case of the latte, when he explains changes in social imaginaries, he gives substance to his interpretation by using a variety of sources: descriptions of popular culture, institutionalization of practices, legal dispositions, the history of ideas, and the development of art, particularly literature, etc. Qualitative studies in the field of cultural anthropology are not ruled out provided that they fill the requirements stipulated by Taylor's hermeneutic view of the sciences of man.

Following Abbey's opinions (Abbey: 362–63), I would argue that Taylorean social theory follows Taylor here when he uses a form of "transcendental argument," by which he (Taylor) starts

---

[12] Here, one finds an account of Taylor's view on social change.

from some feature of our experience which they [transcendental arguments] claim to be indubitable and beyond cavil. They then move to a stronger conclusion, one concerning the nature of the subject or the subject's position in the world. They make this move by a regressive argument, to the effect that the stronger conclusion must be so if the indubitable fact about experience is to be possible. (Taylor 1995: 20)[13]

As a consequence of what has been said, the strength of these strategies of verification does not rely properly on methodological considerations in the first place, but on their end result: the creation of narratives that would provide a more perspicuous interpretation than any rival one, the articulation of an experience with such clarity (in our case, the description of the outcomes of secularization in the three meanings of secularity about which Taylor speaks) that his meta-narrative (by which he interprets such experience of secularization) must be accepted. All this means that what adjudicates the validity of Taylor's interpretations over others is (a) the exhaustive phenomenological description of the object of study—one that becomes indubitable for the audience since it articulates its experience with great clarity—which is based on (b) an interpretation—narrative—which appears to be more universal and with deeper explanatory powers than any rival theory. What is implied here is the "transcendental argument" by which (b) must be true for (a) to exist (as it is, without doubt).

In the end, it is assumed here that arguments can be challenged at any time and the facts provided by the methods of study can always be subject to different interpretations, which makes Taylorean social theory a thoroughly open-ended endeavor.

6.2 Taylorean Social Theory and Social Change

Taylor's narrative of secularization is one of social change. It is, without doubt, a complex and nuanced account. His meta-narrative can be schematically summarized in Fig. 6.3 (next page), where causal relations are represented by filled arrows. Ideal-type landmarks in the process are linked by dotted arrows. The darker areas represent social changes, whereas the lighter ones refer to cultural transformations. Time flows from the top to the bottom of the chart, passing through two cultural crises that mark the shifts from the Ancién Regime to the Age of Mobilization, on the one hand, and between the Age of Mobilization to the Age of Authenticity, on the other.

However, the process of social change—which manifests secularization in the West—happens in Taylorean social theory through the transformation of social imaginaries. This is represented by the uneven thick black line (and its attached label) that crosses the chart from left to right. Such a line is supposed to go downwards in time, representing the fact that all causal relationships in the process occur through social imaginary transformations. Lastly, the thick double arrow at the bottom represents the fact that, at present, the process of secularization understood as religious decline has turned itself into a scenario of mutual fragilization between

---

[13] The quote is from the piece titled *The Validity of Transcendental Arguments*.

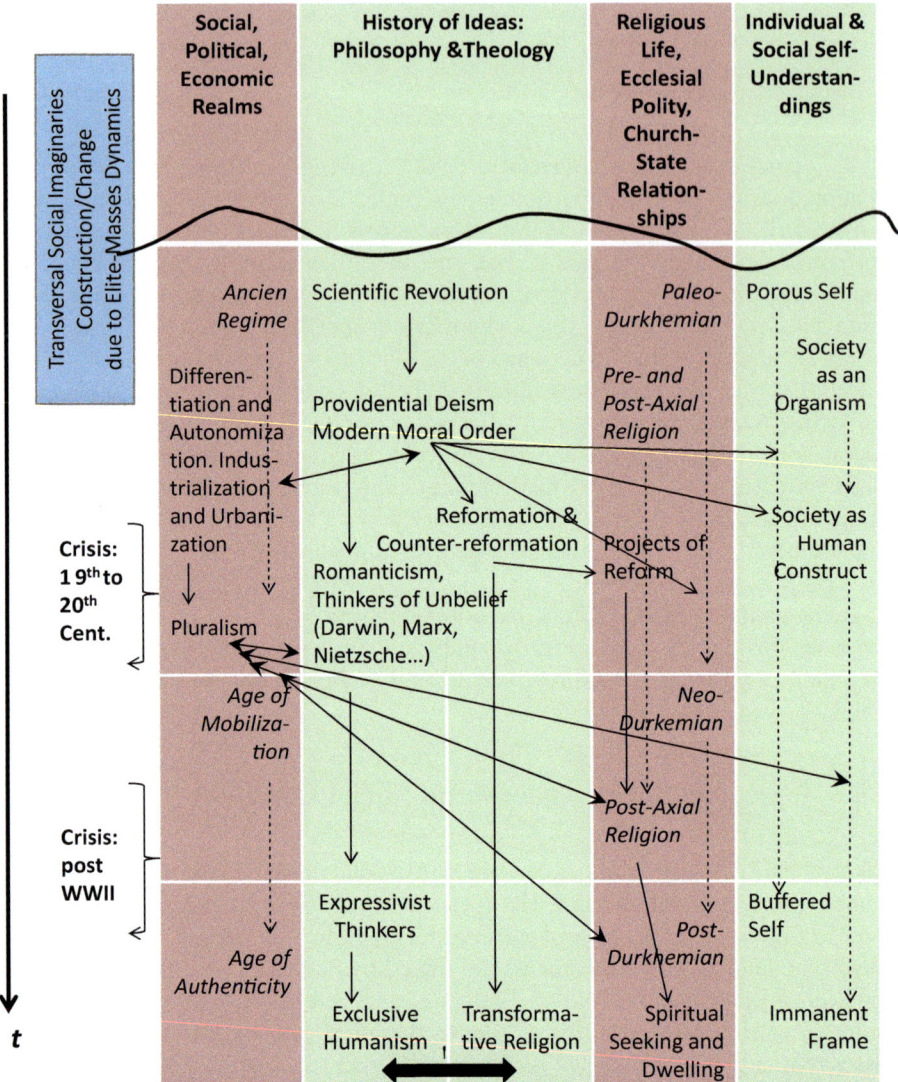

Fig. 6.3 The general causal process of secularization in the West

exclusive humanism and transformative religion at the individual level, which has triggered a gamut of intermediate spiritual/religious possibilities. However, the terrain is uneven when it comes to making decisions because we live in an immanent frame. Figure 6.3 also shows how religious organizations are relocating themselves within society and the public sphere at the societal level, in ways in which their influence is somewhat relevant for both dwellers and seekers.

To better understand the process described, it is necessary to bear in mind that, in Taylorean social theory, secularization in the West is in reality one of religious transformation: old religious forms decline but give place to new ones. This double dynamics happens both in the Age of Mobilization and in the Age of Authenticity, although in each case due to different sets of causes.

Taylorean social theory's account is one of a process of social change. What approach to social change is at work here? It can be characterized by the following elements (Sztompka 1994: 12–23).

(a) The process of change is directional both in its social and cultural aspects up to the present time. It is not necessarily irreversible, but in some aspects it may go back *in toto*—although this is very unlikely. Although cumulative in some aspects, in others the past stages have not been completely superseded but are still present, although in changed ways, as one sees with regard to transformative religion, which keeps living in tension and mutual fragilization with exclusive humanism.

(b) The future of the process of social change, however, does not appear to be aimed in any particular direction. Secularization is a non-linear, zigzag-shaped process, and one full of unintended consequences (Taylor 2007: 95).

(c) The driving forces of the process of social change come from within and without the social and cultural aspects of the process.

(d) The outcome of secularization has been a kind of morphogenesis: a qualitative change in the social and cultural structures, in religion itself, and in the way the sacred is located within personal and social life (e. g. the immanent frame).

(e) Human agents have not been completely aware of the process at the social level, but it has been very much manifest in regard to its cultural aspects, particularly among intellectual and religious elites.

(f) Causation processes seem to be concrete, contingent and involve many factors in Taylor's view. As we have seen, his account vouches for a multi-causal approach, in which "material" conditions—such as technology, economics, politics, demographics and stratification—as well as "non-material" ones—such as religion and ideology—are potentially independent variables that may influence each other and the life course of society (Taylor 2004: 31–32, 63–65, 72–73, 149–52).

(g) Human agency is very much stressed both in its spontaneous ways (e.g. mobilization, search for authenticity) and its planned expressions (e.g. reform initiatives within Christianity). It is so, moreover, because of his conviction that human self-understanding (e. g. "porous" and "buffered" selves) and social imaginaries play a key role in shaping social changes. Both individual and group actions are taken very seriously.

6.3   Social Imaginaries and Elite-Masses Dynamics

Since, in Taylorean social theory, change occurs through the transformation of social imaginaries by means of elite-masses dynamics, this section is focused on answering two questions: How do social imaginaries concretely change? And how do elites and masses participate in such changes? In answering these questions, particular references will be made to *Modern Social Imaginaries*, which is the most important source on the matter in the Taylorean corpus.[14]

(a) At each step of the process of socio-cultural change, social imaginaries take elements from the material (socio-structural) and non-material (cultural-structural) causes at work as their sources, and produce a given shared self-understanding, which is linked with concrete shared social practices. This happens through human agency, particularly through the works of particular groups such as ruling elites, religious elites, activists and the intellectuals.

Changes in social imaginaries can be triggered both at the level of self-interpretations and at that of practices, as Taylor says in *Sources of the Self*:

> There are cases where the genesis of change can be identified with new ideas. But change can come about in other ways as well. Ideas and practices may come to be out of true with each other, because one or the other fails to reproduce itself properly. Some of the original rationale may be lost, just through drift or through the challenge of some new insight; or the practice may alter as it is inadequately handed down.
>
> Above all, practices may be constrained or facilitated, may take on less or more space, for a whole host of reasons which are unconnected to their rationales. (Taylor 1989: 205)

So, changes in social imaginaries can originate in either of the above-mentioned poles. Mutations and developments in ideas (and self-interpretations), including new visions of things, and creative insights bring alterations, ruptures, reforms or revolutions in social practices. Taylor speaks of the creation of new social practices and about the transformation of existing ones by giving them a new meaning, as two strategies for changing the social imaginary starting from practices (Taylor 2004: 109–115). Conversely, drift, constrictions or flourishing of social practices give place to the alteration, flourishing and decline of ideas (in self-interpretations).

Changes like these are gradual and are not exhaustive, which means that previous existing socio-cultural structures may coexist as "survivals" along with the new ones, held by the majority (Taylor 2004: 143–54).

(b) Elite-mass dynamics, in this context, refer to the actions carried out by groups of human agents, and the ways in which that can further changes in social imaginaries by getting the masses involved in them. There is a host of forms in which this happens. They vary depending on the groups that take action. On the one hand, one finds ruling elites, who have political power per se, as well as access to resources. On the other hand, one finds religious elites, activists and the intellectuals, to whom other kinds of power and resources are endowed. Another source of variation in elite-mass dynamics relies on the purposeful or non-purposeful character of the actions that lead to change.

Among the different ways in which elites-masses relationships may occur, one can find the following as the most common in Taylor's narrative:

---

[14] Charles Taylor, personal communication to the author, 2 Oct 2013.

- Diffusion by ruling elites. These elites may collaborate with intellectual, economic or religious ones. In this case, changes are promoted either by the dissemination of ideas or social practices "from top to bottom," through the means of political power. Among many examples, Taylor mentions the establishment of policies for standardized education, universal literacy, higher levels of schooling, and conscription into the army in France during the eighteenth and nineteenth centuries (Taylor 2007: 424ff; 2004: 42–46).
- Diffusion by non-ruling elites (intellectual, economic, religious). These elites promote their own agendas through the means they have at their disposal—with the collaboration of ruling elites, and sometimes without it. For example, there are changes in religious life and spirituality carried out by the Catholic Church in France in the nineteenth century. It included a greater acceptance of popular piety and was more centered on the heart and more compassionate in the approach to the believer's moral life (Taylor 2007: 444–45).
- Rejection by elites of the social practices of the masses which, in turn, causes an estrangement between the two, which would also have consequences at the level of ideas and on the sense of identity of the latter. The fact that elites (political, intellectual or religious) assumed a distance from popular culture or popular religiosity as in eighteenth century France and the United Kingdom is an example of this. The consequence was that new elites appeared as representatives of the estranged segment of the population—as, for instance, in the rise of Methodism.
- Rejection by the masses of the self-understandings offered by religious elites, as when urbanization took place in the United Kingdom and France in the nineteenth century due to industrialization. By then, generally speaking, the churches backed the bourgeoisie in maintaining their privileged economic situation, which alienated great numbers of laborers from organized religion and fostered their drift into "exclusive humanist" ways of providing for their desires of human fulfillment (Taylor 2007: 442–43).
- Mobilization of the masses by social activists against ruling elites. Activists here are non-ruler elites in need of building their own political relevance, that is, of creating their own means of exercising social or political power. A case in point was the Jacobin organization of the sections of Paris, the aim of which was to recruit a larger and larger base in the context of the French Revolution (Taylor 2004: 30).
- Improvisation by social activists against ruling elites. Again, these activists are non-ruler elites seeking to acquire political relevance. However, different from the previous case, here the means for such acquisition are not wholly planned but improvised, taking advantage of unintended consequences of their actions. A good example is the establishment of the public sphere as social practice in the eighteenth century by bourgeoisie elites (Taylor 2004: 30), which started as a network for sharing information in regard to news and commerce, and turned to be an open space for the public debate on issues regarding to the common good of society, one that could challenge the established political power. In this case, in time, a given social practice gained a different interpretation, which in turn changed the ways it was performed.

What is at stake in each of these examples is that changes at the level of society or culture, carried on by elites or activists, with endowed or acquired power and access to resources, affect the social imaginary that gives sense and norms to socio-cultural life.

6.4 Taylorean Social Theory as Morphogenetic

At this point, I will address the question of the basic characteristics of Taylorean social theory as a theory of socio-cultural change, an interpretation of Taylor's meta-narrative of secularization in the West. In order to do this, I will explain its four basic concepts which reflect the non-metaphysical human constants explained in Chap. 4, as well as what has been said so far in this chapter. In a following section I will show how these basic elements taken together give an account of Taylor's meta-narrative in sociological terms.

It is possible to speak, in Taylorean social theory, of a "system" as a complex of elements or components directly or indirectly related in a causal network, such that each component is related to at least some others in a more or less stable way within a particular period of time. The particular kinds of more or less stable relationships between components that become established at a given time constitute the system as structure, thus forming a "whole" with some degree of continuity and boundary.[15] However, it is important to remember Taylor's insistence on affirming that systems should always be open because their boundaries are relative. He uses the notion of systems in this way to refer to structures. He also uses the word "matrices" in a similar sense (Taylor 2007: 438, 461, 464, 516). The key approach is to think about them as necessarily open-ended realities, subject to constant change in themselves from within or from without the social/cultural system.

In the light of the above, it makes sense to speak of Taylorean social theory as morphogenetic, as assuming that socio-cultural structures are always in a process of redefinition, are always being changed through the impact of human agency on them. Such structural redefinitions can aim at their reinforcement (morphostasis) or their transformation (morphogenesis). In this context, the sociological account of secularization in the West entails an explanation of the (morphogenetic) transformation of the place occupied by the sacred within the socio-cultural structures, which has happened in the last five centuries. In what follows I draw on the scholarship of Margaret Archer, who works on "morphogenetic sociology."[16]

---

[15] Here I am adapting the broad definition by Walter Buckley (1967: 41). I am avoiding here entering into the distinction between system and structure for the sake of the clarity of my analysis.

[16] Archer's approach seems the best choice for interacting with Taylor's meta-narrative because (a) it provides the closest philosophical underpinnings to those of Taylor's view, (b) it stresses the bond between society and culture, (c) it shares a similar approach than Taylor's on the relationship between structure and human agency, and (d) it has a focus on relationships between social groups and their effects on structural change.

It is important to mention here that none of the figures presented below have any other aim that being pedagogical resources for the sake of clarity of my argument and in no way intend to portray Taylorean social theory as a brand of sociological systems theory or anything like it.

6.4.1   Basic Concepts

(a) **Vertical and Horizontal:** The "Situated" Agent as Linking Agency and Structure.

This is a cluster of concepts on "actual" agency as concretely lived by individuals and groups. This is considered both "vertically," as keeping defined relationships with agency as such and with structure; as well as "horizontally," as redefining, in time, structure and agency through a given event. It is because these frameworks are inescapable for actual agency operating through a particular event that I am naming it "Situated" Agent. This is expressed in Fig. 6.4.

The vertical axis expresses how a (individual or group) "Situated" Agent, operating through a given event in T_1 (an Agency-event), does so in a way that relies completely on the previously "received" characteristics of Agency$_1$ as well as on the

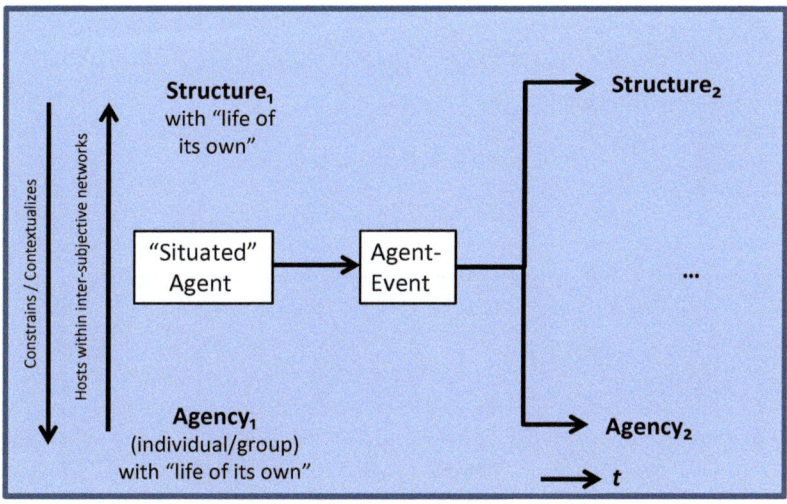

Fig. 6.4   Vertical and horizontal interactions of the "situated" agent

---

There is a certain parallelism between this view and that of the "integrated sociological paradigm" by George Ritzer (1981: 205–238; 1990: 347–70). However, this author does not separate the social and cultural realms and starts his analysis from a micro/macro standpoint.

Another theoretical approach with important similarities with Archer's is that of "relational sociology," developed by Pierpaolo Donati (2011).

constraints and context of possibilities "inherent" in a Structure$_1$. Among the former, one should count the degrees of freedom of individuals and groups, as well as all their resources for action, which in any concrete situation may or may not be completely available to the "Situated" Agent (thus the reason for the distinction). Among the latter, we should mention all kinds of conditioning coming from non-agential sources such as institutions, norms, roles, etc. It is important to mention, in this regard, that in the end, structures live nested in inter-subjective relationships and should not to be reified. This fact is, I think, something that can be deduced from Taylor's choice of social imaginaries (as self-understandings embodied in social practices or, better, as social practices kept alive by shared self-interpretations) as his basic unit of analysis.

The horizontal axis shows how a (individual or group) "Situated" Agent, operating through a given event in T$_1$, and enframed by agency and structure, in turn redefines them in T$_2$. This is also consistent with the fact that social imaginaries are conceptualized as fluid realities in which changes in the agent's self-understanding modify their sense of "identity" as well as affect shared social practices. As a result, we find, in T$_2$, both a redefined Agency$_2$ and also Structure$_2$. It is within this new context that "Situated" Agency will operate again, starting a new cycle.

(b) **Sloped:** Socio-Structural Change in Time due to Agency.

This concept shows the interplay of agency and structure in time. What is assumed is that for any Agency-event carried on by an individual or groups in T2, there is a previously existing Structure1 in T1 which conditions the former, as it can be seen in Fig. 6.5.

However, as we have seen before, one of the consequences of such an Agency-event is the redefinition or "elaboration" of structure in T$_3$, which appears as Structure$_2$. The latter, in turn, becomes a conditioning framework for the following Agency-event that would take place, starting a new cycle of the dynamics.

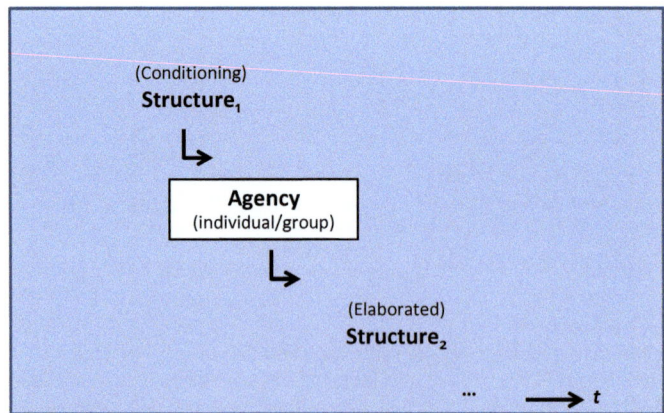

Fig. 6.5 Socio-structural change in time

Structural change is not always the consequence of agency. The way in which the latter affects the former can be described as a redefining process, by which the outcome can be either structural stability of structural change.

Figure 6.5 shows the relationship of structure and agency in time by making use of right angle-shaped arrows.

(c) **Parallel:** The Culture Realm Conceptualized Similarly to the Social.

Given that changes in social imaginaries are agency-driven (although structurally conditioned) and link both the social and the cultural realms, we could naturally ask if the concepts previously developed could be of use for the analysis of a "Situated" Cultural Agent in its relations with both Cultural Structure and Cultural Agency, and for the explanation of Cultural-Structural change in time through agency. Borrowing from Archer's thought (Archer 1988: 103–307), I think the answer is affirmative. It is possible to speak, then, of a Double-Sloped Scheme, one explaining Socio-Cultural Change in time by paralleling the change dynamics in the social realm with that in the cultural realm.

(d) **Structural Elaboration at the Social and Cultural levels:** Conditions for Change.

The basic concepts just explained gain more analytical power if the conditions for structural change are explained at both the level of structure and agency. Besides, following Taylor's focus on elite-masses relationships, in what follows I will identify agency with "agency performed by groups." The analysis will first be carried out in regard to the social realm and then to the cultural.

Before moving ahead, it is important to state that in the social and cultural realms, it should not be assumed that the structure—because of the relative stability of its components for a period of time—is characterized per se by the integration of all its constitutive elements. On the contrary, there are many instances in which social structures present tensions within (Lockwood 1964).[17] A similar thing should be said about cultural structures, which are not supposed to be considered as necessarily leading to integration in principle (Archer 1988: 1–21).[18]

In the *social realm*, social structures are not mere reflections of social agency and, conversely, social agency is not a passive reaction to structural conditioning. Both elements are distinct and to be considered as dialectically integrated. In this context, and as it is described in Fig. 6.6 (next page), one can postulate that, at a given time, structural integration could be high or low. One can also postulate that agential integration could be high (orderly relationships between groups and also between elites and masses) or low (conflictive relationships between those just men-

---

[17] The author distinguishes between orderly or conflictive relationships at the level of the actors (individuals groups), which he calls social integration, and orderly or conflictive relationships between different structures (social, political, economic, etc.), which he calls system integration. Going beyond the differences in terminology, the important point here is the abandonment of integration as a necessary characteristic of the relationships between structures.

[18] Here the author criticizes what she calls the "myth of cultural integration."

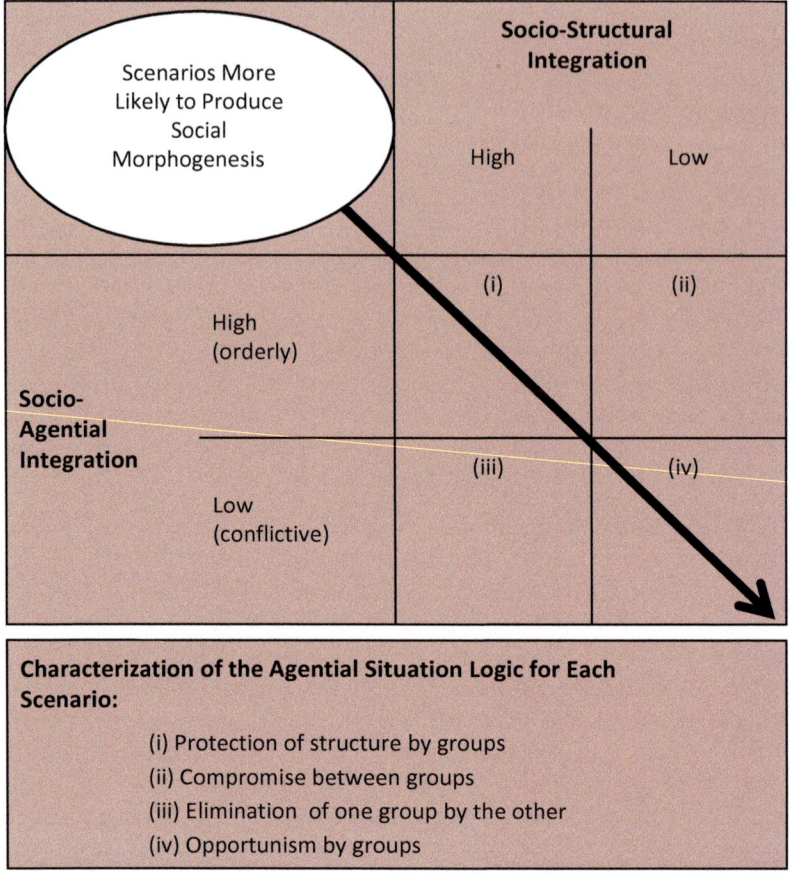

Fig. 6.6 Social morphogenesis

tioned), as well (Archer 1995: 218–229). Figure 6.6 also shows the scenarios that may derive from these possibilities.

The most likely scenarios for morphogenesis are (iv), followed by (iii) and (ii). It is just logical to expect that Taylorean social theory, being focused on secularization in the West as social transformation in the last five centuries, would try to show how these scenarios (particularly the first two) came to happen over that span of time.

In order to understand what this means for agency, it is important to say that the ways in which groups face scenarios of high or low social structural integration depends on the following factors (Archer 1995: 195–218):

- Their specific "social" placement, which includes a number of "received" features such as how groups fare in terms of the distribution of social goods in society, particularly of power, and social roles with their endowed advantages and disadvantages.

- The vested interests groups may have, which vary among all groups in society and are also "received" and structurally-enduring. These constitute motivations for agency.
- The interpretation groups may have about the best course of action to be chosen, which includes: their ethical stance, an analysis of the costs of not following vested interests and of the benefits of doing so, and the balance between the two. These also constitute motivations for agency.
- The strategies groups may follow to carry out a given action for which they are motivated (which relate to their self-awareness of the above elements and their interpretation by agents).

Taking all these factors into account, from the standpoint of social agents, the "situation logics" they would follow in each scenario is that also described in Fig. 6.6. To properly understand these scenarios, it is important to keep in mind the fact that, along with the constrains that social structures do place on agency, human agents are capable of resisting, circumventing, repudiating or suspending structural tendencies in unpredictable ways (Archer 1995: 195; 1988: 103–42).

- Scenario (i). High Structural Integration, High Agential Integration. Here each group has something to lose from disruption, so they assume a logic of "defense" of the structure.
- Scenario (ii). Low Structural Integration, High Agential Integration. In this case, where there is structural disruption, groups tend to balance their diffused vested interests, and their logic is one of "compromise."
- Scenario (iii). High Structural Integration, Low Agential Integration. Here each group looks for the "elimination" of the other. There is an entrenchment of their positions. For instance, the struggle between capital and labor in nineteenth century, during the very beginning of industrialization in the West.
- Scenario (iv). Low Structural Integration, Low Agential Integration. Before disruption at the structural level, vested interests of groups push towards compromise to ensure "opportunistic group survival."

Taylorean social theory, while explaining secularization in the West, shows how the conditions for social morphogenesis actually occurred, as well as how social agency (expressed in terms of elite-masses relationships) actually followed the above mentioned "situation logics," particularly those of Scenarios (iii) and (iv), since such a process of secularization implied a structural transformation.

In regard to the *cultural realm*, a similar analysis to that of the social should be done (Archer 1988: 227–73), which is summarized in Fig. 6.7 (next page). This is justified because human agency in Taylorean social theory operates in and through social imaginaries that per se link both the social and the cultural. For both realms there are analogous keys for analysis.

In the case of culture, as in the case of the social, structures are not a mere reflection of cultural agency and, conversely, cultural agency is not a passive reaction to structural conditioning. Both elements are to be distinguished and to be considered as dialectically integrated. In this context structural integration would refer to the

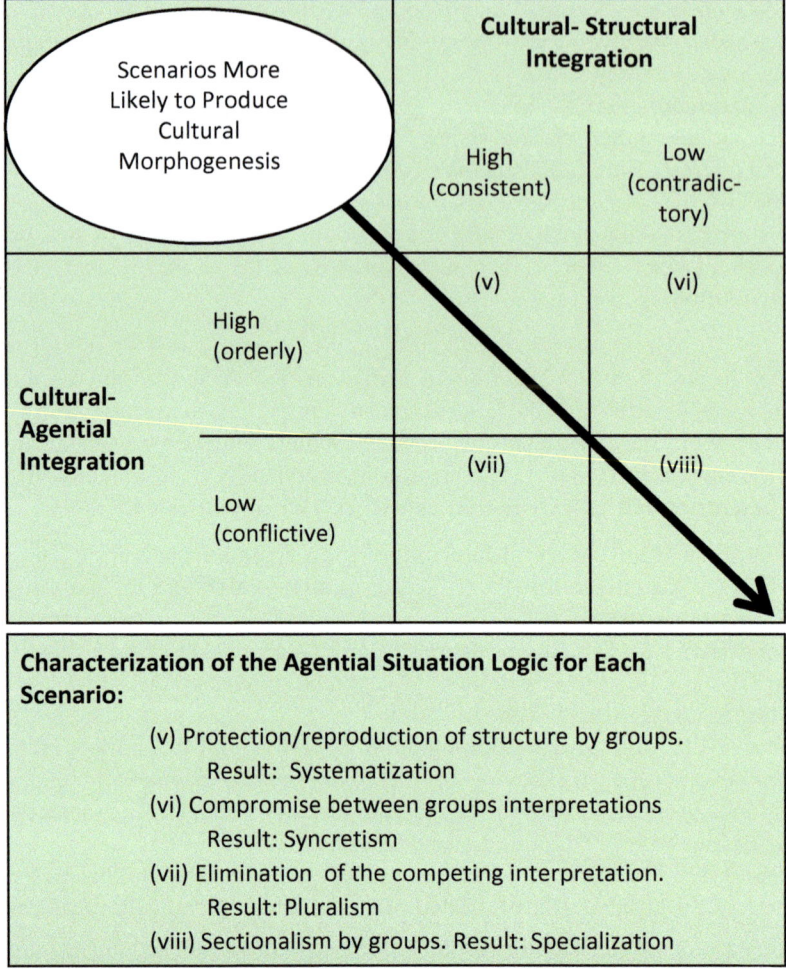

Fig. 6.7 Cultural morphogenesis

coherence and diffusion of a given interpretation of the world as the context for specific cultural agency, which includes its logical consistency (that is, its avoidance of affirming contradictory elements at the same time). We may recall how Taylor speaks of the ways in which some interpretations of the world are more perspicuous than other interpretations.[19]

To affirm there is a cultural structure operative in a given society does not amount to affirming it is thoroughly integrated. On the contrary, even in a situation charac-

---

[19] See Chap. 4. In this regard, there is need to show that (a) the cultural structure as sets of interpretations that have consistency in themselves and are not mere reflection of cultural agency, and (b) that such structures are amenable of comparison in Western history for the past five centuries.

examples?

terized by higher integration, there are contradictory elements in operation, either as "survivals" from past forms or as seeds of new ones.

For its part, cultural-agential integration means the degree of orderly relationships between groups representing different (and often competing) self-interpretations, particularly between intellectual and religious elites. Groups can promote and impose their ideas, receive new ones or challenge those held by others.

The possible cultural morphogenetic scenarios are noted in Fig. 6.7 by Roman numerals as before. Among them, the most likely scenario for morphogenesis is (viii), followed by (vii) and (vi).

To follow up the analogy with what has been said about the social realm, the particular ways in which groups face scenarios of high or low social structural integration depends on these factors:

- The cultural placement in the "received" general landscape of theories, beliefs and self-interpretations.
- The degree of inner logical consistency and "perspicuity" of the theories, beliefs and self-interpretations each particular group has.
- The drive each group has for diffusing its own views in society. This is a motivation for action.
- The strategy used by groups to cope with the weak points and logical contradictions of their views and self-interpretations. This is also a motivation for action.

The "situation logics" that groups may follow in each possible scenario at the cultural level is also explained in Fig. 6.7.

- Scenario (v). High Structural Integration, High Agential Integration. The cultural structure is perceived as logical and highly perspicuous, and groups' particular views are complementary and comfortable within the former. The situational logic here is one of "defense" and "reproduction" of the structure, which gives place to the intellectual systematization of the cultural structure.
- Scenario (vi). Low Structural Integration, High Agential Integration. In this case, two elements at the structural level appear as contradictory in a necessary way (which means that there is no way to escape the tensions the situation raises) in a well integrated group arrangement. There is an urge to repair the damage this produces to the groups involved. The results may be abandonment of the group's position or skepticism. A group in tension could correct its own views, or ask the other group to do so. Another possibility is that the two correct their views to avoid contradiction. The situation logic becomes one of "syncretism."
- Scenario (vii). High Structural Integration, Low Agential Integration. Elements at the structural level appear as consistent in a loosely-integrated group arrangement. The positions of different groups are in conflict, but people will choose between them. In the end, in spite of the desires of the opposed groups to eliminate their opponents, there is a drive towards "pluralism."
- Scenario (viii). Low Structural Integration, Low Agential Integration. Groups vouch for novel particular views in regard to the cultural structure and other

group views. There is a drive to build a synthesis on the new realm along specialty lines. This results in sectionalism by groups and a logic of "specialization."

6.4.2   Taylorean Social Theory and Social Change in the Process of Secularization

I have just described and justified the basic analytical concepts in what I have called Taylorean social theory, which should serve as elements to be used in the elaboration of a hermeneutic assessment of the socio-cultural processes involved in Western secularization. It is appropriate now to show how they are able to express Taylor's meta-narrative of secularization. This constitutes an exercise of re-interpretation of the multilayered narratives present in *A Secular Age* and secularization-related works in a way closer to our current sociological language. Figure 6.8 (next page) shows a process of structural morphogenesis through agency both in the social (darker area) and cultural (lighter area) realms. These realms always appear as linked at any given time, due to the dynamics happening in social imaginaries (represented with the ∞ symbol). This means that changes in socio-cultural structures may occur at any given time due to a predominantly social or cultural factor.

Such a process, in Taylor's view, starts with the integrated socio-cultural structure proper to the Ancien Régime (AR), which existed about five centuries ago (Structure$_{AR}$). It develops in time (from top to bottom in the figure), through a series of Agency-events (in white boxes), into a new structure (Structure $_{AM}$) that crystallizes as the matrix of the Age of Mobilization (AM) by the end of the eighteenth and the beginning of the nineteenth centuries. New Agency-events (again, in white boxes) lead the process to the consolidation of a new structure (Structure $_{AA}$) in the post-WWII/post-60s age, in which we live now: the Age of Authenticity (AA).

Figure 6.8 simplifies the process by which a given structure is transformed into a new one (morphogenesis), through a series of Agency-events in time. Actually, each white box gathers a large number of them that are both conditioned by a given structure and are also transformative of such a structure. Moreover, the transformations in social structures can produce changes in the cultural structures and vice-versa, since both realms are "circularly" linked in social imaginaries. These Agency-events are carried out by social and cultural elites and by the masses.

Besides, it should be said that the passing from a given structure into a new one through agency entails the decline of some forms of religious life and the appearance of new ones. Lastly, the set of causes that produce such changes in religious life is different in each stage (Taylor 2007: 444, 446).

6.4.3   Taylor's Meta-narrative Expressed in Terms of Taylorean Social Theory

In this section, I show with more detail how Taylorean social theory recasts Taylor's meta-narrative. In order to do this, I will develop each of the elements that constitutes Fig. 6.8. This includes a definition of the structures that are integrated in successive stages of the process, and an explanation of the elite-mass dynamics for each of the Agency-event blocks. It also entails linking the social and cultural realms throughout, just as much as it helps the purpose of this section.

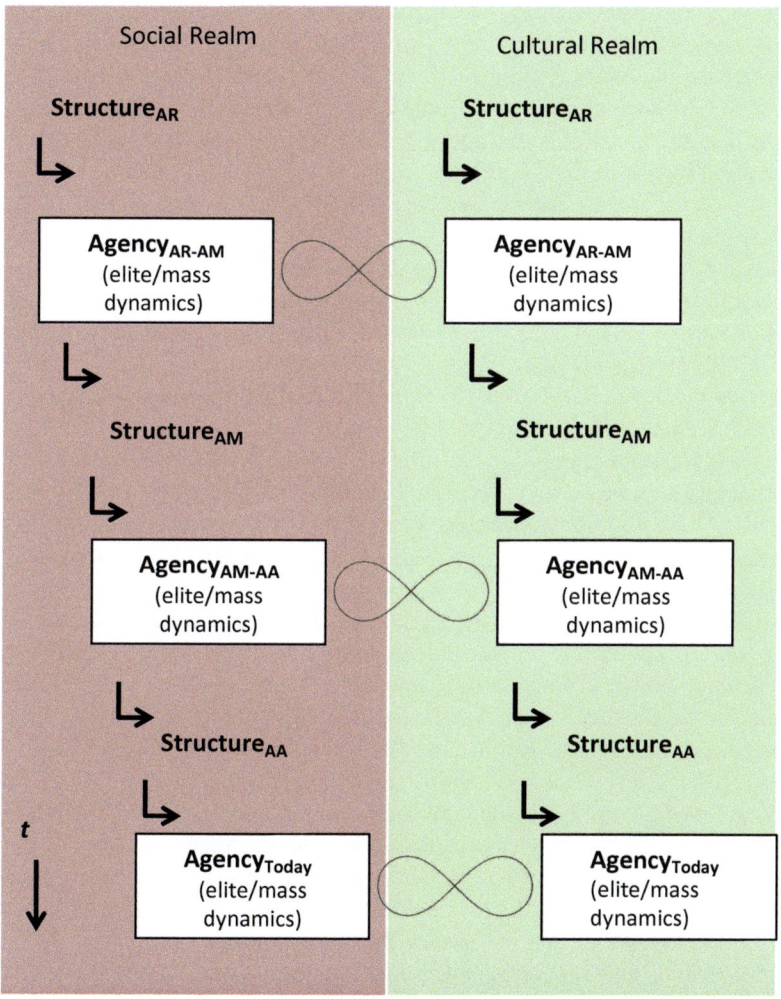

Fig. 6.8 Socio-cultural change in secularization in the West

However, I will not provide a very detailed explanation for cultural agency (groups and masses) because Taylor himself described changes in the social realm in terms of elite-mass dynamics, whereas he does not do so as much in the cultural realm. I will assume here that cultural changes are usually triggered at the level of ideas, which only involve elites and which frequently reach the masses through venues in the social structure (education, media, etc.).

It is only natural to refer to Taylor's meta-narrative, already exposed in Chaps. 2 and 3, to substantiate the account below. For the most part, references will be avoided, unless they refer to sections of *A Secular Age* or *Modern Social Imaginaries* not previously explained.

(a) Socio-Cultural Structure$_{AR}$. The Ancien Régime structure is described as having the following features in the cultural realm: an idea of the cosmos and a higher time, a view of forms defining the nature, status and role of each entity in such a cosmos, and an enchanted view of the world. In Western culture, Christianity is, for the most part, the over-arching interpretation of man and the world. At the social level, society is seen as an organic reality, where "belonging" happens through different orders and smaller social groups; there is a predominant Paleo-Durkhemian dispensation by which the Church gives strength to all social norms and institutions through an "enchanted" worldview; there is symbiosis between Pre-Axial and Axial religious practices.

Such a structure is bound to change through a number of Agency-events, which will be described starting with those in culture. This is because the process of secularization starts with new theoretical insights at the level of intellectual elites.

(b) Cultural Agency$_{AR-AM}$. Taylor shows how a host of intellectual changes occurred at this level, particularly in *Modern Social Imaginaries* and in the first two parts of *A Secular Age* (Taylor 2007: 25–295).

The first work mentioned above fully develops Taylor's explanation of the cultural changes implied in the advent of modernity in the eighteenth and nineteenth centuries. Along with the appearance of modern science, one of the most important elements here is the advent of the Modern Moral Order (MMO), which in time replaces any form-based understanding of society (Taylor 2004: 9–10). Human self-understanding starts to shift out from its embodiment in culture, society and cosmos, bringing about a disembodied agency (Taylor 2004: 51–59, 62). A more rational (and, hence, disenchanted) view of the world is promoted by Christianity towards the dominance of an Axial-religious view, along with ideals of Reform (Reformation and Counter-Reformation) (Taylor 2004: 49–67).

Among the elites, there was a shift from a courtesy stance into civility, which in theory included a more benevolent attitude toward the masses, and the passing from war-centered policies of power expansion towards commerce-centered ones (Taylor 2004: 70–76). The notion of the public sphere appears as a place for conversation on political matters that is also a benchmark for political legitimacy (Taylor 2004: 86, 96 and 99). The distinction between the public and the private (family, economics) appears and unfolds, particularly encouraged by Protestant theology (Taylor 2004: 101–102). Political structures start to be considered as depending on the idea of nation as a collective agency existing in secular time and an egalitarian-horizontal one (Taylor 2004: 155–61).

In regard to the views on the place of religion in society, Taylor mentions the changes carried out by Providential Deism (Taylor 2007: 221–69) and the appearance of the Impersonal Order perspective (Taylor 2007: 270–95). These elements, along with MMO, provided the basis for the gradual development of "exclusive humanism" as an option first available to the elites as an alternative to the Christian worldview. The development of a critique against revealed religion in favor of "natural religion" also facilitated with the drive into "exclusive humanism" (Taylor 2007: 288–95). In general, criticism against the Christian faith intensifies in the eighteenth century and focuses on its irrational character, its authoritarianism, the fact that it poses intractable problems to theodicy or tries to avoid them (particularly that of evil), and the fact that it threatens the order of mutual benefit proper to MMO (through practices of self-denial of the body and sensual satisfaction, or the mortification of others in similar terms, or threatening those who promote MMO) (Taylor 2007: 305). Another line of criticism was directed toward the theological justification of the clergy and their prerogatives.

It is not too difficult to see how many of these developments correspond to the Scenario (vii) already described: for instance, the quarrel between Protestantism and Catholicism and the Impersonal Order's view. Others belong to the case of Scenario (viii): for example, the early appearance of modern science and MMO in the context of Providential Deism, or the early notion of the public sphere. In time, this kind of cultural agency would show its enormous morphogenetic potential.

(c) Social Agency$_{AR-AM}$. A number of Agency-events by political, secular, social and religious elites, as well as reactions by the masses, characterize the social process at this level. Generally speaking, social structural changes include the appearance of political democratic revolutions, the development of capitalism (Taylor 2004: 69–82), the application of "civilized" policies as the expression of state-disciplined societies (2004: 33–50), the gradual establishment of the media as networked outlets for the discussion of public issues (2004: 83–84, 92–93). At the level of the family as an institution, there is a shift from a patriarchal-organic view into a hierarchical complementary one (Taylor 2004: 144–45).

Chronologically, the most important steps leading to structural morphogenesis in regard to the place of religion in society, according to Taylor, are:

- Secularized intellectual elites start by diffusing their views among elites in general.
- Elites diffuse the new views into the masses through standardized education, literacy, larger levels of schooling, and army conscription.
- Religious elites challenge their secular counterparts at the level of ideas.
- Religious elites implement practices aimed at "purifying" religion form Pre-Axial forms. They distance authentic religion from the masses' religiosity. Similarly, secular elites promote the eradication of superstition and magic. As a consequence, there is mutual estrangement between elites and masses. However, popular religious celebrations remain as a source of identity for the latter.

- The masses change the forms of their religious life due to the challenges of industrialization, urbanization, migration and loss of community life.
- Religious elites seek to revitalize the spiritual life of the masses, who react positively (at least for some time, particularly in rural France) to a more compassionate approach, the acceptance of more practices of popular religiosity, and a heart-centered piety. Moreover, mobilization of the masses through voluntarily-joined lay associations is also very well received. (All these elements would constitute the new religious forms that appeared at this stage).
- In France, the political and religious elites during the Restoration modify the strongly hierarchical social order with one (in theory) much more based in the complementarity of the social orders.
- While industrialization progressed, masses and the middle-classes distance themselves from organized religion because it became identified with an unjust economic and social statu quo. Class conflict, urbanization and industrialization exacerbated this. The masses find in varieties of exclusive humanism ways to fill the void they felt as a consequence.

The social dynamics just described correspond to the previously mentioned Scenarios (iii) and (iv). Most of them belong to the former, since they refer to struggles to eliminate the opponent in a still integrated structure. The above mentioned role played by the union/labor movement corresponds to Scenario (iv) inasmuch as it was a novel reality and it triggered a time of structural disintegration. As it happened with the developments at the cultural level, these social events had an important morphogenetic potential.

(d) Socio-Cultural Structure$_{AM}$. The previously described socio-cultural process crystallizes in the Age of Mobilization (AM) structure in the nineteenth century. From the standpoint of culture, the MMO idea becomes well established as an order promoted by human will. The ideal of mutual benefit becomes something to be actualized *hic et nunc*. There is a stress on the importance of choice, also in the religious realm, in contrast with religiously-ascribed belonging. There is also a stress in the alliance between religion and a given "civilizational order" defended and promoted by the state. The view of a disenchanted world to be shaped by human willed, organized and disciplined activity becomes increasingly widespread.

From the perspective of social structure, there is an "immediate access" of the individual to all levels of society, politics and economics. All such structures are aimed at mobilizing individuals through persuasion or coercion. National structures gain strength (along with nationalistic ideals). The place of religion in the social corresponds now to a predominantly Neo-Durkhemian dispensation in which it legitimates a given political order and a national identity.

Structure$_{AM}$ will change, in turn, due to the Agency-events described below.

(e) Cultural Agency$_{AM-AA}$. During the nineteenth century, trajectories of unbelief are multiplied and enriched prior to their diffusion (Taylor 2007: 377–419). At the beginning, they gained momentum due to the ways in which new developments in Biblical criticism undermined traditional Christian beliefs and, more importantly, through a materialistic stance towards reality inspired in Darwin's theory of evolution. This materialistic outlook was seen as proper to adulthood, as an option that reflects the right ethical position of man towards life, whereas religion was considered childish (Taylor 2007: 361–76). Later, these trajectories toward unbelief grew in diversity. Carlyle, Arnold and Ward, in the United Kingdom, embraced Impersonal Deism, whereas J.S. Mill did the same and espoused a materialistic view of life in which altruism was considered an integral part. In France, we have Saint-Simon and Comte's "religion of man" and anti-clerical Republicanism, with the latter radicalized in Marxism. The post-WWI times witnessed the rise of Nietzschean-inspired Nazism and Fascism, both of which despised religion (Taylor 2007: 352–419).

Parallel to these events, there is a sense in which the eclipse of the transcendent would mean that something has been lost (a loss described as a lack of weight, thickness, depth, or as fragility of meaning, the flatness in the celebration of rites of passage in our existence, or as emptiness in the ordinary life). There is also the realization that the translation of Christian-inspired charity and benevolence into versions of Deism/humanism is too pale in comparison, their sources being mere self-interest or sympathy. The growing awareness of the insufficiency of the identification of the good with accomplishing sets of rules is also worth mentioning (Taylor 2007: 307–21).

Another source of criticism of Christianity is Romanticism, with its sense of the need of harmonious integration of inner desires and the sense of a higher goal, which is achieved in a special way through the access to beauty. In this way, protests against rational Deism rise, as well as critiques to Christianity's doctrines of sin and its consequences in human life (Taylor 2007: 313–17).

In post-WWII times, the appearance of expressive individualism as found in the works by Marcuse, Camus and Sartre, proposed an "ethics of authenticity" that greatly impacted the masses through mass media and the consumer society. This development also posed challenges to religion.

Scenarios (vii) and (viii) correspond to what has been described, particularly the former, since, for the most part of the period of time here covered, religion was kept as part of a Neo-Durkhemian dispensation while increasingly becoming the object of intellectual critique from non-believers. To this criticism one should add that which increasingly came from within Catholicism itself calling for a theological reflection more deeply rooted in the Scriptures, the tradition of the Church Fathers, and Church's liturgy, as well as concerned with engaging in dialogue with industrial society, the increasingly secularized mass media culture, and with other Christian churches and denominations.

(f) Social Agency$_{AM-AA}$. As it has been said, Agency-events by political, secular, social and religious elites, as well as reactions by the masses, characterize the social process at this level. Chronologically, according to Taylor, they are the following:

- Protestant denominations thrive in this order inasmuch as congregations are chosen and lack the hierarchical structure of churches. The masses and the middle-class find in them ways of living their religious life as well as ways of reinforcing their identities and interests (in contrast with the elites). This was less the case in Catholic, Lutheran and Calvinist countries.

- Minority groups keep their allegiances to a given religion also as a means of keeping their political identity.
- Protestant elites promote in the masses an "ordered life" ethos through the avoidance of idleness and wasteful behavior. This, in turn, better prepared the masses to cope with the demands of free market economy.
- The beliefs of the masses are maintained by the Neo-Durkhemian identification of religion with the state. This is notorious in the United Kingdom and the United States, with their sense of "civilizational superiority" and of "American exceptionalism," respectively.
- Catholic religious elites are able to mobilize vast sectors of France's rural population during part of the nineteenth century.
- Efforts at reform (including the Reformation, Counter-reformation, evangelical revivals and the French post-Restoration Church) generate resistance from the masses.
- Masses mobilized by the elites enjoy new kinds of spiritual practices: sodalities and guilds, devotions with strong emotional appeal, disciplined methods for meditation and prayer, certain kinds of liturgy and a more positive ethos.
- Intellectual elites who espoused versions of exclusive humanism diffuse their views not only to other intellectuals and elite members but also to the masses through different institutional means (political, educational, media). Post-WWI nihilism also begins to spread.
- In Europe, the post-WWII emerging middle class, with its rapidly expanding experience of affluence, along with the appearance of the mass media society, and the enhancement of individual freedom in regard to social conventions, finds itself gradually alienated from religion due to its interest in the enjoyment of life *hic et nunc*, since that option is now available.

Whereas a good number of the above mentioned social dynamics are aimed at structural integration, the last Agency-events show also signs of Scenarios (iii) and (iv).

(g) Socio-Cultural Structure$_{AA}$. The socio-cultural process just described leads to the establishment of a new socio-cultural structure—that of the Age of Authenticity (AA)—in the post-WWII times, particularly in the 60s and conspicuously in 1968 through the May Revolution in Europe. This matrix is characterized, from the standpoint of culture, by the breaking of the link between civilizational order and religion. Expressive individualism crystallized as a mass phenomenon by way of an "ethics of authenticity." Criticisms of the dominant "system" until then included those against mechanistic ties between people, the prevalence of instrumental reason, the belief of the superiority of reason over the body, and the divisions between reason and feelings, study and work, and of work and play.

From the standpoint of the social, consumer culture practically touches each and every structure. The rise of the middle class, its affluence and greater social and geographical mobility, the appearance of suburbia with its focus on the nuclear family and the loosening of its community ties, and the risk of overwork and stress due to the drive towards two income households, are all new phenomena that impacted society as a whole. Particularly important is the spread of television and the alliance of the media with large businesses. Consumerism as a way of life affected large segments of the population, particularly the youth. Some of these negative effects included self-centeredness, the decline of political involvement, and the predominance of individualistic utilitarian ethics.

In the case of religion in society, we find a Post-Durkhemian dominant dispensation in which religion is disconnected from the political system and is seen primarily as a matter of choice, even as a matter of taste. There are also tensions in this regard since some groups push back towards a Neo-Durkhemian dispensation. However, there are also positive elements coming from the "ethics of authenticity," such as the linkage of the innermost human longings and religion/spirituality, that can be rescued and that can also shape contemporary ways of religiosity.

We also find that at the present time, in regard to religion, we live it in an immanent frame that is de facto tilted towards immanence. The place of religion in the life of society, groups and individuals can be described as complex and ambiguous today. Along with the groups of people who "dwell" in a given religious tradition, and with other groups who profess atheism and agnosticism, there is a large segment of the population that stays somewhere in a myriad of intermediate positions. These individuals are "seekers" looking for a deeper experience of the sacred, one that connects to their own desires and intimations. There is an associated interest in acquiring unity and wholeness. The figures of "pilgrim" and "convert" are close to this existential stance. Many of these persons have previously been affiliated with a particular branch of Christianity. However, they are now keeping a distance from it. When they engage the tradition is primarily for partaking in rites of passage and the like. This is not to say that they do not care at all about organized religion in the way that was traditional in the West, but that while keeping a particular tradition as a point of reference, they do not want to abide by its authority structures.

Taylorean social theory does not stop here but also gives an analysis at the level of agency of what has come after the establishment of a Socio-Cultural Structure$_{AA}$.

(h) Cultural Agency$_{Today}$. Taylor mentions two as the main dynamics in culture in the West today in regard to religion: that of being cross-pressured, and that of facing dilemmas. The first refers to the fact that most people in the West live under the solicitation of two opposing claims in regard to the fullness of human life, one coming from secular humanism and unbelief, and the other from orthodox religion (mostly Christianity). However, these polar positions are not able to offer an apodictic proof of their claims, but fragilize each other by questioning such claims and seeing each other as embracing shallow ethical commitments.

The second dynamic includes the dilemmas both polar positions face, which can be grouped in four general topics: humanism and transcendence; the demand for wholeness for human fulfillment; the relationship between our drives for sex and violence on the one hand, and religious or secular commitments on the other; and the acquisition of meaning. Both polar positions face difficulties in overcoming such dilemmas.

The consequence of this situation is that just a relatively small group of people are able to "break" the immanent frame. Their experiences are diverse and, as such, open a diversity of paths. Some involve a contemplative stance, focused on a larger order different from the ordinarily immanent one; others involve a self-transformation, while others partake of both. There is a realization of the existence of a gap between the larger order and the immanent one, before different stances can be taken, which would also include philosophical, political and cultural positions. New languages are developed by these "breakers" to explain themselves (Taylor 2007: 728–72).

(i) Social Agency$_{Today}$ Expressed in terms of elite-masses dynamics, most important in Taylor's view are (Taylor 2007: 473–504):

- Economic elites use "expressivism" as a means of marketing. The result is an enormous impact on the masses.
- Some elites see the "culture of authenticity" as eroding key institutions in the West and oppose those elites who promote it. Some of the former, particularly in the United States, seek to re-establish a Neo-Durkhemian dispensation.
- Some elites, particularly those involved in the IT industry, move from an "ethics of authenticity" into something much shallower. They focus on sex and sensuality as a means of self-improvement and turn themselves into "money makers."
- Pluralism of all kinds is greatly widened in the West.
- Secular humanist movements in Catholic countries in the West have less success when compared with those in Protestant countries.
- Some masses maintain particular religious beliefs either because they have no access to others, or because they support their identity in such beliefs.
- Youth, generally speaking, is alienated from traditional religion because of clerical reform "from the top" and the moralism and repression of sexual life. This particularly affects young adult Catholics.
- Catholic religious elites remain closed to the demands of an "ethics of authenticity."

In spite of the fact that Socio-Cultural Structure$_{AA}$ has gained a certain degree of stability in the West in the last 50 years, it is not clear that it would not suffer morphogenesis in the near future. Such a possibility is always there due to the surprising ability of human agency to creatively respond to new situations. Moreover, it might be the case that the ethical ideals of modernity (MMO first and "ethics of authenticity" afterwards) may need religion as a source of moral motivation and as an antidote to the Postmodern, Neo-Nietzschean "ethics of affirmation." This might entail a new re-location of religion. It remains to be seen, however, what organized Christianity—which has greatly grown in non-Western areas around the globe—will be able to do in the West.

6.5   Nature and Scope of Taylorean Social Theory

All the important elements pertaining to Taylor's meta-narrative of secularization have been recast in the analytical framework of what I have called Taylorean social theory. By so doing, I have tried to make clear to social scientists what *A Secular Age* may bring to the sociological debate on secularization. As I mentioned at be beginning of the previous section, it becomes apparent that Taylor's meta-narrative needs an elaboration of how cultural changes have been caused by elite-masses dynamics. However, my focus at this point is to clarify the nature and scope of Taylorean social theory.

My first comment is that the strength of Taylorean social theory's conclusions relies in the combination of the kind of morphogenetic analysis developed in the last section with its elaboration into a thick phenomenological narrative. Without it, they just appear to offer a lengthy but too schematic account. On the contrary, it is from the perspicuity of the analysis of the current experience of Westerner living in an immanent frame as expressed in a narrative that the causal explanation of how did it take place draws its validity. However, in the light of what has been said so far, the narrative offered in *A Secular Age* (although greatly erudite) is only one of the several possible interpretations of Western secularization that Taylorean social theory might propose.

Taylorean social theory has a strong cultural-sensitivity. It always pays important attention to the cultural realm, the integration of which, at the structural level, is analyzed by asking about logical consistency, which is a feature proper of Western rationality since its inception (Taylor 1985: 136–39).

Because of its methodological assumptions, Taylorean social theory makes any sociological description of the process of structural change in Western secularization amenable of different interpretations. This is not just because the social sciences are hermeneutic per se. An added point here is the fact that everyone in the West is subject to the modern imaginary framework. In this sense, the concepts and language in which Taylorean social theory is couched should be changed in the future if Western social imaginaries shift dramatically, or when studying other cultural contexts (Taylor 2004: 167–173).

Taylorean social theory is proposed as an interpretive tool for studying Western secularization, which is a macro-social process.

The considerations done so far rise questions about the feasibility of applying my interpretation to non-Western settings, or to meso- and micro-social processes. These issues will be mentioned again later. At this point, it is time to compare Taylorean social theory with other sociological accounts of secularization in the West. Such exploration will take place in the following chapter, where I discuss how Taylorean social theory compares with "orthodox" and "counter-orthodox" theories of secularization.

References

Abrams P (1982) Historical sociology. Cornell University Press, Ithaca

Archer MS (1985) Structuration versus morphogenesis. In: Eisenstadt SN, Helle HJ (eds) Macro-sociological theory: perspectives on sociological theory. SAGE Publications, London, pp 58–88

Archer MS (1988) Culture and agency: the place of culture in social theory. Cambridge University Press, Cambridge

Archer MS (1995) Realist social theory: the morphogenetic approach. Cambridge University Press, Cambridge

Bellah RN (1985) Tokugawa religion: the cultural roots of modern Japan. Free Press, New York

Bourdieu P (1984) Distinction: a social critique of the judgment of taste. Harvard University Press, Cambridge, MA

Bourdieu P, Wacquant Loïc JD (1992) An invitation to reflexive sociology. University of Chicago Press, Chicago

Buckley WF (1967) Sociology and modern systems theory. Prentice-Hall, Englewood Cliffs

Burke P (1980) Sociology and history. George Allen & Unwin, London

Donati P (2011) Relational sociology: a new paradigm for the social sciences. Routledge, London

Dunning E, Hughes J (2013) Norbert Elias and modern sociology: knowledge, interdependence, power, process. Bloomsbury Academic, London

Eisenstadt SN (1963) The political systems of empires. Free Press of Glencoe, London

Elias N (1978a) The civilizing process. Vol 1: a history of manners. Urizen Books, New York

Elias N (1978b) The civilizing process. Vol 2: power & civilty. Urizen Books, New York

Etzioni A (1968) The active society: a theory of societal and political processes. Free Press, New York

Giddens A (1979) Central problems in social theory action, structure and contradiction in social analysis. The MacMillan Press, New York

Giddens A (1984) The constitution of society: outline of the theory of structuration. University of California Press, Berkeley

Habermas J (1987) The theory of communicative action. Vol. 2: lifeworld and system: a critique of functionalist reason. Beacon Press, Boston

Lemert C (2010) What is social theory? In: Elliott A (ed) The Routledge companion to social theory. Routledge, London, pp 3–18

Lipset SM (1967) The first new nation: The United States in historical and comparative perspective. Basic Books, New York

Lockwood D (1964) Social integration and system integration. In: Zollschan GK, Hirsch W (eds) Explorations in social change. Houghton Mifflin, Boston, pp 244–257

Ritzer G (1981) Toward an integrated sociological paradigm: the search for an exemplar and an image of the subject matter. Allyn and Bacon, Boston

Ritzer G (1990) Micro–macro linkage in sociological theory: applying a metatheoretical tool. In: Ritzer G (ed) Frontiers of social theory: the new syntheses. Columbia University Press, New York, pp 347–370

Smelser NJ (1973) Social change in the industrial revolution. University of Chicago Press, Chicago

Sztompka P (1994) The sociology of social change. Blackwell, Oxford

Taylor C (1985) Philosophy and the human sciences, vol 2, Philosophical papers. University Press, Cambridge

Taylor C (1989) Sources of the self: the making of the modern identity. Harvard University Press, Cambridge, MA

Taylor C (1991) The malaise of modernity. Concord, Ontario

Taylor C (1995) Philosophical arguments. Harvard University Press, Cambridge, MA

Taylor C (2002) Language and society. In: Rasmussen DM, Swindal J (eds) Sage masters of modern social thought. Vol. 4: Jurgen Habermas. Sage, London, pp 123–135

Taylor C (2004) Modern social imaginaries. Duke University Press, Durham

Taylor C (2007) A secular age. Belknap Press of Harvard University Press, Cambridge, MA

Taylor C (2008) Akbar Ganji in conversation with Charles Taylor. In: The immanent frame. http://blogs.ssrc.org/tif/2008/12/23/akbar-ganji-in-conversation-with-charles-taylor/. Accessed 28 June 2015

Taylor C (2010) Afterword: Apologia pro libro suo. In: Warner M et al (eds) Varieties of secularism in a secular age. Harvard University Press, Cambridge, MA, pp 300–321

Tilly C (1976) The Vendě. Harvard University Press, Cambridge, MA

Touraine A (1977) The self-production of society. The University of Chicago Press, Chicago

Touraine A (1985) Social movements and social change. In: Borda OF (ed) The challenge of social change. Sage, London, pp 77–92

Not really said much and lacking crucial reference to concrete cases to feel grounded. descriptive summary in the form of analysis.

Chapter 7
Taylorean Social Theory and the "Orthodox" and "Counter-Orthodox" Models

Abstract Taylorean social theory brings new insights to the debate on secularization in the West. In order to articulate them, this chapter compares it with both the "orthodox" and "counter-orthodox" models. In each case, it explores the ways in which my views criticize these theories and furthers the conversation by explaining secularization, I think, more perspicuously and by proposing new issues. In regards with the "orthodox" model, along with criticisms shared by many about social facts not substantiating its claims, it considers that reducing religion as epiphenomenal misinterprets social facts in themselves, sees structural differentiation as not elimination the role of religious motivations, and calls into question the possibility of a strict secular/religious divide. In regard to rational choice theory (RCT), Taylorean social theory main criticism is to its naturalistic methodology, its views of systems as closed, the way RCT privileges instrumental rationality over others, and its interpretation of religious allegiances based exclusively on acts of choice. RCT is seen as unduly stressing structures in detriment of human agency, and social factors in detriment of cultural ones. Taylorean social theory offers positive arguments into the debate when it redefines secularization as religious change, and brings back the cultural factors operative in that social process, as well as the morphogenetic role of human agency (via social movements). Among the pending tasks of Taylorean social theory it needs to produce a clearer set of criteria to incorporate the results of (less hermeneutically-oriented) studies from mainstream sociology, as well as explaining social movements dynamics.

Keywords Theories of secularization • Orthodox model • Rational choice theory • Compared studies • Epiphenomenal religion • Hermeneutics • Structural differentiation • Social movements • Post-secular studies • Naturalistic methodology • Closed social systems • Religious change • Human agency • Morphogenesis

This chapter explores the new insights Taylorean social theory brings to the debate on secularization in the West. In order to articulate them, I will compare it with both the "orthodox" and "counter-orthodox" models. In each case, I will explore the ways in which my views criticize these theories and furthers the conversation by explaining secularization more perspicuously and by proposing new issues. I will also examine the ways in which the "orthodox" and "counter-orthodox" views may

© Springer International Publishing AG 2017   169
Germán McKenzie, *Interpreting Charles Taylor's Social Theory on Religion and Secularization*, Sophia Studies in Cross-cultural Philosophy of Traditions and Cultures 20, DOI 10.1007/978-3-319-47700-8_7

better explain some aspects of secularization. I will also explore some weaknesses I see in my Taylorean social theory. As I have said before, whenever I cite Taylor's ideas in this chapter I am using them to substantiate my own views and not to express aspects of his thought as such.

7.1   Social Theory in Dialogue with the "Orthodox" Model

As a starting point, I will briefly review the main characteristics of social change in the "orthodox" model and compare them with those in Taylorean social theory.

7.1.1   The "Orthodox" View of Social Change

An explanation of the social changes involved in the "orthodox" account of secularization is presented in Fig. 7.1 (next page). There, filled arrows represent causal relationships. Social change happens here mostly through macro-social processes as described in Chap. 1. Although cultural-related phenomenon, such as the Reformation and the appearance of modern science, seems to trigger the process, the following causes in time are mostly socio-structural. In the end, religious pluralism corrodes the universal claims of religion and turns it into something private and relative. The consequence is the irrelevance and marginalization of religion in society.

What kind of process of social change is at work here? Figure 7.2 (second next page) summarizes the answer to this question while comparing it with Taylorean social theory.

Although the process of social change is not linear but multi-linear, it is certainly irreversible, which means that it is also "developmental" in the sense that each stage accumulates the effects of the previous ones. The causes of the process are wholly internal to it (endogenous), operating very much at the societal level and pressing changes at the level of religious organizations and the life of individuals.

However Steve Bruce, following Bryan Wilson, identifies religious pluralism, relativism and privatization as the key forces in the decline and marginalization of religion, the underlying factors that drive religion out seem to be science and technology, and their impact in the way humans understand themselves and the world (Bruce 2002: 16–21). Since religion is a social construct that remains operative inasmuch as it retains some social function, there is little reason for its existence now that science or non-religious ideologies accomplish the same functions even better. The outcome of secularization is a new situation, qualitatively different in regard to the place of religion in human life and society.

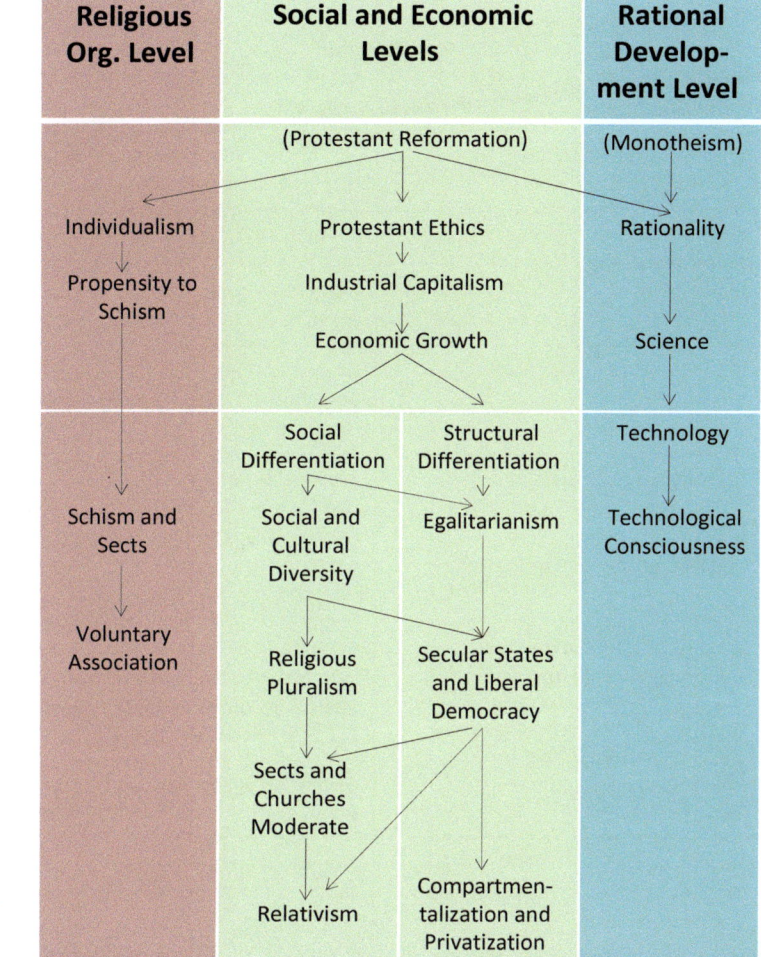

Fig. 7.1   Causal process of secularization in the West according to the "Orthodox" model (Adapted from Bruce 2002: 4)

Many people are unaware of the social process described above, which also suggests very little room for human agency, as individuals have limited power to shape the process of social change. Instead gaining awareness of what is happening, taking distance from it and making decisions on their own, human beings (or social groups) are persuaded of the truth of some ideas or about the good of given ideals primarily by their social interests and social relationships.

Orthodox Model	Taylorean Social Theory
Multi-linear process aimed at decline.	Non-linear, zigzag-shaped process.
Irreversible de facto.	Not necessarily irreversible, but total reversion unlikely.
Cumulative: each stage accumulates the effects of the previous ones.	Partly cumulative, in the case of new religious forms that appear; non-cumulative in the case of older religious forms that survive.
Wholly-endogenous causes.	Causes coming both from within and from without (closed systems do not exist)
The outcome consists of a qualitative change in the place of religion in society (marginalization, irrelevance).	The outcome consists of a qualitative change in the place of religion in society (continuum between religion and exclusive humanism in an immanent frame).
Human agents are unaware of the social process taking place.	Human agents are partly aware and partly unaware of the socio-cultural process happening.
Causation is general and long-lasting.	Causation is concrete and contingent.
Human agency with little influence in the development of the process.	Human agency with great influence in the development of the process.

Fig. 7.2 View of social change implied in the "Orthodox" model and in Taylorean social theory

7.1.2 The "Orthodox" Model Under Critique

Taylor has explicitly criticized "orthodox" theorists at several points in his master-narrative, notably those related to philosophical anthropology and epistemology.[1] However, from the specific standpoint of Taylorean social theory, I want to borrow from him, as from others, the following criticisms that can be derived from my interpretation.

---

[1] Among such topics I would mention: (a) Taylor's idea of humans as self-interpreting beings, who in that very process define ethical goals for their lives; (b) his particular understanding of social sciences as hermeneutical; (c) and his discussion of Close World Structures.

(a) There is no substantive factual support for the affirmation of a necessary and long-lasting set of causes (cumulatively) producing religious decline, as those expressed in Fig. 7.1. Taylor takes pains in showing how facts seem to point to the recognition of different sets of causes operating within particular boundaries of space and in specific and limited timeframes, with different outcomes in regard to religion. This is apparent, for example, in the new forms of religious life which emerged in France in the nineteenth century, after the process of secularization imposed by the French Revolution (Taylor 2007: 444). Another case is the appearance of the denominational system in the United States, which coupled thriving religious forms with modernity (Taylor 2007: 453–54).

Here it is appropriate to recall Taylor's criticism of "substraction theories," those (implicitly) affirming that the cause for a social change was always present, and what sufficed for the phenomenon to occur was the elimination (substraction) of the factors that were preventing such a cause from manifesting itself as such. Taylor criticizes "orthodox" secularization theories for taking this form, without proving the existence of latent causes and their characteristics (Taylor 2007: 26–29, 90, 530–31, 560).

(b) There is no substantive support for rendering religion into an epiphenomenal role in the life of society. This position is methodologically weak, since it renders human motivation as being of very little importance for sociology. In contrast, Taylor—as with Weber—affirms that social sciences should take human motivation as it presents itself and should avoid interpreting it as something else that is regarded as delusional (Taylor 2007: 436). This is not an a priori affirmation of a "religious dimension" in man, but just the confirmation that personal religious interpretations and motivations are social facts and should be taken into account by sociology.

In principle, religious motivation should be considered to be operative in human life, and not as a sole by-product of other forces, nor as epiphenomenal, that is, as being kept alive in human existence by functional imperatives other than religious ones (Taylor 2007: 428–28, 551–580).

(c) There is limited substantial support for affirming a general process of religious decline in the West.[2] While at the societal level there has been a decline in

---

[2] There are, on the contrary, numerous studies that show that at the present time new forms of religious life are appearing in the West, as well as that some of the previously existing religious organizations are undergoing a process of revitalization. In the case of Western Europe as a whole, one could mention McLeod (1997); focused mostly on England, France and Germany one finds Hervieu-Léger (1986: 140–227; 1999: 29–60, 89–155; 2000: 27–41). See also the work by Casanova (1994: 75–91, 135–207).

The British experience is studied by Brown (2001: 16–34, 228–33) and Davie (1994: 45–116). Contemporary religion in France is analyzed by Gauchet (1998: 11–30), Cholvy (1988: 485–95), and Denèfle (1997). This last work is focused on French "nones." The Italian case is the focus of the work by Luca Diotallevi (1999). Contemporary religion is studied in the Canadian context by Reginald Bibby (2004: 55–91, 175–82).

A different case is the United States, which shows high religious vitality, as shown by Kosmin and Keysar (2006: 20–37, 65–88) and Stark (2008: 115–46). For the rise of new religious forms from the 50s on, see Wuthnow (1998a: 1–18, 168–98; 2007: 13–19) and Roof (1993: 241–62; 1999: 294–314).

organized religion's social influence and relevance compared to the past, this does not necessarily amount to its complete marginalization and irrelevance.

At the individual and organizational levels, if the role of religion as provider of meaning is threatened by science, if the universality of religious claims is challenged by rationality, this does not necessarily lead to the demise of the role of religion in the lives of individuals and society. There may well be a "properly religious" operation of religion, at least in the self-understanding of concrete persons and groups who seek it (Taylor 2007: 426, note 5).

(d) The impact of science and technology in modern society, and particularly in the way humans understand themselves and the world, has not completely ruled out religious interpretations. On the contrary, and taking into account modernity and its prolongation in a culture of authenticity, the combination of modern economics and politics with technological dominion over nature has proved to be greatly ambiguous. At the present time, expressivism has also taken new spiritual and religious forms especially in various ecological and holistic movements.

In this context, the establishment of exclusive humanism as an option available to the masses has not been accomplished without uneasiness. The challenges this kind of humanism makes to religion as a source of violence and for impeding holistic human fulfillment just backfires (Taylor 2007: 618–727). Besides, there are human phenomena (like aesthetic experiences) that are not convincingly interpreted by immanent or materialistic perspectives on human life. Furthermore, Postmodernity has brought about an "ethics of affirmation" that puts at risk the dominance of the modern ethical ideas of freedom, human rights recognition, mutual benevolence, and the commitment to diminishing human suffering and to enjoying this-worldly goods.

(e) Pluralism would be corrosive to religion only in the case where a religious tradition would foster uniformity in doctrine and its interpretation. This is not the case, however. Taylorean social theory shares Hans Joas' view of European history, which affirms that religious pluralism has been one of its features, particularly in the case of Judaism and Islam, along with pre-monotheistic religions, which persisted and influenced the way in which Christianity itself was lived in the area (Joas 2008: 24–26).

More significantly, Joas shows how religious institutions that open themselves for discussion, and hence for pluralism, have greater chances for learning and for controlled change. This has been the case of Christianity in Europe for many centuries. Moreover, religious institutions could also embrace pluralisms as a value (and not a necessary threat), which has happened with several branches of contemporary Christianity.

(f) The process of differentiation, along with rationalization as its counterpart, does not entail per se the elimination of religious faith nor religious motivation in

---

Bruce (2002: 60–185, 229–41; 1999: 58–120) interprets the data in the opposite direction, supporting the "orthodox" model by affirming religious decline in England, the precariousness of new religious movements (New Age, Charismatic groups), and considering the advent of Postmodernity as indifferent to the revival of religion.

the life of individuals. With Danièlle Hervieu-Lèger, Taylor affirms that the differentiation of the religious sphere at the societal level, and the concomitant rationalization of norms and interpretation within each sub-system, does not eliminate a situation in which reference to God or to supernatural forces by individuals and groups are ended in regard to their ordinary activities.

Differentiation seems to imply a certain decline of religion only when the latter is bound up with organizational arrangements.

(g) The assumption of a clear-cut divide between the secular and religious in the West, specifically in the public sphere, is not true. It is not even clear in many particular instances where a good amount of effort has been placed on its legal clarification as with the issues related to the church-state separation in the United States, and to the state's *laicité* in France, to mention two examples. This makes it more difficult to affirm that religion (particularly organized religion) has "retreated" from the societal level, since there are various situations in which it still has a strong say in public affairs (in spite of having declined in members and in the rate of religious participation) (Casanova 1994). Besides speaking of ethical matters such as human rights, social justice and the protection of the environment, religion—particularly Catholicism—has also expressed itself in the public sphere on more controversial issues such as abortion, euthanasia, and same-sex marriage. It has still great public influence when it comes to the identities of minorities within Western democracies, which are frequently connected to particular religious traditions.

In several cases in the West, the state relies on religious organization for the accomplishment of specific public roles, due to a variety of cultural and historical reasons.[3] Here, again, a clear-cut distinction between the secular and the religious becomes blurry.

7.1.3 Advantages of Taylorean Social Theory and New Issues

(a) Taylorean social theory contributes to a better understanding of secularization by redefining it as an expression of religious change. This shift recognizes that there has been a relocation of religion within society and individual life. This approach does justice to a number of facts. It concedes the diminution of religion's societal impact. It also acknowledges changes in the relationship between religion and the state and between religion and the public sphere. It also recognizes the decline in personal allegiance to organized religion in the West (except, perhaps, in the United States).[4] However, while doing so, it recognizes that, along with old religious forms that fade away, evidence speaks of the appearance of new ones. So secularization

---

[3] See, for example, in the case of Northern Europe, Casanova et al (2013).

[4] Chaves (2011), however, has been able to document a slow but steady decline of belief in God and, more generally, of religious belief in the United States over the past 50 years.

becomes one aspect of a more complex process of the relocation of religion in society and in individual lives.

(b) Taylorean social theory's view of the relationship between (social and cultural) structure and agency is dialectical and, as such, better reflects what occurs in the process of social change. In this view, on the one hand, human agency is endowed with the capacity to elicit structural changes. More specifically, this is done through the interaction of social groups such as social movements and through processes of social influence carried out by different kinds of leaders. On the other hand, agency is both constrained and empowered by structure. Individual and organizational levels of agency are seen as inherently active and creative within their structural constraints. As a consequence, societal structural changes and their influence on agency, such as those described by the "orthodox" model, are recognized as important, but are complemented with an account of agency aimed at modifying structures. This last element is not sufficiently considered by "orthodox" theorists, as we have seen when analyzing their understanding of social change.

(c) Taylorean social theory links, in its analysis, the social and the cultural realms, through the notion of social imaginary. This is done in a way by which the interplay between both is stressed. Constraints and resources are provided by structures in each realm. It is possible to recognize the development of ideas, language, symbols and ideals without which it would have been impossible for modernity to occur.

This approach complements the "orthodox" model in that it shows how the decline of religion in the West was also a consequence of a complex set of powerful non-material causes. Besides, it also makes room for social influences in the cultural realm. Last but not least, it underscores the importance of cultural changes in the process of secularization, which would not have been possible without the appearance of "exclusive humanism" as an option available to greater numbers of people.

In contrast, "orthodox" theorists convey the image of an agent who is overwhelmed by the pressure exerted on him by social structures. Cultural factors such as the Reformation and the appearance of modern science and the technologies it inspires are mentioned just at the beginning of the process, whereas societal forces account for the most part of it, particularly during the present time. However, as *A Secular Age* shows, the process of secularization in the West cannot be understood without the constant presence of cultural changes all along the way. Thus, for example, the process that occurs from the Ancien Régime, through the Age of Mobilization, to the Age of Authenticity and the present time, would not been possible without the radical change in the passing of people's self-understanding from that of "porous" selves to that of "buffered" ones.

(d) Taylorean social theory assumes the discussion on secularity 3, the condition of belief of individuals at the present time, which should be taken into account in micro sociological accounts of secularization. This has opened new ways of understanding religious and spiritual life, insights that were alien to the "orthodox" model. Among them, is the idea of living in an immanent frame, being cross-pressured between the two poles of transformative religion and an exclusive humanist stance. Besides, the notion of mutual "fragilization" of such poles and the myriad of different middle (and unstable) positions embraced by most people (the Nova and Supernova Effects) provide theoretical tools for further analysis.

7.1.4   What to Keep from "Orthodox" Theories?

I think the "orthodox" focus on religious decline, its causes, processes and outcomes, is still relevant for the debate on secularization, and the scholarship developed to date should be taken into account. Decline at the societal, organization and individual levels has been an integral part of the process of religious change in the West, and its proper analysis certainly benefits sociological understanding (Taylor 2007: 530).

However, the "orthodox" model's insights on the impact changes in societal structures have at the organizational and individual levels of religion would need reassessment. The tasks for such reassessment would be, I think, (a) the reinterpretation of "orthodox" studies in the light of a more thoroughly hermeneutical understanding of the social sciences, (b) the discernment of the ways in which the "disappearance" and "epiphenomenal" biases, "substraction theory" and Closed World Structures may be distorting the results of such studies, and (c) the assumption of some of the framework provided by Taylorean social theory.

7.2   Taylorean Social Theory in Dialogue with the Rational Choice "Counter-Orthodox" Model

The "counter-orthodox model," or Rational Choice Theory's account of secularization, is based on a closed-system approach aimed at the explanation of religion in general, regardless of time, geographical or cultural settings (Stark and Bainbridge 1987). Its insights are drawn from a strong parallel with the dynamics of the economic system. A change in the religious system occurred in the West that imposed a Christian "religious monopoly" since the fourth century. With modernity, and particularly with the Reformation, this situation changed again, this time into one of religious pluralism in the context of a "free market of religion." According to Rational Choice Theory (RCT), the secularization process occurs within this last stage in a self-limiting manner (Stark 2011: 175–81).[5] I will begin by reviewing the main features of social change for "counter-orthodox" theorists and will compare them with those in Taylorean social theory.

---

[5] In his view, Roman Emperor Constantine I initiated this shift in the West first with the Edict of Milan of 313 AD, which tolerated Christianity in the Empire, and then turned it into its official religion (although tolerating other religions). In time, political and ecclesiastical events lead to an exclusivist view on the part of Christianity.

7.2.1   The "Counter-Orthodox" View of Social Change

Figure 7.3 (next page) helps one to better understand how the secularization process in the West is explained by RCT theorists.[6] There, as before, filled arrows represent causal relationships.

Social change happens here at two levels. One is the passing from a religious monopoly to a religious free market or vice versa. This is described on the right side of Fig. 7.3 in three stages in regard to the West: the initial situation of religious pluralism—which was mitigated by the fact that it was mandatory to worship the Caesars during the Roman Empire until Constantine I; that of the gradual establishment of a Catholic "religious monopoly" from the third century on; and a new phase of religious pluralisms (in different degrees) as a result of the Reformation and modernity. The factors that explain how we have reached our current situation are presented in Fig. 7.3. However, this kind of change is not the most important one in terms of RCT, although it ensures a greater "efficiency" of the religious system. Stark puts it concisely: "Religious monopolies are not the *normal* state of affairs in societies, although they have been the *usual* state" (Stark 2011: 309).[7] When the passing from a "religious monopoly" to a "religious free market," societies become "desacralized,' which means that social sub-systems become differentiated, affecting the existing organizations (the supply side) with a relative decline, triggering new organizations without diminishing individual religiosity—the demand side, which is taken to be constant (Stark and Finke 2000: 200).

The second kind of social change that is crucial for the explanation of religious behavior, occurs within the religious system at the individual and organizational levels. This consists of the interplay between religious supply and demand which determines the levels of religious vitality in churches, sects and cults. This is noted at the bottom left of Fig. 7.3 by a bracket, labeled as "religious free economy," that encompasses the church to sect/cult dynamics (Stark and Finke 2000: 141–68), and the movement from cult to church (Stark and Finke 2000: 259–76).

Having described the ways in which RCT theorists have interpreted the last five centuries of religious changes in the West, it is appropriate to discern the process of social change at work here. Since the first level of change from monopoly to free market is related to the degree of efficiency of the religious system, but does not explain how the latter works, I will focus on the second level of changes, namely those happening within the religious system. In such a context, it is appropriate to recall that secularization is seen as a self-limiting process, by which religious organizations lower their tension with the surrounding culture and undergo "internal

---

[6] In what follows, I will use the RCT acronym as a synonym of "counter-orthodox" theorists. However, "rational choice theory" is a complex reality that has taken different shapes due to the works of scholars such as George Homans (strongly influenced by behaviorist psychology), James Coleman, Gary Becker and Jon Elster. For an explanation of these changes, see Jan de Jonge (2012: 3–127). Rational choice theory has been applied not only in psychology, economics and religion, but also in political theory, law and ethics.

[7] Rodney Stark, personal communication to the author, 5 June 2014.

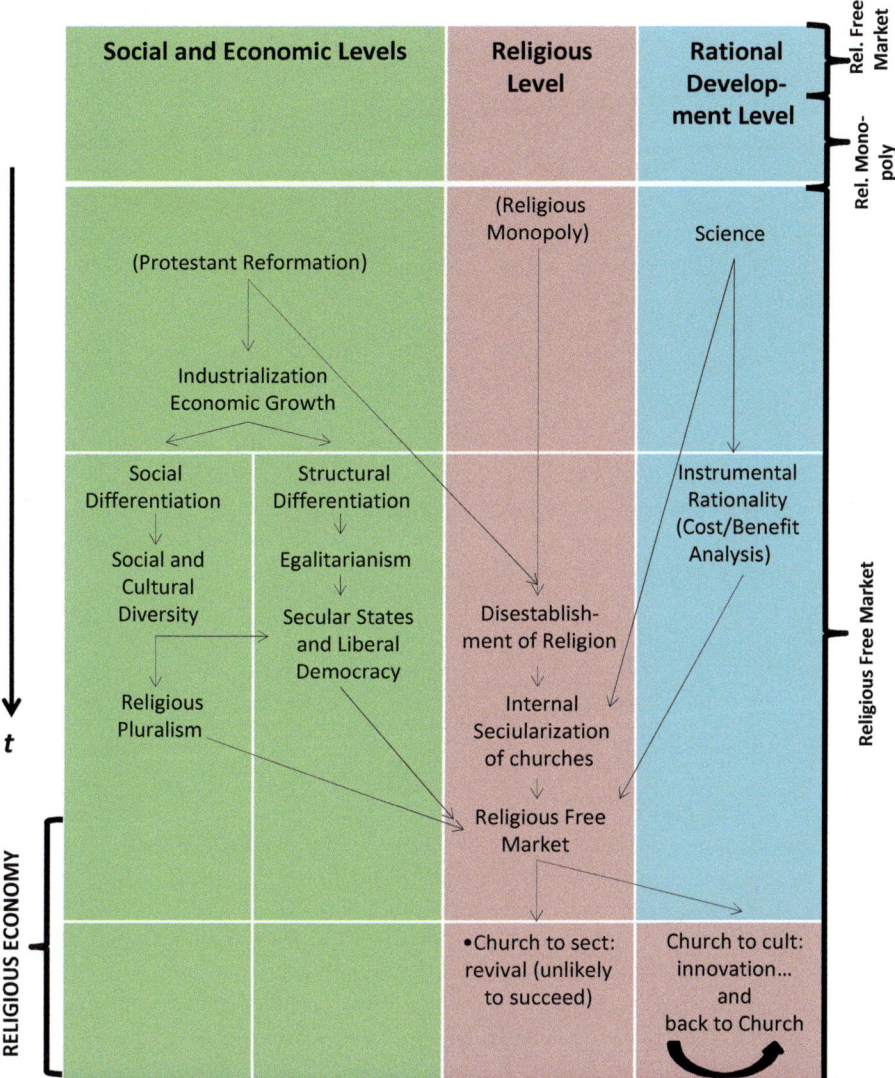

Fig. 7.3 Causal process of secularization in the West according to the "Counter- Orthodox" model (Created from Stark and Finke 2000: 144, 193–217)

secularization." As a result, efforts to go back to higher levels of tension appear within these churches, some of them taking the form of "sects" aimed at revitalizing the existing organization and others becoming "cults" which abandon an existing church and focus on creating a new organization. In time, these reactions tend to turn themselves into churches that again go through a long-term process of secularization. And the process starts again.

RCT sees secularization as a process of change characterized as non-linear and reversible. The forces that drive the social process are endogenous to it, most likely manifest to the agents, and rooted in the human desire to freely choose the kind of other-worldly spiritual compensator they see fit. RCT, in appearance, gives room for human agency inasmuch as "religious choice" is its basis. It also gives a prominent role to the voluntary nature of individual participation in religious organizations.

Figure 7.4 (next page) compares these views by RCT with those of Taylorean social theory. This very same human agency would also be responsible for making secularization a self-limiting process (through the church to sect/cult dynamic), although this outcome as such is latent to the agents. Like other closed-structural systems, the processes of social change within RCT's account of secularization focus on the preservation of the system, establishing equilibrium and safeguarding functionality over time.

7.2.2   The "Counter-Orthodox" Model Under Critique

Taylorean social theory's criticism of RCT will borrow, as it happened in regard to the "orthodox model," from Taylor's own views on the matter. His critique of RCT has not been explicitly developed. Not a word is mentioned about it nor its proponents in *A Secular Age*, except a reference to Finke's work on urbanization and secularization in the United States mentioned in Chap. 5. One needs to go into other works by Taylor to uncover his position.[8] Herein, there are a number of theoretical issues that are in sharp contrast with Taylor's philosophical views and his thinking on the social sciences.

(a) The "counter orthodox" model, as developed by Stark, Finke and Bainbridge claims to be a universal explanation of religious behavior regardless of cultural differences. It is, then, a "grand" or over-arching theory (Stark and Bainbridge 1987: 11). This approach is developed in a way that belongs to what Taylor calls a "naturalistic" view of the social sciences, as was explained in Chap. 4. This is not because RCT is structured as a deductive theory based on a set of definitions and propositions (Stark and Bainbridge 1987: 13–21; Stark and Finke 2000: 277–86), but because it is carried out in a way that parallels the natural sciences. As Stark and Bainbridge put it,

> It is only through the use of abstract concepts, linked by abstract propositions, that science exists. Consider a *physics* that must generate a new rule of gravity for each object in the universe. And it is precisely the abstract generality of science that makes it possible for social science to contribute anything to our understanding of history. (Stark and Bainbridge 1987: 22–23)[9]

---

[8] Taylor (1964) develops a philosophical critique of behaviorist psychology in his first book, which is shown to be unfruitful and confused in many ways, proving the invalidity of at least one kind of mechanistic interpretation of human behavior.

[9] Italics are mine.

Counter-Orthodox Model	Taylorean Social Theory
Non-linear.	Non-linear, zigzag-shaped process.
Reversible .	Not necessarily irreversible, but total reversion unlikely.
Non-cumulative: within a free religious economy aimed at homeostasis.	Partly cumulative, in the case of new religious forms that appear; non-cumulative in the case of older religious forms that survive.
Wholly-endogenous causes.	Causes coming both from within and from without (closed systems do not exist)
The outcome consists of homeostasis.	The outcome consists of a qualitative change in the place of religion in society (continuum between religion and exclusive humanism in an immanent frame).
Human agents are aware of the religious supply/demand process taking place.	Human agents are partly aware and partly unaware of the socio-cultural process happening.
Causation is general and long-lasting in the supply/demand process.	Causation is concrete and contingent.
Human agency is stressed in appearance. However, it is not able to provoke structural change beyond the passing from the monopoly to free market modes and vice versa.	Human agency with great influence in the development of the process and in structural change.

Fig. 7.4 View of social change implied in the "Counter-Orthodox" model and in Taylorean social theory

As we have seen, Taylor thinks that anything like an all-encompassing theory that may predict social behavior as RCT pretends to do is misleading. In contrast, for him, the social sciences should recognize their unavoidably interpretive nature, not just in the sense of interpreting any given set of data, but in recognizing that there is little data which may not need interpretation in itself. More importantly, it is crucial for Taylor to take into account the particular self-interpretations that humans give of their social behavior. Such self-interpretations are part of the specific identity of such human persons and underscore the importance of the context of culture, society and personal morality in which they live. As a consequence, because social facts are always culturally and ethically bound, the knowledge that the social sciences can produce is always particular to the specific group we may be studying and cannot be made into a general theory.

Lastly, Taylor thinks that individual religious motivation, when taken seriously into account by sociology, necessitates a *Verstehen*-oriented methodology, which cannot be separated from considerations on the self-interpretations carried out by the subject of study and also by those of the social scientist. RCT ignores this specific methodological dimension.

(b) Another general criticism is that RCT is a closed system—as is foundational for functionalism and structuralism. Taylor insists that it is impossible to interpret any social phenomenon as a closed system. He has consistently been critical of any view of the social sciences that puts aside what he sees as a constant feature of human beings as "self-defining animals," persons who continuously interpret themselves and their circumstances (Taylor 1985b: 55).[10]

Self-interpretations *de facto* change in human lives and affect human practices, institutions, and ideals in society. This makes the social science enterprise, necessarily and always, an open-ended one. Hence, in Taylor's view, any social theory that would delineate a closed system and place its object of study within is inadequate. In such context, any aspiration to identify and anticipate which social variables would remain constant and which would change, and in this way allow the scientist to work with all the variable combinations of change and stability in such a system and thereby predict knowledge, would necessitate "to have explicited so clearly the human condition that one would already have pre-empted all cultural innovation and transformation. This is hardly in the bounds of the possible" (Taylor 1985b: 57). As a consequence, the use of systems theory in the social sciences should always consider such systems as open.

(c) From what has been said so far, is clear that an important area of divergence is that of the understanding of human beings implied in the RCT approach. It is pertinent to recognize the fact that one of the most attractive aspects of the "counter-orthodox" model is that, by speaking of individual "preferences and tastes" which motivate their rational choices, and by affirming that such choices are taken according to a cost/benefit calculus (Stark and Finke 2000: 85–87), RCT claims to be suitable to studying any particular choice regardless of the substance of the preference or differences due to culture and society.[11] In this way, it appears to be a conceptual tool suitable for general use. It also carries a particular view of the individual, the

---

[10] The reference is to a piece titled *Interpretation and the Sciences of Man*.

[11] This may lead to some paradoxical consequences, such as the interpretation of ethical decisions taken in an Aristotelian or Kantian fashion as being governed by cost/benefit analysis, that is, a utilitarian perspective. The same happens with phenomena like altruism, heroism and ethical decisions which entail a long-term process of enduring difficulties.

influence of his context, the way he discovers the options available to him at any given moment, and the criteria for making a decision.

A first criticism here refers to the radically individualistic understanding of humans that is implied. In contrast to this, Taylor affirms that it is not possible for people to form (and pursue) any specific preference without being and actually living as embedded beings, which means that the sense of who we actually are (which predates any preference and choice we could make) depends on our self-interpretations (nurtured by our own culture and social network) as well as on our ethical understanding ("moral frameworks") of what a good life is (Taylor 1991: 31–69). RCT's strategy has been that of assuming that all these elements can be already found and summarized in the ways in which our individual preferences are construed (Stark and Finke 2000: 86; Becker 1996: 16–18).[12] However, is this really possible? Is the act of choosing according to our individual preference for a particular religious organization—which is also the result of a given culture and language, an understanding of the path to a good and flourishing human life—able to include all these elements for what they are? Or put differently, is it true that the structural constraints on the religious preferences of a human agent are mainly operative when he seeks to maximize them in the outside world through the greater decrease of religious costs? The answer Taylor would give is the negative, considering such understanding as representing an atomistic view of human beings. In contrast, he affirms that social and cultural structures condition not just the very process of religious preference construction, but even the criteria for discerning what "maximizing rewards and minimizing costs" would mean. More concretely, this means that individuals also conceive their preferences and make their decision in reference to collective social or cultural realities.

One could argue that all these cultural and social conditioning factors are already presupposed when an individual, according to RCT, construes his preferences and chooses a course of action. This could even mean that structural elements, for example, conformity to social norms and values, can be preferred and may guide our actions proven that they maximize gains and minimize costs. However, this view does not address the question if structure can be really incorporated into agency in that way. Taylorean social theory affirms, in contrast, that this view of the individual, of the way in which he constructs his preferences and of his subsequent choices cannot be understood as a constant feature of mankind, but as a result of a particular (Western modern/Postmodern) self-understanding which predates it and that has been shaped by social and cultural structures. It also means that if RCT is adequately able to give an account of social phenomena in a given context, it would be because those under study share an atomistic self-understanding.

Second, there is a need for greater precision in regard to what "preferences" are for RCT. While "counter-orthodox" theorists do not differentiate between kinds of preferences, Taylor speaks differently. For him, human beings are driven by purposes or intentions, which give guidance to their actions. However, purposes that have an ethical content have a particular importance, since the moral goods we

---

[12] For a critique of this positions, see Steven Lukes (1968).

pursue constitute our own identity and ensure our human flourishing (Taylor 1985a: 24–25).[13] These goods constitute "moral frameworks" that give direction to other kinds of purposes, which in turn shape our preferences at a given time. Besides, they command respect not because they have been chosen by an individual, but because of their intrinsic worth. Taylor, then, is clearly in sharp contrast with RCT theorists when he affirms humans are "strong evaluation" makers:

> These [strong evaluations] are the qualitative distinctions we make between different actions, or feelings, or modes of life, as being in some way morally higher or lower, noble or base, admirable or contemptible. It is this language of qualitative contrast that gets marginalized, or even expunged altogether, by the utilitarian or formalist [Kantian] reductions. I want to argue, in opposition to this, that they are central to our moral thinking and ineradicable from it. (Taylor 1985b: 234)[14]

In this view, which is inspired by Aristotelean ethics, there is a crucial distinction between ethical goods and all others: the former are considered as having an intrinsic worth apart from the decision-makers interests of the moment. A set of ethical goods, even when accepted as such by the initiative of a free human agent, are recognized by such agent as valuable in themselves and as having the power of eventually asking the former to give up his own less worthy interests. All other preferences are guided by these sets of what Taylor calls "hyper goods" (Taylor 1989: 62–75), God (religion) being one of them. If a specific cost/benefit calculus yields a result which goes against the intrinsic value of such hyper goods, then it will be superseded by them. In this light, RCT would only be able to rightly assess religious behavior if the population under study would share a "strong evaluation" for utilitarianism, if it would have chosen a utilitarian stance as a hyper good. However, this is not the case cross-culturally.

It could also be claimed that the very process of choosing an ethical good as having intrinsic worth is in a way a manner of maximizing self-interest. Taylor would say that this could be the case whenever a utilitarian stance has become part of the "moral framework" of the human agent. However, this argument just shows how self-interpretations predate the actor's choice, and that a different human agent, coming from a different social and cultural context, might define moral goods for which the meaning of their achievement does not come from a result ulterior to it, but in carrying out the particular action for its own sake (Weber 1947: 116).

These differences within RTC's "preferences" show that there is more to ask from RCT theorists than just distinguishing between this-worldly and other-worldly rewards (Stark and Finke 2000: 88–89). Moreover, choosing a particular religion is to choose a hyper good in the sense that such election constitutes who we are and what direction our good life would take, a goal that is an end in itself and which is not amenable of utilitarian calculus unless culturally conditioned in a particular way (Archer 2000: 51–53).

Third, and closely related to what has previously been said, one may question the relevance RCT gives to instrumental reason, which is characterized by cost/benefit

---

[13] The reference is to a piece titled *What is Human Agency?*

[14] The quote is from a piece titled *The Diversity of Goods.*

calculus, over other forms of human reasoning. In Taylor's view, as it has been seen, humans are ethically bounded and are "strong evaluators" who define for themselves a set of hyper goods which, once established, guide all other preferences they may have. Besides, as explained in Chap. 4, Taylor has also affirmed there are different kinds of rationalities operative in human life which should be considered as interdependent. In spite of his differences with Weber in his characterization of rationalization in the West, Taylor agrees with him in accepting the role of different human rationalities in social action, either alone or combined.[15] In this regard, Weber mentions the following ideal types: (a) substantive reason (*Wertrationalität*) is the one that orients action to absolute values, being these duty, honor, religion, morality or beauty. (b) Affective/expressive reason (*Affektuellrationalität*), which includes the conscious release of emotional tension. (c) Utilitarian reason (*Zweckrationalität*), "oriented to a system of discrete individual ends when the end, the means and the secondary results are all rationally taken into account and weighed" (Weber 1947: 117). Lastly, (d) traditional or habitual reason (*Traditionalrationalität*) would consist of the attachment of habitual forms that can be upheld with different degrees of consciousness. In this light, it can be said that in the "counter-orthodox" model, the role played by ethical commitments and emotions is sidelined when it comes to analyzing human choice (Archer 2000: 45–56; Taylor 1991: 93–108).

As a consequence, RCT's insistence on instrumental rationality entails both reductionism and determinism in the way human choice is understood. In regard to the former, Taylor finds that "economic behaviour can be predictable as some game behaviour can be; because the goals sought and the criteria for their attainment are closely circumscribed to a given domain. But for that very reason, a theory of this kind could never help explain our motivated action in general" (Taylor 1985b: 103). In regard to the latter, such a theory assumes a view of the human being as "preprogrammed by a fixed preference schedule... deprived of the ability to reflect morally upon his preference-set" Archer 2000: 53).

(d) The "counter orthodox" account provides a limited and inadequate view of religious choice. If we see religious choices as elections of hyper goods, Taylor finds "moral frameworks" as a "series of beliefs that give overall shape and direction to a person's values and moral options" (Abbey 2000: 33). They are constitutive of human agency. Because of this, the act of human choice per se is also strongly affected by self-interpretation, so it would be difficult to generalize some of the assumptions RCT theorists consider as constants in the determination of human choice (specifically utilitarian analysis), and even more difficult across cultures (Abbey 2000: 35–53).

Taylorean social theory also agrees with Hans Joas' critique of RCT on the above point (Joas 2008: 24–29). The latter insists on the fact that faith is not based primarily on acts of choice. It is instilled in people through the process of their formation as human persons when young, and eventually assumes more conscious delibera-

---

[15] Max Weber, *The Theory of Social and Economic Organization*, 115–118.

tion afterwards, or it is the fruit of an experience of self-transcendence. This last scenario means that religious allegiance is the result of being "seized" by someone and surrendering ourselves to that reality. It is very important to bear in mind that such an experience is recognized a posteriori. This means that, when it comes to commit to a given religion, we usually find that there is no clear display of options, that we need to keep on searching in some direction, which may prove to be fruitful or not. There is a process through which "preferences" in the RCT sense are construed.[16] In addition, Joas and Taylor also contend that cost/benefit calculations are not strong enough to trigger religious commitment. While being present in the process of assuming a particular religious allegiance, they are not the decisive factors. Taylor finds the more important drives in ethical and expressive reasons. This raises another difference between Taylor and RCT theorists: religion does not consist in the first place of general explanations of existence (Stark and Finke 2000: 91–96), ones that would "provide plans designed to guide actions" (Stark and Finke 2000: 87). On the contrary, a religious tradition attracts us because it appears to be a particular path to a greater good. A universal search for meanings (or explanations) would describe the view of a modern-minded external observer of the religious landscape and not that of a religious person (Taylor 2007: 679–80, 717).

(e) There is no reason to suppose that the demand side of the "religious economy" should always be constant, as RCT theorists argue (Stark and Finke 2000: 85–87; Becker 1976: 5). This may or may not be so. Taylor's philosophical anthropology clearly portrays the image of a human agent that is, at the same time, embedded and creative. As a consequence, it is completely possible to have situations in which the decline in religious commitment is not due to the absence of a more appealing spiritual tradition than one's own preferences, but because of social and cultural factors acting through structures or groups. This is not to say that there are not other contexts in which we could assume the demand for religion as constant. The point here is to keep the door open for factors arising from both the supply and demand sides.[17]

For example, Nancy T. Ammerman calls for bringing back the demand side this way:

> Much of the theorizing to date has over emphasized the supply side, forgetting that supply and demand always interact with each other. Institutions shape preferences, and preferences shape institutions. And more important, preferences are not an undifferentiated universal out there waiting to be shaped by whatever institutions may come along. (Ammerman 1997: 125)

(f) This last criticism can also be carried out by Taylorean social theory in relation to the dialectic between structure and human agency. In spite of stressing individual choice and the ways the supply-side of the "religious economy" changes in function of the latter, the "counter-orthodox" model turns human agents into

---

[16] Martin Hollis (1987: 64–73) argues against a view of "preferences" which are already given, complete, consistent and determining.

[17] Bruce (1999: 44–54) develops a similar criticism providing several examples in the sociology of religion to illustrate his points. See also the work by Wilson (1966: 15–16).

extremely passive entities. It is not only that agents appear to be "pre-programmed by a fixed preference schedule" always governed by utility, as mentioned before. In addition, there is no possibility for human agency to trigger changes at the structural level in ways not foreseen by the closed system. Even when RCT theorists have extensively studied religious movements in the form of "cults" and "sects" (Stark and Finke 2000: 141–68, 259–76), they have done so that makes their itineraries predictable within their closed system.[18] This could be seen as a positive feature of such theory. However, such a view puts aside the often radical indeterminacy of the goals pursued by such movements and the sometimes non-negotiable nature of the religious purposes of the movement, often pursued as ends in themselves and in a non-utilitarian manner.

In contrast, Taylorean social theory affirms that structure both constrains and enables human agency and that such agency is able to produce systemic changes. This is not the same as saying, as RCT theorists do, that the requirements of the demand-side in the "religious economy" are responsible for changes at the level of religious organizations. In this case, in the end, the system as a whole remains unaltered. In contrast, what is meant here is that the agent "reflectively weighs his or her current circumstances against the attainment of his or her goals, and [...] determines whether the price can be afforded" (Archer 2000: 48). It is the agent who, taking into account his position within social and cultural structures, decides and does so in a way that leaves open the possibility of choosing a path to the transformation of such structures as a real option. In the "counter-orthodox" model, in contrast, "if we recall that preferences are 'given', then it will be seen that the agent is simply a throughput" (Hollis 1987: 68).

What is implied in this criticism is that RCT's understanding of agency is not endowed with the creative power to generate substantive changes in religious social systems. This is clear in the differences I have already pointed out in Fig. 7.4 above, between the "counter-orthodox" model and Taylorean social theory in regard to social change.

(g) Similarly to what has just been said about the social realm, culture is not taken into consideration by RCT as a relevant context in which the individual is inextricably situated, but as being already incorporated in the particular shape of the preferences held by an individual. There are no cultural systemic considerations in regard to humans. However, Ammerman points out the need to consider cultural factors when exploring the conditions under which religious pluralism might foster religious vitality. For her, while religious economy explanations are plausible, they remain partial: "It is culture that defines the value of various human activities and culture that defines the costs and benefits of participation" (Ammerman 1997: 121). It should be added here that, in Taylorean social theory, culture could also redefine the terms in which religious preferences are construed through a wholly non-utilitarian approach.

---

[18] These cannot be understood, as Taylor affirms in *Irreducibly Social Good*, unless social goods are conceptualized as greater than the sum of the individual goods of all participants (1995: 127–145).

Paradoxically, it should be said that instrumental rationality as we know it as applied in economics, a key element in RCT's explanation of human behavior, is a cultural product and not something "naturally" endowed to humans. "It took a whole vast development of civilization before the culture developed in which people do so behave" (Taylor 1985b: 103).[19]

(h) Facts used by RCT to back up their affirmations can be convincingly explained in different ways through the use of non-RCT theories. This argument becomes more important when one considers the "counter-orthodox" claims of being a universal and trans-cultural theory of religion, one better than others. In this case, external explanations that may give a better account of a set of phenomena would question such claims (Martin 2005: 127–28). Bruce makes the case for analyses at the micro-level on denominational mobility, the typical age of converts, the usual pattern of inter-religious marriage and levels of religious participation in marriages, all through factors which would explain these phenomena with equal or better arguments than those marshaled by RCT (Bruce 1999: 54–56).

For his part, Martin affirms that RCT's drive to become all-encompassing makes it go beyond mere observation and leads to the exclusion of a great number of other theories which appear to be equally trustable and comprehensive. This makes Martin to become "hermeneutically suspicious." As with Martin, Taylor has also considered other theorizing, even when he disagrees significantly with it (an example being the work of Steve Bruce). The absence of "counter-orthodox" works in *A Secular Age*, is compensated by Taylor's assessment and critique of the economic approach as applied to the social sciences (Taylor 1985b: 104–105).[20]

(i) Facts do not unanimously support RCT's claims on religious economy dynamics cross-culturally. This "counter-orthodox" theory seems to have better empirical support in studies carried out in the United States, but does not adequately explain religion in other countries. A case in point is that of religious vitality in several European countries where the Catholic Church has been traditionally predominant (Belgium, Italy, Poland, Portugal), which in 2002 was higher than that in countries with two equally competing churches (Hungary, Netherlands and the United Kingdom) (Dobbelaere 2002: 194–95).[21] This contradicts what RCT theorists would predict. Similarly, Mark Chaves and Phillip S. Gorski have shown how the empirical evidence does not support RCT's claim that religious pluralism fosters religious vitality in the cases of Southern and Eastern European countries (Chaves and Gorski 2001: 270–74).

For Taylorean social theory, in contrast, cultural differences are very much taken into account when developing a theoretical matrix relative to the process of secularization.

---

[19] The quote is from a piece titled *Social Theory as Practice*.

[20] The reference is to a piece titled *Social Theory as Practice*.

[21] The same issue is commented by Bruce (1999: 51–52). For a comparison between RCT theory and the Italian case which shows the former unable to satisfactorily explain the latter, see the work by Diotallevi (2001) and Cipriani (2003).

7.2.3   Advantages of Taylorean Social Theory and New Issues

Generally speaking, I think the advantages and novelties that Taylorean social the-ory has brought viz-a-viz the "orthodox" model can also be mentioned in regard to "counter-orthodox" theorists. However, there are several points that need further elaboration. To this end I will draw from the already mentioned criticisms by Ammerman: the need of "bringing back" both culture and the demand side.

(a) Taylorean social theory explains better than RCT how cultural differences affect secularization. For the former, culture plays a large role in the self-understanding of individuals. This needs to be taken into account to properly under-stand their social behavior and preferences. Culture as structure provides constraints on and resources for human agency. As such, it affects the processes of preference-building and constitutes the context in relation to which goals are also weighed. Human agency, in turn, is capable of transforming social structures via social move-ments and social persuasion.

As a consequence, as has been explained before, culture enters into sociological analysis not as expressed in the individual's preferences in the first place, but prior to them as an inescapable personal context which predates choice and is also modi-fied by it. The relocation of the sacred in society in a scenario of religious decline should, in this light, be explained both by cultural and social structures, as well as by the work of human agency at the level of individuals and groups. For this reason, any general process of secularization should be studied as "deflected"—to use Martin's terminology—by the history, cultures and sub-cultures of a given country.

(b) Taylorean social theory brings the demand side back into the analysis. In this sense, it honors the facts by giving greater space to human agency-related factors than the "counter-orthodox" model does. This is done through the recognition not only of the role of instrumental rationality, but also of ethical and expressive ratio-nalities in the discernment of choices. In this way, realities such as affections, goods in themselves, social goods, and self-transcendence experiences are included among the number of factors operative in human agency (and, hence, in human choice). From this perspective, religious change can either occur by changes in the supply side, or in the demand side, or in both.

(c) Taylorean social theory explains better than RCT the relative decline in reli-gious affiliation and religious participation that has characterized secularization in the West. This is something that the "counter-orthodox" model conceives very dif-ferently, considering the phenomenon as a temporary phase of "desacralization" due to the passing from a situation of "religious monopoly" to a "free religious market" (Stark and Finke 2000: 199–201). The pressure that RCT assumptions bear on its analysis makes it very difficult for RCT to consider such a decline as real. However, it is true that changes have occurred not only at the level of secularity 1 (that is, the unlinking of religion from the political system), but also at the level of secularity 2 (religious belief and practice). In the latter case, Taylorean social theory finds not only the appearance of new forms of religious and spiritual life (as in new religious movements), but also a decline of older forms, which correlates, at least in part, with a relative decline in religious belief and practice. Solid evidence of this is the growth of the number of "spiritual but not religious" people in Western Europe and North America.

(d) Taylorean social theory is a thoroughly open-ended endeavor, which contrasts with RCT's "closed system" approach. If one adds to this the insistence by "counter-orthodox" leading theorists such as Stark and Bainbridge that their view is universal and all-encompassing (Stark and Bainbridge 1987: 11–21), it is seriously challenged every time empirical findings do not conform to its assumptions—as happens with any social theory modeled after the natural sciences rather than a hermeneutic stance.

Taylorean social theory does not pretend to have a general methodology for the social sciences, but just a set of basic concepts and guiding principles to be applied ad casum, hermeneutically, on phenomena well limited in time and space. Besides, it is mostly a *post eventu* affaire, which does not presume to entirely predict social human behavior, but only to a certain degree and always for scenarios specifically determined and through a strong discipline of cultural sensitivity. The resulting sociological analyses are, because of such characteristics, immune to the pressures mentioned above. Any narrative reflective of such analyses can be challenged by a rival one that may have interpreted the social data in a different way. However, it draws from Taylor's view on the human sciences to avoid subjectivism and relativism by providing a set of criteria to compare rival interpretations and to determine which one offers more real epistemic gains, as it was been explained in Chap. 4. The best account would be that more capable of offering a more profound explanation of phenomena and of covering more specific cases. It is also one that resolves the contradictions found in rival theories and brings to the fore hidden aspects. Lastly, when inspiring the concrete practice of human agents, such an explanation leads to a fuller realization of the goods that define them.

Given the fact that human self-understandings vary in time, Taylor affirms that social theories should change accordingly (Taylor 1985b: 1–3). Hence, Taylorean social theory should also do so. In the end, as Abbey argues, the social sciences "are necessarily open-ended hermeneutical endeavors and [...] the sort of knowledge they yield is inevitably more uncertain and labile than the knowledge aspired to by the natural sciences" (Abbey 2000: 155).

7.2.4   What to Keep from "Counter-Orthodox" Theories?

For Taylorean social theory, any economy-based thinking such as RCT still has positive elements, although its usefulness is limited. In this regard Taylor affirms that

> the model of theory as of an independent object, or as bearing an object resistant to our self-understanding, has at best only partial application in the sciences of man. It can apply only in a certain rather specialized domain, where behavior is rather rigid, either because

largely controlled by physiological factors, or because a culture has developed in which what is done in a given department is controlled by a narrow range of considerations, as in games or (to some degree) economic life. (Taylor 1985b: 104)[22]

I think that "counter-orthodox" theories need to be reassessed, as does the "orthodox" model, in the context of Taylor's hermeneutical understanding of the sciences of man.

It seems that the RCT-inspired view could be useful, in the first place, in cultural or sub-cultural contexts in which instrumental rationality has made significant inroads, and in which heightened individualism and "commodification of religion" have taken place in large sectors of the population.[23] In these case studies, RCT-inspired analyses at the individual and organizational level would be useful as hermeneutical tools.[24]

7.3   Some Sociological Criticisms of Taylorean Social Theory

Having reached this point in my analysis, a number of weaknesses and voids in Taylorean social theory should be mentioned.

(a) A noticeable theoretical limitation of Taylorean social theory is the lack of a better understanding of social movements, their lifecycles, the ways in which they interact with other movements, structures individuals and organizations. Taylorean social theory still needs to articulate the way in which "elite-mass" dynamics occur in the social realm, which is one of the phenomena that is crucial for understanding religious change in the West. Analytical tools for the study of the dissemination of the agenda of social movement leaders and their impact on the masses are also needed. Taylorean social theory needs to be complemented by some kinds of social movement[25] and network theories.[26]

---

[22] The quote is from a piece titled *Social Theory as Practice*.

[23] For an analysis of these kinds of contexts, see Robert Putnam (2000), Robert Wuthnow (1998b) and Vincent J. Miller (2005). Although modernization trends can be found worldwide at the present time, particularly due to globalization, it is important to take into account, as Berger (2002) points out, that their reception in non-Western cultures has taken many different and original paths, as an expression of strategies of acceptance, resistance, localization, hybridization, alternative globalization and sub-globalization.

[24] An example of how the "counter-orthodox" model could be used in the context of an hermeneutically-oriented sociology is the already mentioned work by Ammerman (1997). She does so at the level of individuals and organizations.

[25] For instance, from a perspective amenable to that of Taylor, see Smith (2003: 30–79) whose study is focused on the secularization of American public life through the action of intellectual elites. Also, within a Neo-Marxist framework, see the work by Touraine (1977) and Foss and Larkin (1986).

[26] For example, see the studies on social influence processes in Stanley Wasserman and Joseph Galaskiewicz (1994: 3–109).

(b) Although Taylorean social theory studies secularization, its basic concepts and guiding principles seem to be applicable to other social processes. The reason for this is that, on the one hand, they are based on a philosophical account of non-metaphysical human constants, as well as on general views on the interpretive nature of the social sciences. On the other hand, because of the general applicability of morphogenetic theory, as reflected in such basic concepts, in the study of changes in social and cultural structures through the interaction of social groups. This, however, is remains to be explored.

(c) Taylorean social theory is primarily one about secularization in the West. Its current analytical tools are designed for studying specific geographical areas. This is particularly true when one recalls that in the cultural realm, integration at the structural level is analyzed by asking about logical consistency, which is a feature proper to Western rationality since its inception (Taylor 1985b: 136–39).[27] However, one may also say that it could provide principles for a comparative sociological approach to socio-cultural structural change. For instance, Taylor's view on cultural structures as amenable of trans-cultural comparison by way of a shared human reason opens the door for a sociological view that may enable the study of cultures with different canons for rationality (Taylor 1985b: 134–51). This notwithstanding, in keeping the methodological views contained in the first part of this chapter, Taylorean social theory's basic concepts and guiding principles are always to be applied ad casum. As a consequence, it would be necessary to broaden such a theory, taking into account the mentioned insights of Taylor's philosophical anthropology and from others, to make it applicable to any culture.

(d) Taylorean social theory is mainly a macro-theory. However, analytic tools for meso- and micro-sociological studies are also necessary, even within the West, particularly in the case of minorities and their sub-cultures.[28] In this regard, studies developed by the so-called "critical realist" approach to the social sciences[29] seem to be good points of reference for this enterprise since the assumptions operative within this view are close to those in Taylorean social theory. It also seems appropriate to cite here several case studies that make us of "relational sociology."[30]

---

[27] The reference is from a piece titled *Rationality*.

[28] For example, one could ask if Latino Catholics in the United States, with their own shared social imaginaries, do inhabit the same immanent frame Taylor conceptualizes and how, as well as if they offer an alternate mode of modern Catholicity as that he proposes (Lopez-Menendez 2008).

[29] This is an English-born approach to the sciences of man, which has been developed since the 90s by a number of scholars gathered around the philosophy of Roy Bhaskar and the *Journal of Critical Realism*, such as Alex Canillicos, Douglas V. Porpora, Jonathan Q. Tritter, Andrew Parker, Ian Procter, Carol Wolkowitz, Peter Ratcliffe, Margaret Archer, and others. The topics of interest range from social theory to issues as varied as race biases, marriage decisions, decision-making in schools and universities, crimes against humanity, etc.

[30] This is an approach that wants to overcome the dualism between structure and human agency through a focus on social relations as the basic analytical focus for sociology, Its proponents, among others, are François Dèpelteau, Mustafa Emirbayer, Stephan Fuchs and specially Pierpaolo Donati and Nick Crossley. For an overview see Donati (2011) and Crossley (2011).

(e) Taylorean social theory should better define the ways in which its approach is amenable to incorporating the findings of "mainline" sociology, which in many cases it would consider as insufficiently hermeneutical in their design and analysis. As we have seen, Taylor has praised and incorporated in his meta-narrative the work of some contemporary sociologists who make use of "mainstream" sociology methods (Bellah, Martin, Casanova, Joas). However, Taylorean social theory still needs to provide specific criteria for assimilating such studies into its own perspective at the risk of intellectual isolation. Besides, consideration needs to be given to the more recent developments in mainstream sociology towards views with a more hermeneutic stance.

If mainstream sociology could be characterized at the present time as the task of studying social facts by establishing correlations and interrelations between variables and, to a lesser degree, in predicting social trends, then two areas of concern for Taylorean social theory could be defined. First, that of the theoretical frameworks used by mainstream sociologists, in that they could have assimilated unwarranted presuppositions such as those present in "substraction theories," epiphenomenal views of religion, Closed World Structures and the like.

Also problematic would be the definition of variables without developing a "language of contrast" which would enable social scientists to make sense of the cultural context of the subjects under study in order to properly understand their motivations. As I have mentioned before, this demands from such scientists a high degree of knowledge of themselves and of their context, an intuition of the intersubjective language and common meanings they share with their own societies, of their own social imaginaries, and of the social self-understanding prevalent in their own cultures. They would need to be able to contrast all the elements just mentioned with the corresponding ones from the subjects under study, and to establish the contrasts that would allow a deeper and broader interpretation of social phenomena related to the latter.

Another concern for Taylorean social theory in regard to its "mainstream" counterpart would refer to the definition of indicators and to their operationalization in ways in which the meanings human agents give to their social behavior would pretend to be appropriately expressed through quantitative means. Whereas quantitative analysis would not be problematic in the case of "hard" variables (such as age, gender, social class, education, etc.), it will when it comes to studying variables with much more complex meanings (such as, for example, "obedience to religious authority").

Concrete ways of evaluating the vast scholarship developed in terms of mainstream sociology, particularly of the issues described above, should be devised so it could benefit the development of Taylorean social theory.

References

Abbey R (2000) Charles Taylor. Princeton University Press, Princeton
Ammerman NT (1997) Religious choice and religious vitality. The market and beyond. In: Young
    LA (ed) Rational choice theory and religion: summary and assessment. Routledge, New York,
    pp 119–132
Archer MS (2000) Homo economicus, homo sociologicus and homo sentiens. In: Tritter JQ,
    Archer MS (eds) Rational choice theory: resisting colonization. Routledge, London, pp 36–56
Becker GS (1976) The economic approach to human behavior. University of Chicago Press,
    Chicago
Becker GS (1996) Accounting for tastes. Harvard University Press, Cambridge, MA
Berger PL (2002) Introduction. The cultural dynamics of globalization. In: Berger PL, Huntington
    SP (eds) Many globalizations: cultural diversity in the contemporary world. Oxford University
    Press, Oxford, pp 1–16
Bibby R (2004) Restless gods: the renaissance of religion in Canada. Novalis, Ottawa
Brown CG (2001) The death of Christian Britain: understanding secularisation, 1800-2000.
    Routledge, London
Bruce S (1999) Choice and religion: a critique of rational choice theory. Oxford University Press,
    Oxford
Bruce S (2002) God is dead: secularization in the West. Blackwell Publishers, Malden, MA
Casanova J (1994) Public religions in the modern world. University of Chicago Press, Chicago
Casanova J et al (eds) (2013) Secular and sacred. The Scandinavian case of religion in human
    rights, law and public space. Vandenhoeck & Ruprecht, Göttingen
Chaves M (2011) American religion: contemporary trends. Princeton University Press, Princeton
Chaves M, Gorski PS (2001) Religious pluralism and religious participation. Annu Rev Sociol
    27:261–281. doi:10.1146/annurev.soc.27.1.261
Cholvy G (1988) Histoire religieuse de la France contemporaine 1930/1988. Éditions Privat,
    Toulouse
Cipriani R (2003) Invisible religion or diffused religion in Italy? Social Compass 50:311–320.
    doi:10.1177/00377686030503005
Crossley N (2011) Towards relational sociology. Routledge, New York
Davie G (1994) Religion in Britain since 1945: believing without belonging. Blackwell, Oxford
De Jonge J (2012) Rethinking rational choice theory: a companion on rational and moral action.
    Palgrave Macmillan, Basingstoke
Denèfle S (1997) Sociologie de la sécularization. Ê sans-religion en France à la fin du XXème
    siècle. L'Harmattan, Paris
Diotallevi L (1999) The territorial articulation of secularization in Italy: social modernization,
    religious modernization. Archives des sciences sociales des religions 107:77–108. doi:10.3406/
    assr.1999.1164
Diotallevi L (2001) Il rompicapo della secolarizzazione italiana: Caso italiano, teorie americane e
    revisione del paradigma della secolarizzazione. Rubbettino, Soveria Mannelli
Dobbelaere K (2002) Secularization: an analysis at three levels. Peter Lang, Brussels
Donati P (2011) Relational sociology: a new paradigm for the social sciences. Routledge, London
Foss DA, Larkin RW (1986) Beyond revolution: a new theory of social movements. Bergin &
    Garvey, South Hadley
Gauchet M (1998) La religion dans la démocratie. Parcourse de la laïcité. Gallimard, Paris
Hervieu-Léger D (1986) Vers un nouveau Christianisme? Seuil, Paris
Hervieu-Léger D (1999) Le pèlerin at le converti. La religion en movement. Flammarion, Paris
Hervieu-Léger D (2000) Religion as a chain of memory. Rutgers University Press, New Brunswick
Hollis M (1987) The cunning of reason. Cambridge University Press, Cambridge
Joas H (2008) Do we need religion? On the experience of self-transcendence. Paradigm Publishers,
    Boulder

Kosmin BA, Keysar A (2006) Religion in a free market: religious and non-religious Americans: who, what, why, where. Paramount Market Publishers, Ithaca

Lopez-Menendez M (2008) Memory, faith, and social action. Int J Polit Cult Soc 21:87–91. doi:10.1007/s10767-008-9036-6

Lukes S (1968) Methodological individualism reconsidered. Br J Sociol 19:119–129. doi:10.2307/588689

Martin D (2005) On secularization: towards a revised general theory. Ashgate, Aldershot

McLeod H (1997) Religion and the people of Western Europe, 1789-1989. Oxford University Press, Oxford

Miller VJ (2005) Consuming religion: Christian faith and practice in a consumer culture. Continuum, New York

Putnam RD (2000) Bowling alone: the collapse and revival of American community. Simon & Schuster, New York

Roof WC (1993) A generation of seekers: the spiritual journeys of the baby boom generation. HarperSanFrancisco, San Francisco

Smith C (2003) Introduction: rethinking the secularization of American public life. In: Smith C (ed) The secular revolution: power, interests, and conflict in the secularization of American public life. University of California Press, Berkeley, pp 1–96

Stark R, Bainbridge WS (1987) A theory of religion. Peter Lang, New York

Stark R (2008) What Americans really believe: new findings from the Baylor surveys of religion. Baylor University Press, Waco

Stark R (2011) The triumph of Christianity: how the Jesus movement became the world's largest religion. HarperOne, New York

Stark R, Bainbridge WS (1987) A theory of religion. Peter Lang, New York

Stark R, Finke R (2000) Acts of faith: explaining the human side of religion. University of California Press, Berkeley

Taylor C (1964) The explanation of behaviour. Routledge & Kegan Paul, London

Taylor C (1985a) Human agency and language, vol 1, Philosophical papers. University Press, Cambridge

Taylor C (1985b) Philosophy and the human sciences, vol 2, Philosophical papers. University Press, Cambridge

Taylor C (1989) Sources of the self: the making of the modern identity. Harvard University Press, Cambridge, MA

Taylor C (1991) The malaise of modernity. Concord

Taylor C (1995) Philosophical arguments. Harvard University Press, Cambridge, MA

Taylor C (2007) A secular age. Belknap Press of Harvard University Press, Cambridge, MA

Touraine A (1977) The self-production of society. The University of Chicago Press, Chicago

Wasserman S, Galaskiewicz J (1994) Advances in social network analysis: research in the social and behavioral sciences. Sage Publications, Thousand Oaks, CA

Weber M (1947) The theory of social and economic organization. Free Press, New York

Wilson BR (1966) Religion in secular society. Penguin, Baltimore

Wuthnow R (1998a) After heaven: spirituality in America since the 1950s. University of California Press, Berkeley

Wuthnow R (1998b) Loose connections: Joining together in America's fragmented communities. Harvard University Press, Cambridge, MA

Wuthnow R (2007) After the baby boomers: how twenty- and thirty-somethings are shaping the future of American religion. Princeton University Press, Princeton

Chapter 8
Conclusion

In this book, I have elaborated what I have called Taylorean social theory. As such, it offers a theoretical understanding of the social processes and social agents involved in Western secularization. Its sources are Taylor's views on philosophical anthropology and on the method of the social sciences, on the one hand, and other sociological sources as those used by Taylor himself in his meta-narrative as well as the work of other sociologists among which the more important is that by Margaret Archer.

After presenting its basic concepts and guiding criteria and principles, I used it to explain Western secularization. The hermeneutic result of Taylorean social theory could be found in Taylor's (most erudite) meta-narrative or in any other interpretation of the kind consistent with the former's own principles. At last, I compared Taylorean social theory with those that have been predominant in the contemporary debate over secularization, showing the ways in which the former could help to move the conversation forward. The following is a summary of my conclusions.

(a) A consistent Taylorean social theory can be proposed, one which provides with a macro approach circumscribed to the study of Western secularization. Such social theory can be characterized by considering both the social and cultural realms as of similar importance in the explanation of social and cultural change. There is also a particular stress on both the structural and agential perspectives as intervening in socio-cultural change. In this it is a reaction to mainstream sociology which it sees as too much inclined to socio-structural explanations of phenomena, while giving less importance to culture and human agency.

Taylorean social theory also considers history more closely in the socio-cultural analysis he carries out, strives always to complement quantitative data with qualitative approaches and with expanded cultural sensitivity on the part of the social scientist, all of which is blended together into a comprehensive narrative, a thick phenomenology. The strength of such a narrative is measured in the way it is more perspicuous than rival theories, and in its use of "transcendental arguments."

© Springer International Publishing AG 2017

Germán McKenzie, *Interpreting Charles Taylor's Social Theory on Religion and Secularization*, Sophia Studies in Cross-cultural Philosophy of Traditions and Cultures 20, DOI 10.1007/978-3-319-47700-8_8

Taylorean social theory sees secularization as a process of social change, the trajectory of which is not linear but zig-zag shaped. Such a process is not necessarily irreversible but its total reversion is unlikely. It consists in the decline of old religious forms and the apparition of new ones. Causes for these changes come from within the social system and also from the outside (closed social systems are deemed impossible to exist). The outcome of this process is a qualitative change of the place religion occupies in society, a change strongly driven by human agents. This does not mean that all members of society are fully aware of the process, but that the action of political, social, cultural and religious elites is able to persuade the whole of the population in ways that are sometimes evident, and other times not so.

(b) Taylorean social theory elaborates on the basis of Taylor's philosophical views of the human person, of knowledge and of the social sciences as hermeneutic. It also assumes Taylor's main sociological sources on secularization: among the classical sociologists, Weber, specifically his *Verstehen* methodology and his use of ideal-types as heuristic devices. Among contemporary sociologists, David Martin, Robert Bellah, Jose Casanova and Hans Joas in the specific ways that have been studied. Lastly, it draws from Margaret Archer's morphogenetic theory.

(c) Taylorean social theory understanding of secularization in the West has characteristics that enable it to overcome the somewhat stalled debate between the "orthodox" and "counter-orthodox" models, opening new venues for the analysis of secularization.

In regard to the "orthodox" theories, Taylorean social theory builds on some criticisms widespread among scholars today, such as the empirical recognition of the resilience of religion in the West, the critique of considering religion as epiphenomenal, and of the existence of a clear-cut distinction between the secular and religious. However, it adds insights of his own, such as its criticism of "substraction theories," his understanding of the process of differentiation as not necessarily causing decline in religious practice at the individual level, and his insistence on the important role exclusive humanism has played in Western secularization.

However, Taylorean social theory still values "orthodox" theories in that they point to a decline in religious practice and belief that has really happened, and because of the insights they could offer for understanding this phenomenon.

In regard to the "counter-orthodox" or RCT model, Taylorean social theory offers more challenging insights. Among the stronger criticisms against RCT worth mentioning are the fact that it tries to model itself in a similar fashion to the natural sciences, and that it uses a closed-systems approach, both of which are methodological flaws. Taylorean social theory also sees RCT as portraying a passive view of human agency, in spite of appearances, and as sidelining cultural factors, particularly cultural structures. It also says that there is no compelling reason to suppose that the demand side of the "religious economy" should always be constant. In short, Taylorean social theory criticizes RCT's view of religious change as inadequate, but recognizes the validity of the "counter-orthodox" paradigm for specific subcultures in which utilitarian views of religion are prominent.

(d) In its more constructive facet, Taylorean social theory redefines secularization as referring to changes in the place religion occupies in Western societies, which includes the decline of religious forms and the rise of new ones. Such a process is also partially understood as manifesting itself as the emptying of religion from the autonomous social spheres, the falling of religious belief and practice, and the change of the conditions of belief in our times, in which religion is simply considered as one option among others and also a challenged one. However, in this context, it sees religion as still operative in social sub-systems, and as reappearing in new kinds of religious beliefs, practices and communities.

It interprets Taylor's meta-narrative of Western secularization in terms that allow to see more clearly how social and cultural structures changed, how did human agency intervene in that process, and by which means. It also shows that the above mentioned narrative is in need of elaborating of elite-masses dynamics in the cultural realm.

Taylorean social theory's narrative can be expressed, at least as one of several possible accounts, in Taylor's meta-narrative. Because of this, its verification powers benefit from the strength of Taylor's phenomenological analysis of our contemporary conditions of belief at the level of individuals. The recognition of the existence of an immanent frame which is assumed as "natural" or "normal," in which two strong poles, exclusive humanism on the one hand, and religious transcendence on the other, create a continuum within which the majority of people situate themselves in a myriad of different positions. Their positions vary during their lifetimes and acquire different degrees of commitment. Most people live as religious/spiritual seekers in this way.

By stressing the role of agency and its powers for structural transformation, Taylorean social theory also gives way to the study of the role of social movements and groups in religious change, as well as of their strategies of persuasion of the masses. In this light, secularization also happens through the action of political, cultural and religious elites with their agendas, resources, plans, and means of networking.

(e) In Taylorean social theory, however, there are a number of issues in need of completion and expansion. These include its lack of theoretical elements to study social movements and to articulate "elite-masses" dynamics; its focus primarily on macro-sociology; and its lack of concrete ways in which it might incorporate scholarship coming from mainstream sociology.

Glossary

anticipatory confidence Allegiance to either the religious or the non-religious poles that attract Westerners in the "Age of Authenticity" is understood to be based on an act of the will. In the former case such an act is based on the conviction that "certain truths open to us as a result of our commitment," as well as the claim of making our own choices before the risk of losing truth. In the latter case, it is based on the certitude that "it is better to risk loss of truth than to open a chance for error," and on the imperative of rejecting as immoral any premise that may not be proven through the method of science. In both cases, what takes place is an act of "anticipatory confidence," an *ante facto* commitment.

axial religion The kind of religion that appeared in the last millennium B.C. when various "higher" forms of religion came to be seemingly independently in different civilizations, led by Confucius, Gautama, Socrates and the Hebrew prophets. It is characterized by proposing a transformative goal to its practitioners, and by establishing a group of spiritual virtuosi who are closer to achieving it.

buffered self This describes a view of the self in which it is possible to posit a boundary like a "buffer" that separates the mind from the extra-mental world. The "buffered self" takes away the fear for spirits or moral forces and, more importantly, sees itself as disengaged from whatever is beyond the boundary. It gives its own autonomous order to its life. The absence of fear of spirits or moral forces can be not just enjoyed, but seen as an opportunity for self-control and self-direction.

closed world structures (CWS) They are ways of restricting our grasp of things which are not recognized as such.

enchantment/disenchantment An enchanted world is that which is filled with spirits and moral forces that directly affect human existence. Besides, the meanings of things reside in objects or agents which act independently of us and can impose their influence on us. In contrast, a modern disenchanted world is characterized by the fact that thoughts and meanings are only in human minds and are

© Springer International Publishing AG 2017
Germán McKenzie, *Interpreting Charles Taylor's Social Theory on Religion and Secularization*, Sophia Studies in Cross-cultural Philosophy of Traditions and Cultures 20, DOI 10.1007/978-3-319-47700-8

given by humans to things. There are neither spirits nor moral forces affecting human life.

fragilization This is a characteristic of the contemporary religious landscape by which both the religious and the non-religious poles that attract Westerners are challenged, eroded in their abilities to make the case for their claims.

fragmentation A feature of contemporary religious landscape by which, between the religious and non-religious poles, there exists a myriad of highly nuanced middle-positions.

immanent frame This is the specific order which results from the process of disenchantment (especially in its impact on the human practical self-understanding) and the rise of modern natural science. This particular frame can be understood on its own, without reference to any transcendent reality. The life of the buffered individual, instrumentally effective in secular time, created the practical context within which the self-sufficiency of this immanent realm could become a matter of experience. More precisely, this frame is "objectivized," and appears as including a set of cosmic, social and moral orders, all of them impersonal.

modern moral order (MMO) That which starts with the Enlightment and is still prevalent today. What characterizes it is the fact that it is based on the idea of human beings as disembedded individuals, who came to associate together. Each, in pursuing her/his own purposes, act to benefit others. It was conceptualized in its basic elements by Locke, and had Rousseau and Marx among its radical proponents.

neo-Durkhemian dispensation That in which reality is disenchanted and no church can uniquely define and celebrate the link between the political society and the divine. However, there exists a kind of "religious umbrella" than encompasses different denominations and links with the given political order. It also nurtures a certain "civilizational order" and a certain ethnocentric stance.

nova effect This is the ever increasing multiplication of positions which range from religious to irreligious that occurred after the second half of the 20th century, during the "Age of Authenticity."

paleo-Durkhemian dispensation That in which society is seen as an organism where our specific place defines our duties. The church is that of all society, to which everyone should belong. The force that inheres in social obligations comes from the church, its guardian.

pluralization This is the multiplication of positions which range from religious to irreligious, since the end of the 18th. century, due to the emergence of "exclusive humanism." This happened first among the elites, during the "Age of Mobilization," and was passed on into the masses.

porous self This describes a view of the self in which the source of the more powerful and important human emotions is external to the mind, and in which any boundary between the self and such sources is meaningless. The self is, in this way, thoroughly embedded into an ordered cosmos. Living in this world entails a sense of vulnerability.

post-axial religion That which broke the embedded order: social, cosmic and in relation to human goods, that existed before them.

post-/non-Durkhemian dispensation That in which there is not any allegiance between religion, on one hand, and political identities or civilizational orders, on the other.

pre-axial religion That existing before the last millennium B.C. that kept an embedded order: social, cosmic and in relation to human goods.

secular The term was originally linked with time: there was a "secular" time which contrasted with an eternal, sacred or "higher" time. Specific times, places, persons, institutions and actions that were in close relationship with this kind of time, because of these, could also be considered as sacred. This view happened in the context of Latin Christianity. By the 17th century, a new understanding of the term appears which affirmed the secular by itself and as something that was opposed to any claim made in the name of something transcendent of this world and its interests. Later on, this position would further develop into a Deist and a post-Deist outlook.

secularity 1 The retreat of religion from the public space.

secularity 2 The decline of religious belief and practice.

secularity 3 The conditions for belief of a given historical time.

social imaginaries The ways people imagine their social existence, how they fit together with others, how things go on between them and their fellows, the expectations which are normally met, and the deeper normative notions and images which underlie these expectations. Social imaginaries also help people both to know what they should normally expect from living together as well as to understand how they fit together.

strong evaluation This is the kind of evaluations on moral good that humans perform and through which they discriminate between what they perceive as worthy and of value and what they see as unworthy and base. Taylor thinks this is a fact of all human live, regardless of any possible distinctions.

substraction theory This is said of a theory which affirms that the cause for a social change was always present, and what sufficed for the phenomenon to occur was the elimination (substraction) of the factors that were preventing such cause from manifesting itself as such. Taylor criticizes "orthodox" secularization theories for taking this form without proving the existence of such latent cause for the decline of religion in the West.

Index

© Springer International Publishing AG 2017
Germán McKenzie, *Interpreting Charles Taylor's Social Theory on Religion
and Secularization*, Sophia Studies in Cross-cultural Philosophy of Traditions
and Cultures 20, DOI 10.1007/978-3-319-47700-8

CPI Antony Rowe
Chippenham, UK
2017-02-16 21:59